Byron and Place

Byron and Place

History, Translation, Nostalgia

Stephen Cheeke
Bristol University

First published 2003 by
PALGRAVE MACMILLAN
Houndmills, Basingstoke, Hampshire RG21 6XS and
175 Fifth Avenue, New York, N.Y. 10010
Companies and representatives throughout the world

PALGRAVE MACMILLAN is the global academic imprint of the Palgrave
Macmillan division of St. Martin's Press, LLC and of Palgrave Macmillan Ltd.
Macmillan® is a registered trademark in the United States, United Kingdom
and other countries. Palgrave is a registered trademark in the European
Union and other countries.

ISBN 1–4039–0403–0

This book is printed on paper suitable for recycling and made from fully
managed and sustained forest sources.

A catalogue record for this book is available from the British Library

Library of Congress Cataloging-in-Publication Data

Cheeke, Stephen, 1967–
    Byron and place: history, translation, nostalgia / Stephen Cheeke.
       p. cm.
    Includes bibliographical references and index.
    ISBN 1–4039–0403–0
      1. Byron, George Gordon Byron, Baron, 1788–1824–Settings. 2. Byron,
George Gordon Byron, Baron, 1788–1824–Homes and haunts. 3. Byron,
George Gordon Byron, Baron, 1788–1824–Knowledge–Europe. 4. Translating
and interpreting–England–History–19th century. 5. Literature and
history–England–History–19th century. 6. Place (Philosophy) in literature.
7. Nostalgia in literature. 8. Europe–In literature. 9. History in literature.
10. Setting (Literature) I. Title.

PR4392.S46 C47 2003
821'.7–dc21
                                                                      2002192459

10 9 8 7 6 5 4 3 2 1
12 11 10 09 08 07 06 05 04 03

Printed and bound in Great Britain by
Antony Rowe Ltd, Chippenham, Wiltshire

For my mother and father,
and Donna

Contents

Afterword: Dying in Greece	193
Notes	198
Select Bibliography	233
Index	238

Acknowledgements

Parts of the Introduction and Chapter 1 first appeared as an essay in the *European Journal of English Studies* 6:2 (2002) and are included here by permission of the editors and Zwets & Zeitlinger Publishers. Other sections of the Introduction first appeared as part of an essay in *The Byron Journal* 27 (1999), and the final section of Chapter 1 as an essay in *Romanticism* 7:2 (2001), and are included here by permission of the editors. Thank you also to the editors of the forthcoming *Byron and Freedom: Essays from the Nottingham Byron Conference 2000* for their permission to reproduce earlier versions of parts of Chapter 3, included in their collection. Also thank you to the Bristol University Research Fund Committee for their financial assistance.

I would like to thank and acknowledge the following people for their support, encouragement and inspiration during the writing of this book: Devorah Baum, Bernard Beatty, J.J. Borg, Mike Bradshaw, Lesel Dawson, George Donaldson, Hester Jones, Paula Kennedy, Donna Maclean, Tom Mole, Vincent Newey, Ralph Pite, Emily Rosser, Nick Roe, Diego Saglia, Philip Shaw, John M. Smith, Phill Wilmott. Especial thanks to my friends and colleagues at Bristol whose comments and advice were invaluable: Andrew Bennett, Andrew Nicholson and Timothy Webb.

Acknowledgements

Introduction

Commonplaces

In Rome during the early spring of 1849, over thirty years after Lord Byron had visited the city, Arthur Hugh Clough witnessed events of historical significance while looking at paintings and sculpture. The daily life of the Roman Republic of Mazzini, the French siege of the city, and the eventual capitulation of the Republic in June took place as a backdrop to Clough's busy schedule of sightseeing and art-gazing, while occasionally he would climb the Palatine hill 'to look at the firing'.[1] Writing to his mother on 11 May, Clough takes pains to reassure her that newspaper reports of a 'Roman Terror' were exaggerated:

> The Spectator and perhaps other papers will have told you of the warfare that has been going on hereabouts. However it would seem very small to you if you saw it as I am doing; and except for the nuisance of galleries etc being shut up, I should be very well content. … The only awkward thing that has happened in the city has been the killing of four or perhaps five priests by the mob, about a week ago, soon after the news of the advance of the Neapolitan army.[2]

Allowing for a commendable impulse to set his mother's mind at rest, Clough nevertheless seems to have been surprised that events of historical significance could occur without much disturbance of reality or routine, perhaps even experiencing something like a disappointment with the Roman siege. 'But it is funny to see how much like any other city a besieged city looks',[3] Clough wrote to Thomas Arnold in June 1849, while later that same month he describes seeing a crowd

1

assembled in the Piazza Colonna to watch the 'pretty fireworks' of the French bombardment.

> Ecco un altro! – One first saw the 'lightning' – over the Post Office, then came the missive itself, describing its tranquil parabola, then the distant report of the mortar, and finally the near explosion, which occasionally took place in the air. This went on all night...and this morning as I went to the Pantheon, I heard the whizz of what I suppose was one, up in the air above the Temple of Antonine.[4]

Clough took these odd misalignments of historical event and lived experience as a paradigm for a broader crisis of subjectivity, which he connected to a distinctly Victorian *Zeitgeist*. The curious hexameter poem composed during his months in Rome, *Amours de Voyage*, examines some of the difficulty in responding to the city as a visitor, and the particular difficulty in responding to the events occurring there in 1849. Claude, the anti-hero of the poem, is troubled by most things, but among them history, both in the 'rubbishy' aspect it assumes in the city's structure ('All the incongruous things of past incompatible ages' I.22), and in the immediate unfolding of historical event and action during the siege. The 'awkward' scenes of anti-clerical mob violence that Clough had played down in his letters home reappear in the poem in a passage in which Claude attempts to describe a murder:

> So I have seen a man killed! An experience that, among others!
> Yes, I suppose I have; although I can hardly be certain,
> And in a court of justice could never declare I had seen it.
> But a man was killed, I am told, in a place where I saw
> Something; a man was killed, I am told, and I saw something.
>   I was returning home from St. Peter's; Murray, as usual,
> Under my arm, I remember; had crossed the St. Angelo bridge; and
> Moving towards the Condotti, had got to the first barricade, when
> Gradually, thinking still of St. Peter's, I became conscious
> Of a sensation of movement opposing me, – tendency this way
> (Such as one fancies may be in a stream when the wave of the tide is
> Coming and not yet come, – a sort of poise and retention);
> So I turned, and, before I turned, caught sight of stragglers
> Heading a crowd, it is plain, that is coming behind that corner.
> Looking up, I see windows filled with heads; the Piazza,
> Into which you remember the Ponte St. Angelo enters,

Since I passed, has thickened with curious groups; and now the
Crowd is coming, has turned, has crossed that last barricade, is
Here at my side. In the middle they drag at something. What is it?
Ha! bare swords in the air, held up! There seem to be voices
Pleading and hands putting back; official, perhaps; but the swords are
Many, and bare in the air. In the air? They descend, they are smiting,
Hewing, chopping – At what? In the air once more upstretched! And
Is it blood that's on them? Yes, certainly blood! Of whom, then?
Over whom is the cry of this furor of exaltation?

(II.7.162–86).

Here the difficulty of *witnessing*, both in the immediate sense of experiencing an event, and in the subsequent effort to narrate that experience, is given full sinuous expression in the hexameter's own wave-like
'poise and retention', while the complexity of the relationship between
an event and its narration reveals itself in a simple shift to the historic
present when Claude begins to relive the experience in the telling: 'So I
turned, and, before I turned, caught sight of stragglers / Heading a
crowd, it is plain, that is coming behind that corner'. 'It is plain' is of
course not true of the narrative itself, which bears witness to nothing
being plain, but is true to the sense of *something* being witnessed,
something that *should* be plain and cannot be obfuscated by language.
Nevertheless, the obligation to speak as plainly as possible upon this
subject of all subjects – seeing a man killed – is complicated by the possibility that seeing a man killed may simply be 'an experience... among
others', and hence vulnerable to all the ordinary approximation of representation. In such circumstances, the temptation to seek refuge or
guidance in more plainly transparent modes of language must naturally be great. Claude is carrying under his arm 'Murray, as usual', that
is John Murray's *Handbook for Travellers in Central Italy, including the
Papal States, Rome, and the Cities of Etruria* (1843). 'Passing away from
the place with Murray under my arm, and / Stooping, I saw through
the legs of the people the legs of a body'. Murray is still there then
when Claude catches sight of the victim, although the 'legs of a body'
suggests an unreality about the murdered priest which is in contrast to
the personhood of the handbook, held close as Claude hurries away.
The passage closes in a different mode:

Through the Trastevere walking last night, at nine of the clock, I
Found no sort of disorder; I crossed by the Island-bridges,
So by the narrow streets to the Ponte Rotto, and onwards

Thence, by the Temple of Vesta, away to the great Coliseum,
Which at the full of the moon is an object worthy a visit.

(II.7.212–16)

That closing line, 'Which at the full of the moon is an object worthy a visit' is a pastiche of the language of the travellers' guidebooks, and a sly reference to the entry upon the Coliseum in Murray's 1843 handbook, which was a little more expansive:

> The scene from the summit is one of the most impressive in the world, and there are few travellers who do not visit the spot by moonlight in order to realise the magnificent description in "Manfred", the only description which has ever done justice to the wonders of the Coliseum...[5]

The handbook then quotes an extract of 34 lines from the third act of *Manfred* (the lines beginning 'I do remember me...'), so that the traveller who had gone to Rome without a copy of Byron's poems, and who had also forgotten to purchase Murray's pocket-size *Lord Byron's Poetry*, purposefully designed for the tourist, might nevertheless enjoy this magnificent description upon the very spot itself. Clough's poem interrogates then not only the bourgeois sensibility of the traveller/tourist, but the grander and earlier shades behind John Murray's handbook – most especially the Romantic experience of place, which, having become in some sense commodified by booksellers such as Murray and son in the previous decades, seemed a very distant phenomenon by 1849. More particularly, *Amours de Voyage* is in tension with Lord Byron and Byronism, and the pat evocation of the Coliseum in moonlight is meant to recall not merely the passage from *Manfred* celebrated in Murray's handbook, but the equally famous passages from the fourth canto of *Childe Harold's Pilgrimage* which also helped to make the visit a 'worthy' one for later travellers. *Childe Harold's Pilgrimage* and *Manfred* offer accounts of the Coliseum in moonlight which witness an intense communion with history and the spirit-of-place; *Childe Harold* responds to a 'dread power' in the ruin, which is so tangible that 'we become a part of what has been, / And grow unto the spot, all-seeing but unseen'(IV.138.); Manfred speaks of a mysterious transformation in the moonlight, 'till the place / Became religion, and the heart ran o'er / With silent worship of the great of old!' (III.iv.37–8). Such experiences do not seem available to Claude, who vacillates between suspicion and envy of their transcendental claims, but who is also aware of the ways in which these ecstasies had become attitudes for the 'middle-class people…not wholly / Pure of the taint of the shop', who surround him in Rome. The Coliseum, after all, was the place to go in ancient Rome not for aesthetic pleasure, but to enjoy the experience of seeing a man killed. Conscious then of his own painful distance both from the intensity of Byronism, and from the clichés and commonplaces that Byronism had bequeathed its Victorian followers, Claude takes strength from the certain knowledge that he lacks Byron's strength, but that he didn't quite believe in it anyway. Most importantly of all, Claude represents a suspicion that Byronism even in its original and undiluted form may contain a certain predictability, conventionality and emotionalism which suggest that the seeds of the later clichés were in fact contained *within* it; and moreover, that this weakness was most apparent in Byron's response to places such as the Coliseum in moonlight. By turning to the moonlit Coliseum at the end of a passage describing seeing a man killed and by allowing the sanitised language of the handbook to close the section, Clough is offering an implicit critique of Byronism and its afterlife, a critique which in fact runs throughout *Amours de Voyage*, questioning the authenticity of Byron's claims not only to transcendent or ecstatic communion with the spirit of place, but also to 'experience', and to heroic self-sacrifice for an unequivocal cause.

Any study of Byron and place must take these suspicions seriously, not least because they arose from the very beginning of his career. Byron's sharpest contemporary critic, William Hazlitt, for example, repeatedly suggested that Byron's poetry consisted of fine-sounding commonplaces, and observed that the author of *Childe Harold's Pilgrimage* described 'the stately cypress, or the fallen column, with the feeling that every schoolboy has about them'.[6] Hazlitt's judgement, which would be shared by Victorian writers such as Clough, suggests an explanation both for the popularity of Byron's verse during his lifetime and for the kind of posthumous fragmentation of the work into the 'magnificent' passages appended to guidebooks. The notion of the commonplace – the second-hand and inauthentic emotional response – shadows Byron's writing in all its phases, particularly in its relationship to places of historical significance and fame, such as the Coliseum, partly because this was precisely the subject Byron frequently wrote about, i.e. *famous* historical places. Authenticity then is a central topic of this study, part of the argument of which will be to suggest not only that an anxiety about responding to places of historical fame is a central part of Byron's imagination, but that the idea of the commonplace becomes transformed in the use Byron makes of his actual experience and direct knowledge of such places gained in his travels. I will suggest that in fact the notion of *being there* represents the most powerful and complex aspect of Byron's work, even as it is perhaps the most obvious and immediate element of Byron's enduring fame – everybody knows this at least, that he had been there (and seen it and done it). Indeed it is part of the point in offering the traveller fragments of Byron's poetry that such passages would not only reverberate more powerfully when read in the actual places they describe, but that reading them would somehow constitute a participation in or recreation of Byron's presence in the same place. If Byron inaugurates a sense of being connected to history through being there on the very spot, then this is reprocessed by Murray in the promise of being connected to Byron upon the very same spot. What does it mean, however, to 'grow unto the spot' of places such as the Coliseum? What significance is there in *being there*?

One corollary of this large investment in the authority of experience would of course be a lifelong suspicion of the travelling English and a fierce belief in the distinction between travel and tourism.[7] The last piece of prose Byron wrote before leaving Italy for Greece in 1823, which was probably intended for inclusion in Leigh Hunt's *The Liberal*, describes an Italian carnival, and opens with a passage about the English abroad:

> In the year 18- a young Englishman had resided for some time in the Italian City of T. — for the Geography of which the reader is referred to the Map – and for the description to the Guide Book. – It is possible that he may derive no great information from either of these sources – inasmuch as it is but little frequented by the second-hand Society of half-pay economists – no pay dandies – separated wives, unseparated *not* wives — the Starke – or Invalid – or Forsyth – or Eustace or Hobhouse travellers – as they are called according to their Manual – neither had the great Irruption of Welbeck Street broke loose – as yet invaded it's [sic] venerable precincts. – In short the middle ton – which is a very distinct thing from the *bon ton* which England possessed – (and may perhaps still possess –) had neither disgusted the natives – nor dishonoured their Country – perhaps Rome and Naples can say the same – or Florence,– Ask them.[8]

Mariana Starke, Joseph Forsyth, John Chetwode Eustace and Henry Matthews (*The Diary of an Invalid* (1820)), were the authors of popular Italian travel books of this period (Eustace is the name Clough gives

Claude's silent correspondent), while John Cam Hobhouse was of course Byron's close friend, had been his travelling companion both in the East and through parts of Italy, and was the author of *Historical Illustrations to the Fourth Canto of Childe Harold: Containing Dissertations on the Ruins of Rome; and an Essay on the Italian Literature* (1818). For Byron to include Hobhouse in this list was to recognise the process by which his own poetry was being commodified for the growing middle-class market in travel, the great 'Irruption of Welbeck Street' who invaded Italian cities and experienced them through the medium of the guidebook, or 'Manual', to which Byron's publisher John Murray would shortly add his own name with spectacular success. Byron's disgust for the English 'middle ton' anticipates Claude's prejudice in *Amours de Voyage*, although it is part of Clough's critique of Byronism to have Claude fall in love with a member of that particular class and grow to be ashamed of his initial snobbery. For Byron, however, a determined belief in the distinction between his own experience of other countries (in particular Italy), and the experience of the majority of English travellers, remained with him to the end of his life, and was no doubt correct, but at the same time Byron understood better than anyone else the kind of temptations *Childe Harold's Pilgrimage* had offered its readers. It is partly therefore a measure of his own distance in 1823 from earlier work such as *Childe Harold* that there is an apparent revulsion for those following in his footsteps with Hobhouse under their arm. Nevertheless, Byron's responses to places of historical significance *had* often been ecstatic, and had often suggested that there was a particular kind of historical knowledge available through the experience of *being there* on the spot. This book is about that suggestion and what it might mean.

Geography

The interdisciplinary romance between the social sciences and literary theory which began in the middle of the 1980s produced, among other things, a broad field of enquiry called the 'new geography' or 'cultural geography'.[9] These large terms shelter a range of cognate disciplines (urban and environmental studies, geopolitics, ecocriticism, postmodern geography, etc.) all of which have embraced either specific parts of literary theory, or have more generally taken the theoretical 'turn' literary studies is said to have made in the 1960s. Most significant perhaps has been the sustained rethinking of philosophical questions of space and place, a rethinking which has itself taken place in different modes and styles. One strand has been a 'poetics' of space, post-Heideggerian, phenomenological, and most closely associated with the name of Gaston Bachelard.[10] Another strand, associated most closely with Henri Lefebvre, has emerged through Marxist cultural analysis and has sought to foreground the 'affective and social experience of space', the ideological encryptions of maps, or city streets, or gardens, or any 'produced' space.[11] These are different emphases, rather than antagonistic approaches, and literary studies has adopted elements from both the 'poetics' and the cultural critique of social space, as it has pursued the complex relations of writing and place. Central to this project has been the reorientation of philosophical thinking about the human subject in relation to place and space. Locality, spatiality and situated embodiment have re-emerged as preoccupations in recent philosophical thought which has sought to argue, for example, that 'the structure of subjectivity is given in and through the structure of place', rather than vice versa.[12] Predicating the structure of the subject upon its temporal and spatial situatedness has significant implications for the study of those literary texts which most often present subjectivity within its setting or situatedness, or 'scene'. In particular, this re-emphasis inscribes the human subject with the reality of its physical environment, as conversely it marks that environment with human experience and culture at a deep level. Geography then is both over-written and written-through with lived experience, with memory and subjectivity, with human inscription – in short, with history. In literary terms the governing metaphor for this relationship might be the palimpsest, a figure for the hidden layeredness of historical experience within a singular place, or text. It is a favourite Romantic trope (Thomas De Quincey famously used it as a metaphor for the human mind in his *Suspiria de Profundis* (1845)), and it hovers behind Byron's own notion of the 'one page' of human history. Freud was to make a tentative analogical link between the archaeology of Rome and the structure of the psyche, *materialising*, as it were, the sense of memory in place, and although he quickly retreats from the metaphor it seems a useful one for my purposes since it suggests that just as the mind is layered and striated with memory and experience, so too is the physical structure of a city.[13] In other words, if the mind is like a palimpsest text, which is like a layered place, an archaeological treasure-trove, so, too, places are structured like human psyches, and reveal to us cross-sections of buried experience, of historical subjectivity. Lord Byron was particularly interested in just such a relation between the materiality of place and the buried life of the historical subject, and responded to places as if they promised the recovery of what had been lost or erased. What form would such a recovery take, and what might it mean?

Romanticism is perhaps the most problematic and interesting among the various fields of literary studies in its relation to the new cultural geography, in that it has traditionally been burdened with the notion of a particular orientation towards the natural world which may at first seem most resistant to the kind of geo-historical excavation I have been describing. Indeed it has partly been the desire of unmasking claims to transcend the geographical and the historical that has driven historicist criticism over the last twenty years, and which shares something of Hazlitt's suspicion of the Romantic commonplace. Nevertheless, a Wordsworthianism inevitably preconditions our thinking about Romanticism and place, offering its own forceful notion of the interstructuring of subjectivity and situation, and eclipsing most others. In fact it is hard either to resist or escape the paradigms of psyche-in-place offered by *The Prelude*, the example of which has been central not only to recent ecocriticism but to critical arguments surrounding the praxis of New Historicism about the politics of local knowledge, regionalism, the 'particular', etc.[14] New practices of cultural geography will discover in Romanticism a foundational struggle over the meaning of place, in that Wordsworth's claims to have experienced the transcendent and universal amid the scenes of 'local' Cumbria are passionately contested by a counter-vision of cosmopolitan experience, developed by Lord Byron.[15] It would be wrong, however, to see this as a conflict between a natural supernaturalism on the one hand, and an enlightened scepticism on the other. Byron's engagement with place is not one emptied of the 'something far more deeply interfused'; quite the opposite in fact, as the trope of the *genius loci* is regularly invoked to suggest the mysterious, the supernatural or the ecstatic in Byron's writing. Byron's sense of mystery, however, emerges from different sources than Wordsworthian nature, deriving instead partly from an awareness of the strangeness and power of being in places of historical fame, being physically present where history has occurred; partly from the cult of the 'real' which develops in and around Byronism, the desire for accuracy, for re-enactment, and for the material *facts*. But also because Byron is drawn to the aura, or as he preferred, the 'halo' of the past as he perceived it in place, and is fascinated by the possibility of an unmediated connection or communion with the *genius loci*.

History

Byron's 'grand passion' was for history, and to read him is to be
exposed to a vast range of historical knowledge, materials and narratives.[16] Furthermore, Byron has been central to the work of Jerome
McGann, who has in turn helped to make history central to Romantic
studies, so that placing Byron within history we have come to see not
only how much 'history' is Byron's own subject, but how complex the
relations are between historicist readings and Romantic historiogra-
phies. Does Byron have a theory of history, and if he does, how does
his theory relate to the kind of historiographical ecstasies I have been
describing above? And where does Byron stand in relation to other
Romantic theories or practices of history given the cultural commonplace (perhaps even embodied in Byron himself) that the beginning of
the nineteenth century witnesses history writ large?[17]

The sheer force of Byron's 'grand passion' distinguishes him from
other writers of the period with the exception perhaps of Sir Walter
Scott, but its tendency to take different forms, its tendency indeed to
emerge as passion rather than system may obscure any sense of an
overarching theory. If we do think of Byron as a theorist of history
then we tend to cast him in a deeply pessimistic or tragic mould, citing
his Calvinist upbringing or his family history of manic depression, or
some such uncertainty, which veils any specific vision of history in a
more general sense of Byronic gloom.[18] Malcolm Kelsall's study of the
configurations of a Whig vision of history in Byron's work, although
persuasive, also seems oddly isolated in Byron studies.[19] Much more
typical is a certain kind of a-political characterisation of Byron's vision
as essentially a Gibbonesque one of history as repetition, fatalism, and
patterns of decline:

> There is the moral of all human tales;
> 'Tis but the same rehearsal of the past,
> First Freedom, and then Glory – when that fails,
> Wealth, vice, corruption, – barbarism at last.
> And History, with all her volumes vast,
> Hath but *one* page...

> (*CHP*, IV.108)

These lines from the fourth canto of *Childe Harold's Pilgrimage* recall the
epigraph to the first canto from Fougeret de Monbron's *Le Cosmopolite*:
'L'univers est une espèce de livre, dont on n'a lu que la première page

quand n'a vu que son pays...', and disturb the optimism of that opening with the sense that the first page is also the last page.[20] They reflect, with detachment, upon the bloody similarities in the separate histories of the European nations rather than offering any kind of historicist methodology. Byron's personifications of 'History' ('the grand liar', *Don Juan*, IX, 81) are always negative, but there is something in the very process of summary and of personification which tends to freeze history in a negative or tragic aspect. History as subject matter, on the other hand, as disparate material, as detail, may be something quite different from the 'blind series of cycles'[21] which emerges when Byron thinks of it abstractly. In other words, how Byron engages with historical documents and materials as imaginative sources may be quite contrary in spirit and emphasis from his occasional pronouncements about the meaning of 'History'. History as subject matter, material, place, subjectivity, is vital, rather than moribund, in his writing.

The dichotomy between a dark theory and a bright praxis is, however, a difficult one to resolve. To take one example: the influence of the 'catastrophism' of Cuvier upon the mystery plays *Cain* and *Heaven and Earth* is well documented.[22] Here Byron is engaging directly with a theorist, citing his reading in the preface to *Cain*, and exploiting that reading in the body of his text. Cuvier's notion of a succession of catastrophes by which the world steadily degenerates might be better described, however, as a cosmic theory, or a theory of Time, rather than of history in the human or political sense. Byron's Cuvier is not a model for deciphering the movements and patterns in historical material, nor the motives of historical subjects. It doesn't help us to understand the life of Doge Marino Faliero, for example, and although it may offer a metaphysical endorsement of the lines beginning 'History.../ Hath but one page...', 'catastrophism' is not a template for a kind of 'secular Calvinist' historiography either.[23] The moral aspect to historical material, rather than being obliterated in the blind cycles of time, emerges most vividly in the specific moments and instances of human historical action. If *Cain* is in some sense a play of historical (or cosmic) theory, then *Marino Faliero* (1821) is a play of historical materials, events, persons and places. The Doge is not represented as the victim of blind historical cycles, but is brought back to life and agency (subjectivity) in the reality of his historical moment. Theory and practice are radically separated here: the moral of all human tales may be the same (freedom/glory/corruption/barbarism), but that lesson is not visible in the individuation of specific historical example, when those tales come to be told. This in turn raises larger and more intractable questions as to the role of the historical subject in the larger processes and patterns of history, and the exact relationship between historical material and the models of signification we make that material serve. Byron's 'grand passion' brings these questions into a particular focus.

Connecting Byron with other Romantic writers in all of this doesn't seem easy either. Indeed locating him within any kind of historiographical context seems insecure given the essential contradiction that history is everywhere alive in Byron's work, but is also negatively theorised and personified. Combining the notion of historically repeated cycles of decline with a sense of the expressiveness of specific historical materials, we might align Byron with the work of Giambattista Vico,[24] or with other figures of Enlightenment scepticism such as Pierre Bayle.[25] The temptation to trace philosophical family trees might suggest one that runs through Bayle (whom Byron described as 'the very martyr of impartiality'[26]), through Voltaire to Gibbon. Byron's visit in 1816 to the garden in Lausanne in which Gibbon had walked among the acacia plants on the evening he completed *The Decline and Fall of the Roman Empire* in 1787, and in which Byron plucked a sprig of the same plant to send to John Murray as a souvenir, is the kind of personal connection with literary places through material re-enactment of the past that played such a significant part in Byron's sense of history. We might, like Peter Thorslev, see Bayle and the historical rationalism which influenced Byron as in some sense the forerunner of the Higher Criticism, and therefore one of the sources of modern historiography. What all these Enlightenment ancestries do, however, is enmesh Byron in essentially sceptical philosophies of history and historiography, processes of demystification which do not fit comfortably with the ecstatic communion he so often recorded in his writing. Even critics of Byron who stress his desire for historical authenticity or immediacy, usually do so in McGann's sense of an ideological escape into surfaces, or from the figure of Byron the proto-novelist of *Don Juan*: all-including, all-questioning, all-sceptical.[27] Otherwise, Byron is said to dramatise history, that is, to represent history as spectacle or pageant – an aesthetic Kierkegaard would later diagnose as one of the inherent dangers of Romantic irony, and which some would blame for the political ills of the twentieth century.[28] As Manfred describes the Coliseum in moonlight the moment is certainly dramatic, but 'dramatisation of history' isn't a full or adequate description of the kind of mysterious communion occurring here, the place becoming 'religion', or, to borrow the same phrase from T.S. Eliot repeatedly used in Bernard Blackstone's study of Byron, 'grace dissolved in place'.[29] The idea that Byron is 'dramatising' history (as in the notion that he 'dramatises' his own life), is too often a way of registering a distrust of a certain intensity of emotional engagement which doesn't sit comfortably with Byron's overt scepticism. For many readers Byron simply can't be serious when he describes a place becoming religion.

But Byron wrote about historical places, about specific 'spots', as if they were sites in which direct connection with the buried subjectivity of the lived experiences associated with those places was somehow (supernaturally) possible. This, we might argue, is merely a Romantic version of the brightest aim both of the New Historicism and the 'new geography' – the idea of the recovery of lived experience. It also means that Byron's own subjectivity, which has occupied so much critical attention, is perhaps most available to us through place, or most open to our knowledge in those historical locales into which it is written, so that this book also attempts to be the delineation of a life story, or a topo-biographical study.

My opening chapter explores the notion of *being there* during the years 1807–12, most particularly the authority and meaning invested in the notion of direct knowledge and experience of *place* in the period during which Byron travelled in the East, and became famous for doing so in the West. Being in Greece in particular is for the western traveller always a question of authenticity, but also focuses anxiety about belonging to a western imperial power and initiates a struggle with the notion of the classical *genius loci* that will extend throughout Byron's writing life. One consequence of this anxiety is that Byron and Hobhouse 'discover' and present Albania to their readership as a challenge to the hegemony of the classical, the first of many such challenges or questionings in Byron's writing. On returning to England in 1811, Byron's literary orientalism relied upon just such firsthand knowledge, but it was a knowledge or a 'knowing' that was carefully prepared for the reading public's consumption. The first section of the second chapter examines the ways in which Byron's oriental poems are predicated upon the notion that in the East the fantastical could be real, and the real fantastical, and that this relationship could not only be corroborated but in some sense reproduced in the relationship between the poems and their notes. The chapter then goes on to explore the relationship between the body or materiality of significant historical sites and the notion of a spirit of place in the third canto of *Childe Harold*, in particular upon the field of Waterloo and in Rousseau's Clarens. The work immediately following Byron's departure from England in 1816 repeatedly turns over the notion of the mind as its own place, both in its metaphysical and its political aspect, and tests the limits of self-sufficiency against the encroachments of place and situation. During these first years in exile Byron writes dramatic monologues of historical 'prophecy' and vindication based upon his direct experience of places associated with Bonnivard, Tasso and Dante, poems which are meant in some sense to influence contemporary European politics, particularly in Italy. I will argue that Byron develops the notion of interchangeability – the imaginative act of exchanging places – as a method to recover historical subjectivity and to allow such knowledge to disturb the present, a method most evident in the fourth canto of *Childe Harold*, and most achieved in the famous scene of the dying gladiator in the Coliseum. At the same time I will argue that there is again a cross-authentication between the poem and its supplementary notes, which this time is an analogue for the kind of cultural sanctuary and support that is necessary in order to effect an Italian *risorgimento*.

If the first half of my study is concerned with 'place' in its material reality, the second half goes on to explore metaphors of displacement, and the condition of exile. Byron's own exchange of places, his gradual acculturation within Italian society is the subject of Chapter 3, particularly in relation to his role as *cavalier servente* to Teresa Guiccioli. This period is best understood, I shall argue, through the idea of translation, both figurative and real (this is the period during which Byron is translating and being translated), and in which we witness the close and troubled familial interplay of the linguistic, the erotic and the political. My final chapter examines Byron's peculiar susceptibility to and sharp suspicion of nostalgia, in particular his complex nostalgia for England, both for the early years of the regency he had directly experienced and for ideas of a recent English past of which he had no direct knowledge. I will suggest that Byron's return to England in the later cantos of *Don Juan* should be read in relation to the wider examination of the pathology of nostalgia, homesickness and place-attachment which runs throughout the writings of 1821–23, and which interrogates both the nature of the memorialising process and again the notion of the classical, the *genius loci*. Byron's temporal and geographical distance from England results in a sense of the period 1811–16 in particular as a unique fragment of English history, but one which may appear strange or even monstrous to posterity. If my study begins with 'place' and the notion of *being there*, and then pursues Byron through the processes of his 'translation', it culminates in the powerful sense of *having been there* which shapes the work of 1821–23. Being there, being in-between, having been there – this then is the broad trajectory I perceive in Byron's writing life, and which provides the structure of this book.

1
Being There: 1807–12

1.1 Newstead and Harrow

Since most readers of Byron begin with the year 1812, a date coincident with the emergence of Byronism, one consequence is that we have not paid much attention to the years before the poet became famous. Indeed it seems hard to imagine this period, when George Gordon Lord Byron was an unknown writer who lived his life without the accompanying celebrity. Was there ever, in fact, a Lord Byron without the long shadow of Byronism pursuing him? In a sense, perhaps there wasn't, not simply because Byron's pre-fame writings seem especially sensitive to questions of reputation, name, and reaction (Byron often talks of his own 'fame' in letters pre-dating 1812), but because the representational potencies of Byronism are such that it may be impossible not to discover this phenomenon at each and every stage of the poet's life and work, at least *in potentia*. The seriousness of Byron's investment in geo-history (that is, in the experience of places where historically significant things have happened) seems especially evident from the beginning of his poetic career, even before he had travelled in the East. 'Place' is where Byron's writings begin, and around which Byronism first begins to take shape. That fact is announced by the opening poem of his first public collection, *Hours of Idleness* (1807), entitled 'On Leaving Newstead Abbey', even as it makes the valedictory gesture that would also become distinctly Byronic.

The poem takes its epigraph from Macpherson's Ossian's 'Carthon: A Poem': 'Why dost thou build the hall, Son of the winged days? Thou lookest from thy tower to-day, yet a few years, and the blast of the desart comes, it howls in thy empty court.'[1] Macpherson's poem is about a young warrior 'coming to man's estate' who avenges the

15

destruction of his home, and the quoted lines provide Byron with the requisite lament for a ruined place, whilst registering an *Ecclesiastes*-style warning against the vanity of castle-building. Answering the world-weariness of the epigraph, Byron fills the empty courts of a decaying Newstead with the history of his ancestors and their vivid and violent historical places: crusader-knights who journeyed from 'Europe to Palestine'; a medieval minstrel who followed his master to the siege of Askalon (1157); dead soldiers at Crècy (1346); a Royalist at Marston Moor (1644). On leaving the single place (Newstead Abbey), in which these separate names are mingled, Byron vows that he himself will live in 'emulation', or 'perish' in like manner, i.e. directly involved in heroic military action for a just cause.

This is a complex notion of identity, ordered and split around two places, one of which is being left behind while the other is proleptically imagined; split too around a history at once *there* at Newstead, and elsewhere. Such a duality of place and time is instinctive to Byron, as are the modulations of nostalgia revealed here: the poem desires, promises, and foretastes the future moment when the poet's own occupation of Newstead Abbey will enter the roll-call of the heroic past, his aristocratic place *here* assured by an heroic death elsewhere. In this manner Byron's lordship will always be drawn to the imagined battlefield where glory and legitimacy fall into their proper place. The historically significant sites remembered in his writing are most frequently those authenticated in some sense by violent action, or, alternatively, by miraculous protection from violent destruction. Letters of early August 1807 (two months after the publication of *Hours of Idleness*) announce that Byron has been writing a poem on the subject of 'Bosworth Field', which he intends to extend 'to 8 or 10 books'. This projected national epic will be 'finished in a year'[2] (later '3 or four years, & most probably never *concluded*').[3] By 26 October Byron had written 560 lines.[4] None of the poem is extant.

Nevertheless, the topography of ancestral home and battlefield, each in some sense authenticating the other, is developed in a further poem upon Newstead in this first collection (a sister-piece probably dating from pre-1807), 'Elegy on Newstead Abbey', a poem preoccupied with dying in places. Again fantastically conjuring the crusader knights, the elegy retraces their 'progress, through the lapse of time' to Judea; returns to the monastic period, visits the dissolution of the monasteries, the civil wars (in particular the battle of Newbury), the years of neglect and spoliation, the death of Cromwell, and the happy return of Newstead's 'noble line'. Byron's footnotes (though not always accurate) supplement the historical fantasy-journey of the poem with prosaic 'fact', so that the abbey becomes a synecdoche of identity within a broader self-interrogation of the kind Jerome Christensen has suggested underwrites Byron's lordship: '"What does it mean that I am noble? What does it mean to be one who *deserves* that name I have been given? On what basis do I command belief in my right to command?"'.[5] These early poems explore what it might mean to give the single answer 'Newstead' to such questions. It is a method of fashioning the self through the meaning of *place*, answering the needs of identity through physical situation and material historical memory. Of course such a method may also be open to the charge of circularity: being Byron means being Newstead Abbey, and vice versa, and it was precisely this manner of claiming one's place, this assumption that Newstead and its history spoke for himself, particularly as it was couched in Byron's preface to *Hours of Idleness* (which seemed to claim aristocratic privilege both as a reason to admire the poems and to excuse them) that Henry Brougham found most absurd when he came to write his now famous notice of the collection in the *Edinburgh Review*. Brougham made sport of the disingenuousness of the preface, and ended his review by turning to Newstead:

> What right have we poor devils to be nice? We are well off to have got so much from a man of this Lord's station, who does not live in a garret, but "has the sway" of Newstead Abbey. Again, we say, let us be thankful; and, with honest Sancho, bid God bless the giver, nor look the gift horse in the mouth.[6]

The sting of Brougham's review lay in the manner in which it exploited Byron's own uncertainties about his place (the warning against vanity is implicit in the Macpherson epigraph), and presented Newstead as an empty cipher. It is one of the inherent dangers in Byron's method of naming places and one clear from the very first poem in his first public collection, that such a method wrought to the extreme would merely become a form of name-dropping, part of an easy aristocratic idiom mimicked by Brougham in the phrase 'has the sway'. In probably the most well-known poem of the collection, 'Lachin Y Gair', the mountain of the Northern Highlands is recalled in order to summon Byron's maternal ancestors the Gordons, in turn to remember Culloden. The note to the poem confesses to a process of concentrating history into place and name: 'Whether any perished in the Battle of Culloden, I am not certain; but as many fell in the insurrection, I have used the name of the principal action, "Pars pro toto"'.[7] The flaws in this are obvious. If the part is to stand for the whole, then the part must be fully possessed, not merely taken for granted. To what extent can a place-name stand in for history and identity?

At the time of the publication of *Hours of Idleness* Newstead Abbey had a tenant. A further poem dating from 1807, though discreetly left out of the collection, was entitled 'To an Oak in the Garden of Newstead Abbey, planted by the Author in the 9th Year of his age; this tree at his last visit was in a state of decay, though perhaps not irrecoverable. – 15th March 1807'. Lord Grey de Ruthyn, Newstead's tenant, is the 'stranger' dwelling in 'the hall of my sire' until Byron obtains his majority, and whose neglect explains the drooping state of the tree. Whereas the earlier poems in the collection summoned ancestors and their death-places, this cousin-poem conjures future generations of the family visiting Newstead and remembering Byron:

> And as he, with his boys, shall revisit the spot,
>   He will tell them in whispers more softly to tread.
> Ah! surely, by these I shall ne'er be forgot:
>   Remembrance still hallows the dust of the dead.

> (ll.33–6)

If Byron habitually thinks of place in terms of 'pars pro toto', and in doing so allows 'place' to stand in for recovered historical subjectivity, a process Brougham's review disallowed, there is nevertheless a tension within his writing between an assumed potency in the place-name (the possibility of places standing in for history), and the suspicion that this may merely be a method of name-dropping or a rehearsal of commonplaces. Nevertheless, the most important tool in the synecdochic process of 'pars pro toto' is the little word 'spot' ('And as he, with his boys, shall revisit the spot'), a word almost talismanic in Byron's writing, which emerges from the discourse of the picturesque and particularly from Gilpin's injunction to record landscape impressions 'on the spot' in the 1790 essays. It will later be interiorised and temporalised by Wordsworth, and, partly through Byron, finds its way into the language of tourism as disseminated by the first handbooks provided by John Murray III in the late 1830s/ early 1840s.[8] As such it is a word both uniquely central to Byron's imagination and already something of a cliché. Being there on the spot, having been there on the spot, composing on the spot, having made observations on the spot – the word registers the authority of direct personal knowledge and experience of a place, as well as suggesting a particular concentration of perception. Frequently (as here) it is, as it were, the smallest part standing for the whole: the spot stands for Newstead, and represents the exact place where, in the future, Newstead will stand for Lord Byron.

Byron makes this word work harder than any other in his writing. The 'spot' marks where history happened, and will have happened, and in doing so promises that this history may be recoverable. Often the word is accompanied with a quasi-mystical or magical sense of access to the past; it stands both for geo-historical site and the written *topos*, yielding the one to the other. Moreover, the word both releases and is bound up with the cross-currents of nostalgia. These 'spots' are places of historical inscription where the past marks the present and can be *read*, but they are also places where the present will be most vividly recollected as the past, as history; moreover, they are places where the present or recent past will be imaginatively reconstructed as a future to the deeper past. Dante's Ravenna, Tasso's Ferrara, Doge Faliero's Venice: particular 'spots' in each of these cities inspire Byron to write poems set in historical moments and places, and to prophesy the future for those places. The idea of the 'spot' is one of immediate access to an inter-subjective experience of history.

Treading softly on certain special 'spots' then, in places hallowed or haloed, is a motif vividly present at the beginning of Byron's writing-life and never to disappear. The father enjoining his sons to tread softly around Newstead Abbey is moreover an eerie anticipation of the fourth significant poem Byron addressed to the abbey on his return to England from the continent in 1811, shortly after receiving news of his mother's death. This darker untitled poem fails to take comfort in either ancestral or projected lineage, it cannot summon ghosts from the past or the future, and the footsteps it listens to belong solely to Byron: 'And the step that o'erechoes the gray floor of stone / Falls sullenly now, for 'tis only my own' (ll.9–10). The sullen echo is partly explained by the fact that Newstead had been under threat for two years from the lawyer John Hanson's repeated encouragement to sell the estate, so that the symbolic interchange of identity between the young poet and the abbey had come to seem like a desperate last stand. Writing to his mother in March 1809 Byron had made perfectly explicit, as he would again and again in his letters from the East, that the rhetorical strategies of the poems in *Hours of Idleness* were serious; the part stood for the whole:

> What you say is all very true, come what may! *Newstead* and I *stand* or fall together, I have now lived on the spot, I have fixed my heart upon it, and no pressure present or future, shall induce me to barter the last vestige of our inheritance; I have that Pride within me, which will enable me to support difficulties, I can endure privations, but could I obtain in exchange for Newstead Abbey the first fortune in the country, I would reject the proposition. – Set your mind at ease on that score. Mr Hanson talks like a man of Business on that subject, I feel like a man of honour, and I will not sell Newstead.[9]

Newstead, like the Coliseum to Rome, stands with and for the young Byron (he has lived upon the spot and fixed his heart upon it). But it is important to remember that this was a metonymic exchange that was threatening to break apart for a large part of Byron's writing career. Byron writes with the sharpest personal knowledge that the interchangeability of self and place is insecure, even as his work is a form of resistance to such knowledge. And if the celebrated notion of *mobilité* gives us any useful insight into Byron's 'personality' then it does so in a literal sense as much as any other: place was central to Byron's fashioning of himself, and Byron's places were constantly changing.

There may also of course be more than one place at one time. While the patrimonial link of name and place seemed in some *de facto* sense ruined in Newstead, the other place foregrounded in Byron's first collection, namely Harrow school, represented an alternative model of identity. Pastoral, feminised Harrow (or 'Ida! blest spot...'[10]) offers a classical counterpart to Newstead's Gothic, and as such completes the structure of subjectivity around which *Hours of Idleness* is organised. Byron originally had plans to publish his first collection with a frontispiece plate either of Harrow or Newstead, but in fact only the successor volume, *Poems Original and Translated* (1808) carried a lithograph of Harrow school.[11] It is possible that he chose not to make up his mind between the two candidates for this honour earlier since *Hours of Idleness* works partly around the principle of contrast and complementarity between the worlds of Harrow and Newstead – feudal ancestry and classical education; violence and leisure; patrimonial imperatives and boy-friendships – while it is an important effect of the whole collection that these two nexi are mutually inclusive. If Byron thinks in terms of 'pars pro toto', it is equally important to grasp the paradox that there are quite different parts standing for the same whole.

For Harrow, the collection develops a languid nostalgia for his old school as an Arcadia, the nourisher of a cult of boy-friendship and a deep sentimental attachment to the 'spot' or the 'scenes' of Byron's youth, 'A home, a world, a paradise to me' ('Childish Recollections' l.218). As with Newstead, Byron's attachment is figured in valedictory terms – Harrow is first in the list of places to which Byron says farewell in 'The Adieu. Written under the impression that the author would soon die'; the others, in order, being Cambridge, Loch na Garr, Newstead and Southwell. 'Lines Written Beneath an Elm, in the Churchyard of Harrow on the Hill' relishes the thought of dying just there, a prospect Byron would privately entertain when close to fighting a duel with a certain Mr Twiddie in January 1808.[12] When Allegra died in 1822, Byron would try to have her buried in the graveyard of Harrow church. The attempt was blocked by the church warden.

But like Newstead, Harrow is a place where it may be impossible not to discover a Byronism already highly developed, and developed precisely through the synecdochic process of investing meaning and identity in certain 'spots'.[13] Byron's identity becomes most immediately vivid, most available through these exchanges with place and place-name, and many of the later strategies of his authorship are encoded, as it were, within the shorthand of such a process. In particular the erotico-sentimental cult of male attachment remained something most closely associated with the name of Harrow school and its 'blessed spot' throughout Byron's life. From the beginning such a cult is being constructed in terms of nostalgia, as if it lay in a distant past remembered from a distant point in the future. Harrow provides a sense of *generation*, belonging to a peer group bound to a particular historical moment which is both an identity and an allegiance of sorts (marked out for Byron in Harrow, rather than Cambridge). On repeated return-visits to the school Byron quickly perceived the sense of having become 'obsolete', but the perception of accelerated obsolescence and its relation to nostalgia would become an important part of later works, central to the English cantos of *Don Juan*, as I shall argue.[14] In fact Harrow stood for a particular kind of nostalgia, a complex sense of belonging while no longer belonging; belonging to a place which survives both the departure from that place and the keener separation of historical obsolescence. The shared language in which Harrovians would reveal this allegiance to each other and mourn its being-in-the-past, was the literary language of Latin and Greek, most especially within its own mode of nostalgic longing. This produces a strangely inlayered form of nostalgia-within-nostalgia, which, again, would become (or is from the very beginning) distinctively Byronic. Writing to an old-Harrovian friend, William Harness, about his travels of 1809–11, Byron drew upon this shared language of male friendship and lament in explicitly nostalgic terms:

> Be assured I have not changed, in all my ramblings, Harrow & of course *yourself* never left me, and the
> –"dulces reminiscitur Argos"
> attended me to the very spot to which that semi-line alludes in the mind of the fallen Argive.[15]

The phrase is in fact 'dulces moriens reminiscitur Argos' ('dying remembers sweet Argos'), reported of Antores, Argive friend of Hercules, in Virgil's *Aeneid*, X, l.781. Byron, who wanted to die at Harrow rather than anywhere else, may have elided that 'moriens' ('dying') consciously or not. But here, Harrow, and male friendship, shared knowledge of Virgil, Virgil's own representation of nostalgia, and Byron's authority in having visited Argos, are all gathered and concentrated in the notion of the 'very spot', as if only *there* can the potency of this nexus be comprehended and experienced. As if the 'very spot' is the ground of the authenticity of all these values and emotional investments: a place which is both Harrow and Arcadia, and the absence of Harrow and Arcadia. Byron had been *there* on that very spot. In fact the 'classical' for Byron will always be most vividly (and later most problematically) connected to specific places or spots, very many of which in some sense point to an originary nostalgia experienced for Harrow and the Latin and Greek authors read there. It was a fine slip of the pen or tongue which produced the rumour late in 1811 that Byron's forthcoming production would be titled 'Childe of Harrow's Pilgrimage'.[16]

1.2 'I was present'

From the beginning of Byron's writing life, then, the place, or more specifically the 'spot' which stands for the essence of the place, simultaneously speaks for itself *and* for Byron, so that geo-history and self-identity are interchangeable, or assumed to be so. Inevitably, however, some spots speak louder than others. The preface to *Hints from Horace* (written 1811; revised 1821; posthumously published 1831) puts it like this:

Though it be one of the obnoxious egotisms of authorship to state when or where a work was composed, I must incur this censure by stating that the following Imitation was begun and finished at Athens the only spot on earth which may partly apologise for such a declaration[17]

There was no such faux apology at the head of *The Curse of Minerva*, which vaunted the exact *where* and *when* of composition as 'Athens: Capuchin Convent, *March 17, 1811*', even though most of this particular poem had in fact been drafted in November 1811, i.e. when Byron was back in England. Clearly the claim to Athens as the spot of composition is one which carries especial authority, and not merely Athens, but the famous Capuchin convent which stood at the heart of the city at the foot of the Acropolis, and from which the first map of ancient Athens had been produced – a kind of topographical centre.[18] It was a location and setting Byron had described more exactly in a letter to Francis Hodgson of January 1811:

I am living in the Capuchin Convent, Hymettus before me, the Acropolis behind, the temple of Jove to my right, the Stadium in front, the town to the left, eh, Sir, there's a situation, there's your picturesque! nothing like that, Sir, in Lunnun, no not even the Mansion House.[19]

The Curse of Minerva, printed in a limited run for private circulation, but later pirated, is a neglected though crucial document of Byron's consciousness as a traveller in the East because it is a poem about finding oneself in this situation.[20] Ostensibly written in angry reaction to the activities of Thomas Bruce, seventh Earl of Elgin, the poem is not merely an exercise in invective (although as such it is extreme), but a subtle and conflicted meditation upon the responsibilities of imperial power. The celebrated opening section of the piece describing an Athenian sunset, which Byron had plans to publish separately as 'A Fragment' and later placed at the beginning of the third canto of the *The Corsair*, expands the 'situation' the poet had described to Hodgson to include a wide expanse of the Morea, the islands of Aegina, Hydra, the gulf of Salamis, Delphi, Hymettus and the Aegean. This 'magic shore' is a spot where, for Byron, the 'past returned'. Alone among moonlit ruins he confronts the broken figure of Minerva who directs the poet to observe his surroundings ('*These* Crecops placed, *this* Pericles adorn'd'); and then to note Elgin's graffitoed name upon the ruins he has plundered. A careful distinction is drawn between England (variously identified as 'Britain' or 'Albion') and Scotland – Elgin belonging to the latter, or Caledonia (described in relation to Britain as Boeotia is to Greece). In fact Elgin, like Byron, was half-Scottish, and more importantly, Byron, like Elgin, was a peer of the British imperial realm. Therefore although Scottishness is the first ostensible target of the poem – a long passage of anti-Scottish animus portrays that 'bastard land'(l.131) as a place of 'niggard earth'(l.135), 'A land of meanness, sophistry and mist'(l.138), the Scots 'Foul as their soil and frigid as their snows'(l.142) – Scotland is merely something to which Byron *in part* belongs, and as such disguises and deflects the poem's hidden anxiety about also partly belonging to the imperial projects of one's own nation, which would include the policy of propping up the Ottoman empire in Greece against the threat from Russia.[21] From the merging of national character with natural landscape, the poem turns to prophetic survey of Britain and the British Empire, Minerva's curse falling upon the dilettantish philhellenism of the London art-world in a parody of the social rituals surrounding the viewing of the Elgin marbles. Elgin's plunder of Greece is then specifically compared to British imperial interests and activities, and in a move Byron frequently repeats in his writing, the present is represented *as if* it were a prophecy of the future. So, Minerva 'predicts' British foreign policy disasters in the Baltic of 1807–8; refers to insurrection (possibly the Madras mutiny of 1809) in Central India;[22] suggests that the victory at Barossa (1811) may not have been the glorious conquest many had claimed it to be; and finally turns to 'home' and English domestic politics, particularly the financial crisis of 1811. Minerva describes a Britain bankrupted by war, the continued hostilities with France merely preliminary troubles after and due to which European conflagration will be revisited upon 'Albion'. The extraordinary final passage of the poem transposes and re-imagines the opening Athenian sunset in terms of a London skyline set alight by revolutionary fire:

> Would flying burghers mark the blazing town?
> How view the column of ascending flames,
> Shake his red shadow o'er the startl'd Thames?
> Nay frown not, Albion! for the torch was thine
> That lit such pyres from Tagus to the Rhine:
> Now should they burst on thy devoted coast,
> Go, ask thy bosom who deserves them most.
> The law of Heaven and Earth is life for life,
> And she who rais'd, in vain regrets the strife.

(ll.304–11)

That the transportation of marbles from the Acropolis by a (half) Scottish peer should somehow signal the collapse of the British Empire at home and abroad, may seem radically over-reaching in its web of cause and effect, responsibility and guilt, violence and counter-violence. But the poem is centrally concerned not with the 'local' question of Lord Elgin, but with the very inter-connectedness of localities in a global matrix of imperial interest, and the wide-ranging campaigns of war. Elgin himself is, as it were, a synecdoche – he stands for brutalising imperial interests achieved in the name of higher ideals, and it is precisely the darker significance of the part–whole relation that *The Curse of Minerva* uncovers. The despoliation of the Acropolis (and the fact that it was not prevented) is an image of the political misuse of power on a global scale, in particular the British policy of supporting Turkish interests in Greece. At the same time Athens, which in some sense 'stands for' Western civilisation, is reduced to the vulnerable status of a local conflict of interests – no longer a whole, but fragmented and reduced. There may even be an aesthetic analogy here with Byron's own negative reaction to the marbles themselves, which in their 'mutilated' and fragmented condition offended his neo-classical tastes.[23] What is beyond doubt is that Byron's venom towards Lord Elgin is partly explained in terms of his instinct for taking the *pars pro toto*, but also by a broader sense of impotence in the face of British imperial power; moreover, by the curious sense of divided identity experienced by a classically educated liberal-minded English nobleman living in Athens. Venom towards the activities of British peers abroad had already surfaced in *English Bards and Scots Reviewers* in the form of anti-antiquarianism, and poured out in the notes accompanying the first canto of *Childe Harold's Pilgrimage*. Antiquarianism is overtly linked with class-interest and customs, with the leisure activities of the aristocracy, and so with a grand-tourism which is represented as an insidious form of imperial conquest:

> While he [Elgin's agent Lusieri] and his patrons confine themselves to tasting medals, appreciating cameos, sketching columns, and cheapening gems, their little absurdities are as harmless as insect or fox-hunting, maiden-speechifying, barouche-driving, or any such pastime: but when they carry away three or four shiploads of the most valuable and massy relics that time and barbarism have left to the most injured and most celebrated of cities; when they destroy, in a vain attempt to tear down, those works which have been the admiration of the ages, I know no motive which can excuse, no name which can designate, the perpetrators of this dastardly devastation.[24]

The curious self-implications of the first part of this passage are striking. Byron had himself maiden-speechified in February 1812, had frequently toured sites and dined with Lusieri in Athens – it was with Hobhouse and Lusieri that Byron first visited the Acropolis in January 1810 – and had himself hired an artist to sketch views of Greece.[25] He had also helped his friend John Cam Hobhouse transport marbles out of Greece and had himself stolen a copy of the famous 'Geography' of Meletius from the archbishop of Chrysso in 1809.[26] Elgin's act of scratching his name on to the stones was a common one among aristocratic travellers, and one repeated by Byron in various locations around Greece, perhaps even on the Acropolis itself.[27] We might simply want to call this hypocrisy; or we might prefer to say that Byron's philhellenism is a complex phenomenon, perhaps partly involving a sense of guilt or self-incrimination, or at least involving an uneasy sense of implication. The very notion of *being there*, 'Athens: Capuchin Convent, *March 17, 1811*', becomes ambivalent in this context. For the second edition of *Childe Harold's Pilgrimage* cantos one and two Byron availed himself of information provided by his friend and classical scholar Edward Daniel Clarke to add 'tenfold weight to my testimony' in a note to the famous stanzas describing Lord Elgin's activities. Byron quotes Clarke's anecdote:

> 'When the last of the Metopes was taken from the Parthenon, and, in moving of it, great part of the superstructure with one of the triglyphs was thrown down by the workmen whom Lord Elgin employed, the Disdar, who beheld the mischief done to the building, took his pipe from his mouth, dropped a tear, and, in a supplicating tone of voice, said to Lusieri; *Telos*! – I was present.'[28]

The Disdar's acknowledgement of bearing witness to this destruction is couched in the past tense, 'I was present', as if anticipating the future moment when that fact would be remembered. Naturally, the notion of *being there* is projected forward to a moment when it *will have been* true: 'Athens, Capuchin Convent, *March 17, 1811*', is recorded for just such a future moment. But in the Disdar's case the claim to having been present is partly one of impotent shame and guilt. This stands as a negative or reverse image of Byron's own insistent claims for authenticity in having composed poetry at the foot of the Acropolis, his own reiterated claim to have been present in a more felicitous sense. But just as Lusieri and his patrons seem strangely close to Byron and his Athenian circle, so the Disdar here also seems in a sense to speak directly for the poet himself. The interaction of note and text in this case is delicate, but the very notion of *being there* may, in the case of Athens, partly involve a regret, or an unease, perhaps even an oblique self-incrimination which is displaced and removed, but which nevertheless is registered. Being present, as Byron was, at different times in different locations across the imperial map of Europe produces an ambivalent perspective upon the whole, and creates a sense in which Lusieri and the Disdar assume the part of Byronic *doppelgängers*. The strange apocalyptic conclusion of *The Curse of Minerva* in which the skyline of London burns like an Athenian sunset and the network of responsibility is traced *across* the imperialist map, arises from just this sense of ambivalence. Having been there, 'Athens: Capuchin Convent', is a mark of authenticity in a literary sense, but it also marks the experience of being where imperial interests hold sway, and of belonging, in a national sense, to an imperial power hostile to Greek independence. The debate about Lord Elgin's acquisitions took place in the broader context of rivalry between France and Britain in the rush to gather antiquities, as well as in relation to the perceived hostility of Turkey to such an enterprise. The despoliation (or rescue) of the Parthenon marbles is therefore a struggle of conflicting imperial interests in which the non-imperial power cannot actively participate. Whether one argues for or against Elgin, the claims and significance of the city of Athens amount simply to those of passive victim. The restoration of the freedom and glory of Athens, like the restoration of the marbles to their original wholeness, is not possible in the circumstances – except through simulation (the kind of administrative 'freedom' offered Athens as a Turkish protectorate; or the kind of 'restoration' Lord Elgin had requested Canova to undertake with the marbles).[29] In these circumstances, being in Athens, in this 'situation', would also of course be an experience of the unbridgeable distance between the historic past and the imperial present, as well as representing, in itself, an experience of the contiguous but radically unequal localities of the European imperial map: Byron's joke about the Mansion House in London registers this uneasy contiguity, this interconnection which is also a sign of difference or discontinuity. The neo-classical splendour of the Mansion House may pay architectural homage to Athens, but as a sign of British imperial strength it is also a (self)-parody. This anxiety about *being there* and what that might mean becomes focused for Byron in the idea of the *genius loci* and emerges most directly in *Childe*

Harold's despairing appeal to the tutelary spirits of the Acropolis who failed to prevent its spoliation by Elgin:

> Where was thine Aegis, Pallas! that appall'd
> Stern Alaric and Havoc on their way?
> Where Peleus' son? whom Hell in vain enthrall'd,
> His shade from Hades upon that dread day,
> Bursting to light in terrible array!
> What? could not Pluto spare the chief once more,
> To scare a second robber from his prey?
> Idly he wander'd on the Stygian shore,
> Nor now preserv'd the walls he lov'd to shield before.

(II.14).

Since Hazlitt's observation that the author of *Childe Harold* described 'the stately cypress, or the fallen column, with the feeling that every schoolboy has about them', one tendency has been to read stanzas like this as rehearsals of clichés, or the attitudes of the sentimental traveller.[30] But the very notion of the commonplace (here: the disappearance of the glory of the Acropolis, and the inability of Athenian history to intervene in the present), is radically altered when taken out of a merely textual and a-historical setting (that of every schoolboy) and returned to its actual place. Byron himself had been there and had composed upon the spot. In this context the experience of *being there* and yet being unable to intervene, so forcefully registered by the Disdar, calls into question what being there may actually mean, and is replayed here in the pressure put upon the trope of the *genius loci*. Where were the guardian spirits of place to protect Athens from desecration? Against hostile predators (whether they be art-collectors or invading armies) what meaning has the notion of a spirit-of-place? How strong is this trope when faced with the pressures of imperial interests? Is there anything in the historical palimpsest of memory-in-place that can offer resistance to aggression? And if not, then what is the significance of writing about the 'sacredness' of these 'magic spots'? In what sense are they either sacred or magic?[31] In short, these questions take poetic commonplaces ('Where was thine Aegis, Pallas!'), and deepen their resonance by returning them to their common places in a specific historical context. The questioning of impotent place-spirits then becomes an interrogation of the very act of poetic composition in such a place, indeed an interrogation of the very meaning of the 'classical' – the *genius loci* is perhaps *the* primary trope English poetics had inherited from the ancient world, and so its insecurity becomes self-reflexive. The poet who is a peer of the imperial realm the interests of which were served by Elgin's plunder, the Disdar who witnessed the stripping of the Acropolis, and the tutelary spirits of the Acropolis itself, are all *there* and *not there* at once. They are compelled to bear witness, and to bear witness to their witnessing; but their presence is also cancelled out or neutralised by their relation to imperial power. Such questions are recurrent and central ones in Byron's writing, and are asked unflinchingly. A tension between the sacred and inviolable sense of place on the one hand, and the possibility that the *genius loci* may be an empty and powerless trope on the other, a classical ruin, complicates the notion of a commonplace response to the 'stately cypress and fallen column', but does so only through the reality of having been there on the spot where cliché and commonplace become alive and resonant. *Being there* becomes the indelible marker both of geo-historical continuity and discontinuity, of imperial interconnection *and* inequality. This is the way in which an individual human consciousness experiences what the larger forces of history, familiar to every schoolboy, actually mean for a specific place at a specific time. But it is *only* the fact of being there that enables this tension properly to reveal itself, and to play itself out in Byron's writing.

1.3   Places without a name

To read Byron is to be captivated by this fact. The claim for an authority of direct and first hand *experience* (the 'Chief philosopher' as *Don Juan* puts it) is the most central and consistent aspect of his poetry and prose, letters and journals, and enshrined in the opening sentence of the preface to *Childe Harold's Pilgrimage*: 'The following poem was written, for the most part, amidst the scenes which it attempts to describe'.[32] Byron's maiden speech in the House of Lords, 27 February 1812, against the Bill making frame-breaking a capital offence, was 'founded upon these opinions formed from my own observations on ye. spot', as he assured Lord Holland.[33] When John Murray expressed reservations concerning the stanzas on Spain and Portugal in the first canto of *Childe Harold*, Byron responded with the same claim: 'On Spanish affairs I have said what I saw, & every day confirms me in that notion of the result formed on the Spot'.[34] The very brevity, even curtness of that little word 'spot' puts an end or a stop to the argument. Writing to Charles Dallas at the end of August 1811, Byron reveals his working method in compiling the extensive footnotes to the first two cantos of *Childe Harold*: 'I have found among my poor Mother's papers all my Letters from the East, & one in particular of some length from Albania, from this (if necessary) I can work up a note or two on that subject; as I kept no journal, the letters written on the Spot are the next best.'[35]

But Albania represented a very different experience of 'spots' to Athens, and the joint enterprise Byron and Hobhouse undertook to acquaint British readers with the present state of modern Greece and Albania was partly a response to the uneasy 'situation' of the classical, and its relation to imperial realities. Byron's *Childe Harold's Pilgrimage* appeared before Hobhouse's *Journey Through Albania and Other Provinces in Turkey in 1809–10* (1813), though Byron had supplied Hobhouse with information and helped him organise the materials for his separate prose account, and had diluted his own Romaic specimens in the lengthy appendages to the poem so that there should not be too much overlapping between the two works.[36] Describing Albania as 'untrodden ground',[37] Byron's impulse to supplement his poem with extensive notes, surveys and examples of the present state of society and literature in Greece and Albania was precisely in order to gain an alternative kind of authority to that displayed by classical or antiquarian travel-writing and ancient Greek scholarship. In this case, *being on the spot* would create authority anew, rather than drawing upon an existing guarantee. Rigorously committed to the here-and-now, Byron's notes therefore represent a form of anti-antiquarianism, or counter-connoisseurship, rooted in a present reality of which he and Hobhouse, and few other English travellers, had direct experience. Moreover, the determination to concentrate upon a present reality would counter-check the rhetoric of the 'magic spots' and 'consecrated ground' associated with the trope of the *genius loci*, a rhetoric which in its very mystery and intangibility may have seemed not wholly adequate to the situation in modern Greece. Anxieties about belonging, and responsibility, might also in part be allayed by writing about a place like Albania which escaped the representational categories of the 'classical'. A note to the second canto introduces Albania to English readers ('Albania comprises part of Macedonia, Illyria, Chaonia, and Epirus'), before staking its claim to what amounts to discovery:

> Of Albania Gibbon remarks, that a country 'within sight of Italy is less known than the interior of America'. Circumstances, of little consequence to mention, led Mr. Hobhouse and myself into that

country before we visited any other part of the Ottoman dominions; and with the exception of Major Leake, then officially resident at Joannina, no other Englishmen have ever advanced beyond the capital into the interior, as that gentlemen very lately assured me.[38]

Writing in May 1810 to his Harrovian friend (the son of his ex-headmaster) Henry Drury aboard the Salsette frigate 'in the Dardanelles off Abydos', Byron had pushed the claim even further to suggest that there were parts of this undiscovered country which were worthier of notice than the most famous sites of classical Greece:

Albania indeed I have seen more of than any Englishman (but a Mr. Leake) for it is a country rarely visited from the savage character of the natives, though abounding in more natural beauties than the classical regions of Greece, which however are still eminently beautiful, particularly Delphi, and Cape Colonna in Attica. – Yet these are nothing to parts of Illyria, and Epirus, where places without a name, and rivers not laid down in maps, may one day when more known be justly esteemed superior subjects for the pencil, and the pen, than the dry ditch of the Ilissus, and the bogs of Boeotia.[39]

This sense that knowledge of a discovered country would offer an alternative to the authority of classical topography saturates the notes to the first two cantos of *Childe Harold*, whether championing the superiority of the lesser-known river Laos ('as wide as the Thames at Westminster... neither Achelous, Alpheus, Acheron, Scamander nor Cayster, approached it in breadth or beauty'[40]) or suggesting that events in Albanian history matched those of heroic Greece.[41] The forty-sixth stanza of the second canto phrases it this way:

> From the dark barriers of that rugged clime,
> Ev'n to the centre of Illyria's vales,
> Childe Harold pass'd o'er many a mount sublime,
> Through lands scarce notic'd in historic tales;
> Yet in fam'd Attica such lovely dales
> Are rarely seen; nor can fair Tempe boast
> A charm they know not; lov'd Parnassus fails,
> Though classic ground and consecrated most,
> To match some spots that lurk within this lowering coast.

(II.46)

The phrase 'classic ground and consecrated most' hints at the inertia of places overburdened with historical association, suggests that in ancient fame there is also something debilitating, and again expresses the unease I have been describing in Byron's relation to Greece. Whether 'consecrated' ground means simply 'written-about', or whether it has a more durable, sacred and invulnerable meaning, is uncertain. Can there be a ratio of consecration, as implied by 'consecrated *most*'? Moreover, 'classic ground' serves 'classic' as a moribund adjective, a measure of the gap between an actual place and a famous place-name. Parnassus 'fails' to speak for itself in this instance, while 'places without a name, and rivers not laid down in maps' offer what is perceived to be a healthy escape from the inscriptions of history. The political dimension to such revisionist endeavour is clear; its commitment to the presently subjugated and disenfranchised regions of the Ottoman Empire is linked to Byron's questioning of the trope of the *genius loci* and its significance in the realm of European *Realpolitik*. The notes mean to be recuperative of historical events lost to classical historiography, 'discovering' anonymous places, standing against British aristocratic antiquarianism and the casual imperialism of the grand tour. They represent a latent suspicion of classicism as something complicit with a turning-away from present realities (realities that Byron and Hobhouse *know* directly); or as an ideological disguise for the politics of imperialism. The very insistence that Albania is a country in its own right with a distinct national identity and culture, while partly contained within the borders of what was thought of as classical Greece, is a radical challenge to the hegemony not only of the Ottoman Empire, but to the cultural hegemony represented by philhellenism in the West. Perhaps the most vivid descriptive passages of the first two cantos are those describing Ali Pasha's court at Tepalen: cosmopolitan, hierarchical, exotic, where 'the Albanian proudly treads the ground' (II.59), a pocket of sophisticated court-culture quite distinct from Graeco-Christian traditions. Even among the Greeks it is not Athens, but Joannina that Byron insists is their first city: 'superior in the wealth, refinement, learning, and dialect of its inhabitants'.[42] All this relied upon the fact of having been there themselves, and it was painfully important to Byron and Hobhouse that Albania remained their own special subject in this respect, unthreatened by rival authorities. Going to dine with Dr Clarke, the famous Cambridge classicist who had provided Byron with the anecdote about the Parthenon's metopes, Byron confided with glee to Hobhouse that, 'I find he knows little of Romaic, so we shall have *that department* entirely to ourselves, I tell you this that you need not fear any competition.'[43]

That department had been won through experience and both were fiercely protective of it, enjoying the exposure of other would-be-authority's inaccuracies and errors.[44] This was a pleasure that reached its climax in the third lengthy appended note to the second canto of *Childe Harold*, a note significantly headed with the same dating and placing (only the denomination is a variant) as *The Curse of Minerva*, i.e. 'Athens, Franciscan Convent, March 17, 1811.'[45] Here Byron is responding to an *Edinburgh Review* article of April 1810, in which the reviewer had 'introduced some remarks on the modern Greeks and their literature' and had criticised one of the translators of a French *Geographie de Strabon* for his lack of knowledge of the Romaic. The authority conferred by the convent in Athens as the place of composition is again invoked as a protecting and vindicating frame, its own self-authorisation, but in this case being in Athens does not produce an uneasy sense of the 'classical', but exactly the opposite. The spot of composition is proof of a legitimate knowledge of the modern: 'On those remarks I mean to ground a few observations, and the spot where I now write will I hope be sufficient excuse for introducing them in a work in some degree connected with the subject'.[46] Byron's 'few observations' extend for approximately three thousand words, and treat of modern Greek translators and compilers of grammars and lexicons, education systems, dialects, epistolary style, language history, and a list of British travellers who *might* have provided the same information: 'Sir W. Drummond, Mr. Hamilton, Lord Aberdeen, Dr. Clarke, Captain Leake, Mr. Gell, Mr. Walpole, and many others now in England, have all the requisites to furnish details of this fallen people.'[47] Early stanzas intended for the second canto of *Childe Harold* had named William Hamilton and Lord Aberdeen along with Lord Elgin as 'classic Thieves' for their antiquarian activities in Greece, calling upon them (with irony) to: 'Come pilfer all the Pilgrim loves to see, / And all that yet consecrates the fading scene'. These lines had eventually been replaced by the plaintive appeal to the *genii locibus* of the Acropolis who had failed to offer protection when the Parthenon was threatened ('Where was thine Aegis, Pallas!'). In other words, Byron's vigorous authority in matters Romaic is a direct rebuke to the classicist antiquarianism of such as Aberdeen and Hamilton, which was itself bound up in his own mind with imperialist anxieties and a demystifying of the trope of the *genius loci*. There was a direct connection between antiquarian pilfering and the sense of unease with the spirit-of-place, or with the notion of *being there*, and in this sense the recuperative project to introduce the West to Romaic and Albanian culture stood as both a challenge to classical knowledge and a corrective standard. Byron ends this particular short essay on the Greeks (before moving on to the Turks) with a reiteration of his earlier claim to authority through place:

> The few observations I have offered I should have left where I made them, had not the article in question, and above all the spot where I read it, induced me to advert to those pages which the advantage of my present situation enabled me to clear, or at least to make the attempt.[48]

Again the 'spot' in some sense speaks for itself, or at least commands Byron to speak for it: 'Athens, Franciscan Convent, March 17, 1811'. But in this case Athens is, as it were, speaking for a different self; not for the network of imperialist responsibility and interconnection represented in *The Curse of Minerva*, but for a modern Greece unburdened by the classical.

1.4   Being where?

The fact that the 'spot' of composition in Athens may suggest different things at different times according to Byron's rhetorical purposes says something about the promiscuous and conflicted nature even of those places singled out for an essential or absolute kind of authority. So, too, Byron frequently depicts places as inhering within other places, nesting within, or overlayering, sometimes even contaminating quite different locations, which was particularly the case in the relationship between Greece and Scotland. In the preface to *Hours of Idleness* (1807) Byron had gauchely attempted, among other things, a Scottish version of Cumbrianism, in his modest claim to have spent a childhood with 'nature':

> Though accustomed, in my younger days, to rove a careless mountaineer on the Highlands of Scotland, I have not, of late years, had the benefit of such pure air, or so elevated a residence, as might enable me to enter the lists with genuine bards, who have enjoyed both these advantages.[49]

The examples of Burns and Scott, as well as the English Wordsworth and Southey, and the Irish Tom Moore, hover behind this careless mountaineering, with the result that there is a synthetic feel to the early lyrics of pastoral nostalgia, such as 'Song: When I rov'd, a young

Highlander, o'er the dark heath', or 'Stanzas: I would I were a careless child, / Still dwelling in my Highland cave'. Scotland is never quite Scotland in Byron's early work but a place to be defined in relation to other places, or tinged with the hues of places known about through books, particularly Wordsworth's lakes and Moore's Ireland.[50] Even 'Lachin Y Gair', where Byron remembers his 'footsteps, in infancy, wandered', has a prose epigraph describing the mountain as 'one of the most sublime, and picturesque, amongst our "Caledonian Alps"'.[51] When Byron comes to write *English Bards and Scots Reviewers* (1807–8; published 1809) this embarrassed posturing is abandoned for a Juvenalian relish of the degraded nature of place, and the ready availability of stereotypes. The 'North' is pictured as dark and wild, mock-heroically disturbed and shaken by the events of 1806 when Francis Jeffrey of *The Edinburgh Review* came close to fighting a duel with Tom Moore.[52] The same uncertainty and slipperiness of belonging which later characterises Byron's treatment of Lord Elgin, is already here in the uneasy interchanges of Albion / Britain / Caledonia / Scotland / the North; and most conspicuously in the mock-invocation of a spirit of place when 'Caledonia's Goddess' (l.527) is conjured to intervene in the impending duel. A note accompanies the line:

> I ought to apologise to the worthy Deities for introducing a new Goddess with short petticoats to their notice: but, alas! what was to be done? I could not say Caledonia's Genius, it being well known there is no Genius to be found from Clackmannan to Caithness: yet without supernatural agency, how was Jeffrey to be saved? The national 'Kelpies', etc. are too unpoetical, and the 'Brownies' and 'gude neighbours' (spirits of a good disposition) refused to extricate him. A Goddess therefore has been called for the purpose, and great ought to be the gratitude of Jeffrey, seeing it is the only communication he ever held, or is likely to hold, with anything heavenly.[53]

Scottish culture is here being mocked, of course, the Caledonian Goddess is a *genius loci* without 'genius', but at the same time the mockery itself is of a recognisably Scottish tenor, and the verbal register that of *The Edinburgh Review*. In other words Scottishness is represented as essentially mock-heroic, hardened to reality, 'unpoetical' – the rational and sceptical strain that encouraged the view, first articulated by T.S. Eliot, that Byron's own half-Scottishness represented some sort of key to his writing, particularly his later writing. Undoubtedly this kind of out-and-out demystification of the notion of a metaphysical spirit-of-place anticipates *Don Juan* with its determination to keep its feet firmly on the ground, whether or not we want to call this a specifically Scottish characteristic. But the relation to the mock-heroic is a fraught one, and the refusal to acknowledge the existence of a Scottish 'genius' is not merely a snub to *The Edinburgh Review*, but an example of Byron's own sense of Scotland as a place that can only be experienced in relation to and in terms of other places, a place authentically *in*authentic, but also of course a place constantly recalled by other places, and therefore inescapable and unforgettable. The postscript to *English Bards and Scotch Reviewers* contemplates a forthcoming edition of *The Edinburgh Review* in which Byron wrongly anticipated an attack upon himself appearing. 'What a pity it is that I shall be beyond the Bosphorous', Byron writes, 'before the next number has passed the Tweed. But I yet hope to light my pipe with it in Persia.'[54] This was the pattern of Byron's relationship with Scotland (and with Scottish culture): a pursuit in which the poet makes gestures either of scornful rejection (lighting his pipe), or else is suddenly disarmed by moments of nostalgia. Returning to the subject of Francis Jeffrey in a late addition of some thirty-eight lines, later removed, to the *Hints from Horace*, and still smarting at the review of *Hours of Idleness* which he supposed Jeffrey to have written, Byron recorded his inability to forget Scotland even in the most interesting parts of his travels in the East. The rejected lines anticipate the Scottish nostalgia generated by the South-Sea landscape of *The Island* (1823), in which one place is overlayered and inset with another. As Byron stands upon the plains of Troy he cannot shake off the image of Edinburgh: 'Is it for this on Ilion I have stood, / And thought of Homer less than Holyrood? / On shore of Euxine or Aegean sea, / My hate, untravelled, fondly turned to thee'.[55] Not being able to forget Scotland in this negative sense reaches a feverish pitch in the *Curse* as we have seen, and it is not until the later cantos of *Don Juan* that some kind of *rapprochement* is finally achieved. Scotland won't go away, especially when Byron is furthest from its shores, as its likeness keeps reappearing throughout the itinerary of *Childe Harold*:

> The Arnaouts, or Albanese, struck me forcibly by their resemblance to the Highlanders of Scotland, in dress, figure, and manner of living. Their very mountains seemed Caledonian with a kinder climate. The kilt, though white; the spare, active form; their dialect, Celtic in its sound; and their hardy habits, all carried me back to Morven.[56]

Of course all childhood landscapes haunt the scenes that come after them, and Scotland for Byron, like Harrow and Newstead, would always represent a place of imaginative return. But as a place nested within other places, the 'genius' of which will always in some sense be mock-heroic, Scotland represented a different paradigm to the 'pars pro toto' exchange of Newstead and Harrow, or at least she embodied an extreme version of a general truth, which is that all places are overlayered in our perception with other places, and that the authenticity of the *genius loci* is never wholly secure or pure. Whereas the apparent impotence and invisibility of the *genii locibus* of the Parthenon cause Byron anxiety, the absent or inverted 'genius' of Caledonia offers the exhilaration of satirical summation. Both, however, raise the same essential questions about the meaning of the spirit-of-place. What is its relation to culture? How might it endure? How will it manifest itself ? Scotland, for Lord Byron, offered a burlesque of the solemn communion with the 'magic spots' of classical Greece, an inversion of 'genius' which imposed itself even as he stood upon the plains of Troy. At other moments, Scotland mixed itself in with his sentimental response to places, warming up his sense of a nostalgic ur-landscape recalled in every mountain and moor he saw. The very persistence of Scotland as a place unsettling perception or contaminating the memory, or suddenly taking the breath away, was a lesson in the psycho-dynamics of belonging or half-belonging. Irreducible to the synecdochal 'spot', resistant to the notion of 'genius', Scotland was nevertheless pervasive, and so in quite another sense essential. On the one hand stood the 'magic spots' and 'consecrated ground' of Greece; on the other the 'sophistry and mist' of Scotland. But the latter seemed to penetrate and haunt the former.

1.5   Travel plans

It was to Scotland that Byron's thoughts turned as early as August 1805, in the summer before going up to Cambridge, when, as he told Augusta, he intended 'making a tour through the Highlands, and to visit the Hebrides with a party of my friends'.[57] This is the first indication we have in the letters and journals of travel plans which were constantly to alter and shift during the course of 1805–9, and indeed after 1809 when Byron was abroad. As early as February 1806 Byron seemed to be formulating plans for a continental tour accommodated to the political exigencies of the time: 'Tis true I cannot enter France, but Germany, and the courts of Berlin, Vienna, and Petersburg, are still open', he assures his mother.[58] By August 1807 the Highland tour reappeared in a letter to Elizabeth Pigot, in which Byron describes his plan to proceed in 'a *Tandem* (a species of open Carriage) through the Western passes to Inverary, where we shall purchase *Shelties*, to enable us to view places inaccessible to *vehicular Conveyances*, on the Coast, we shall hire a vessel, & visit the most remarkable of the Hebrides, & if we have time & favourable weather mean to sail as far as Iceland only 300 miles from the Northern extremity of Caledonia, to peep at *Hecla*'.[59] Some of the desire for the difficult and 'untrodden' which was to find its satisfaction in Albania is already apparent here, as Byron anticipates writing some stanzas 'on Mount *Hecla*' where 'on' means both subject and place of composition. So too the recuperative aspect of the Albanian enterprise is anticipated in Byron's intention to gather materials (as Scott had for the Border country), and to publish them in a book: 'I mean to collect all the Erse traditions, poems, & &c. & translate, or expand the subjects, to fill a volume, which may appear next Spring, under the Denomination of *"the Highland Harp"* or some title equally *picturesque*'.[60]

But plans change. Writing again to Elizabeth Pigot in October 1807, Byron expressed his intention to go to sea for four or five months with his relative George Bettesworth, captain of the *Tartar*: 'We are probably going to the Mediterranean, or to the West Indies, or to the Devil.'[61] Four months later, in February 1808, the destination had changed again, as Byron told old-Harrovian James De Bathe: 'In January *1809* I shall be twenty one, and in the Spring of the same year proceed abroad, not on the usual tour, but a route of a more extensive description, what say you? are you disposed for a view of the Pelopennesus? [and a?] voyage through the Archipelago?'[62] By October 1808 Byron was announcing to his mother his 'departure for Persia in March (or May at farthest)'.[63] The following month his mother was told that he would 'sail for India, which I expect to do in March, if nothing particularly obstructive occurs'.[64] John Hanson is informed later that month (November 1808) that the destination was to be India: 'I have written to Government for letters and permission of the Company [East India Company], so you see I am *serious*'.[65] But these plans failed to materialise and early in 1809 Byron is planning to sail 'with Ld. Falkland in the Desiree Frigate for Sicily'.[66] Falkland was killed in a duel before he could set sail, and so in April 1809 Byron is informing John Hanson that he has 'taken the Malta Packet for May'.[67] In May the Reverend Robert Lowe, a cousin of Elizabeth Pigot, is told that 'I sail for Gibraltar in June, and thence to Malta.'[68] Waiting in June at Falmouth to board the Lisbon packet, the *Princess Elizabeth*, Byron writes to his mother suggesting that if his financial situation does not improve he will 'enter the Austrian or Russian service, perhaps the Turkish'.[69] Byron sailed for Lisbon on 2 July 1809.

Byron's plans became no more fixed once he had begun to travel. The long letter written to his mother describing the court of Ali Pasha from Prevesa in November 1809, looks ahead vaguely: 'I shall not enter Asia for a year or two as I have much to see in Greece & I may perhaps cross into Africa at least the Ægyptian part.'[70] From Smyrna in March 1810 Byron was informing his mother of plans to travel to Constantinople, whence he 'shall determine whether to proceed into Persia'.[71] From Constantinople Byron wrote to John Hanson late in June 1810 announcing that he would not return to England 'for two years at least'.[72] At other times he stressed that he had no plans at all to return to England, or would pass through England en route: 'Englonde, Malta, Sicily, Ægypt, or the Low Countries'.[73] 'I am very undecided in my intentions', Byron informed Hobhouse, who had returned to England, 'though stationary enough as you perceive by my date. – [Byron was writing from the Capuchin convent in Athens] I sometimes think of moving homewards in Spring & sometimes of not moving at all till I have worn out my shoes which are all as good as new.'[74] The Capuchin convent offered a situation, or a situatedness, which, as we have seen, was useful to Byron. Nevertheless, even in the letter to Francis Hodgson of January 1811 rhapsodising this particular place ('eh, Sir, there's a situation'), Byron is projecting travel plans beyond his present location, suggesting a tour 'some summer to Wales or Scotland'.[75] Just a few days later he is writing to Hanson to announce: 'As I have just received a firman from the Porte enabling me to proceed to Ægypt & Syria I shall not return to England before I have seen Jerusalem & Grand Cairo.'[76] 'I am off in Spring', he told Hobhouse, 'for Mount Sion, Damascus, Tyre & Sidon, Cairo & Thebes.'[77]

It is not until May 1811 that Byron seems to think seriously of returning home, and even then it is merely 'probably'.[78] Even aboard the frigate *Volgate* on his way home in mid-June of 1811, Byron is writing to Hobhouse with thoughts of travel, teasing his friend for his recent commission into the army: 'If you will be mad or martial ('tis the same thing) go to Portugal again & I'll go with you (for I have some serious thoughts of it if matters are intricate at home).'[79] And to Hodgson (again written from the *Volgate*) Byron is even more decided (in his indecision): 'In short I am sick, & sorry, & when I have a little repaired my irreparable affairs, away I shall march, either to campaign in Spain, or back again to the East.'[80]

Concurrent with these changing plans is the composition of the first two cantos of *Childe Harold's Pilgrimage* (revised when Byron returned to England). In July 1811 Byron submitted the manuscript to the publisher William Miller, who was wary of the effect Byron's unorthodox religious and political views might have, and who seems to have objected in terms of the unevenness of the poem. Byron responded:

> I am perfectly aware of the Justice of your remarks, & am convinced that if ever the poem is published the same objections will be made in much stronger terms. – But as it was intended to be a poem on *Ariosto's plan*, that *is* to *say* on *no plan* at all, & as is usual in similar cases having a predilection for the worst passages I shall retain those parts though I cannot venture to defend them.[81]

There is clearly more than an analogous relationship here between the generic conception of the poem in terms of the wanderings and structural flexibilities of Romance, and the 'no plan' of the actual travel itinerary upon which the poem was based. *Childe Harold* emerges from a two-year journey (planned and re-planned for three or four years), which is characterised by its lack of a consistent plan, its changing directions and shifting intentions partly shaped by the external exigencies enforced by the political map of Europe at this time.[82] One critically orthodox reading of *Childe Harold* is that which takes the generic 'no plan' of Romance as a psychological paradigm for Byron's emerging 'self'. According to this reading the poem interiorizes the eighteenth century topographical poem to reflect the growth of a poet's mind; thus, the diversity of material in the poem, the erratic movement between different places, the shades of difference between Harold and the narrator (and the author), the flexibility of the Spenserian stanza form, are all taken as formal or thematic expressions of the variety of tones or 'shifting sensibilities' in Byron's own mind, a mind which becomes visible over the course of the poem.[83] When Byron returned to England in 1811 a series of personal bereavements caused him to revise the poem in a more singular tone, of gloom and pessimism. As we read the wanderings of Harold, a sense of the author Lord Byron emerges, a powerful individual shaping his materials to the strong contours of his own masculine self, or at least pitting that autonomous self against the forces that would oppose it.[84] If the poem has 'no plan' then at least, according to this reading, it has a destination. Its destination, the place it finally acquires and occupies, is Byron's own mind or personality. Readers who have felt uncomfortable with the teleology of this particular model of self-authorship, who have

felt that the poem's disorder or 'no plan' is in some sense more recalci-
trant and inchoate than this would recognise, have nevertheless dwelt
upon the sense of a poetic mind or psyche, or set of attitudes (even if
they seem confused), which emerge from the experience of reading the
poem. This psyche may be caught up in loops of self-negating desire, an
'enraptured yet fickle travelling'; it may be attempting the 'escapist
gesture' of a flight into immediacy – nevertheless, it is unmistakably *there*
in some sense, demanding that we take notice of it.[85]

But *is* this exactly what it is like to read *Childe Harold's Pilgrimage*? Isn't
there something crucial missing from this account of the authorship of
the poem, something to do with place and the sense in which it has a
primary, we might even say authorial role within the poem? That is to
say, that *Childe Harold* appears to be written not merely by an English
nobleman travelling on the continent, but also by a sequence of places,
or rather a sequence of geo-historical spots with pre-existent narratives,
spots that in some sense speak for themselves. Looking at it this way
round Byron might be seen as a brilliantly individual amanuensis to
whom the European landscape is dictating its histories, while his psychological interiority is an effect that the poem's places produce as their histories are articulated. These histories are inflected through a distinctive
voice, but, essentially, the places *themselves* command as much attention
within the poem as Byron's 'personality' or psyche, or mind. Perhaps
Hazlitt's suspicion that Byron merely reproduced commonplaces and
clichés is one way of registering this effect, this sense of place itself acquir-
ing a distinctly active voice in the poem's authorship, this sense of something *already there* which speaks in the poem. Although this may be a
somewhat bizarre way to think of the publishing phenomenon that made
a young Lord famous, would it nevertheless add something to the
account of what it is like to read the poem? If it does, then of course it
does so because Byron has created this strange *as if*. His achievement in
Childe Harold's Pilgrimage is to suggest that 'place' may somehow supernaturally be dictating its history to the humble poet-secretary, while at
the same time suggesting that there is a poet's psyche or personality to be
discovered somewhere inside this automatic writing. Reading the poem is
both the discovery of an individual psyche emerging through its contradictory materials, *and* like reading a poem without a human author at all,
reading a poem that has somehow always inhered in the European landscape. And this effect primarily relies upon the reality of *having been there*
in person, the authority produced therein, but also the phenomenology
of the encounter between poet and place and the complex ways in which
Byron allows his direct experience of certain 'spots' (in many cases the

strangeness and impossibility of being there) to, as it were, write the poem. In short, *Childe Harold's Pilgrimage* is authored by Byron *in place* – and so rather than being a poem about the growth of a poet's mind, or even about a fantastic journey – it seems first and foremost to be a poem written through the experience of place, a type of experience which may be a more troubled phenomenon than we have assumed. This is best illustrated with one further example from Byron's 1809–11 itinerary, and one which underlines the particular problems caused by being an English philhellene in Greece.

1.6   The 'real' Parnassus

Travelling widely and exotically, even over 'the most interesting scenes of the ancient world',[86] can put strains upon a friendship. In July 1809, at the age of twenty-one, Lord Byron had left England on the Lisbon packet the *Princess Elizabeth* with a friend and fellow-traveller, John Cam Hobhouse, aged twenty-three. For the next year the two travelled together through Portugal, Spain, the Levant and Turkey, until Hobhouse returned to England alone in July 1810, leaving Byron in Athens, which remained his travelling base for almost another year. Edward John Trelawny, who himself travelled with Byron to Greece some thirteen years later, would publish memoirs in which Byron (or Trelawny's Byron) recalled that earlier journey with Hobhouse:

> Travelling in Greece, Hobhouse and I wrangled every day. His guide was Mitford's fabulous History. He had a greed for legendary lore, topography, inscriptions; gabbled in *lingua franca* to the Ephori of the villages, goatherds, and our dragoman. He would potter with map and compass at the foot of Pindus, Parnes, and Parnassus, to ascertain the site of some ancient temple or city. I rode my mule up them. They had haunted my dreams from boyhood; the pines, eagles, vultures, and owls, were descended from those Themistocles and Alexander had seen, and were not degenerated like the humans; the rocks and torrents the same. John Cam's dogged perseverance in pursuit of his hobby is to be envied; I have no hobby and no perseverance. I gazed at the stars, and ruminated; took no notes, asked no questions.[87]

This is a compelling double-portrait: John Cam Hobhouse the classical scholar, the pedant, the connoisseur, the topographer; Byron the wandering Romantic poet, who takes no notes. When the two friends travelled together to Delphi and Parnassus in December 1809, their different pursuits might have been highlighted by the significance of their destination: Delphi, of course, was the site of Apollo's oracle, and Parnassus is the mountain sacred to Apollo and the muses. Byron's journal of 'Detached Thoughts' (1821) remembers seeing a 'flight of twelve Eagles' above Parnassus (an earlier journal numbered them as six) on the day after he had composed the famous lines to the mountain for the first canto of *Childe Harold's Pilgrimage* ('Oh, thou Parnassus! whom I now survey...'). On beholding the birds, Byron recollects that he 'had a hope that Apollo had accepted my homage'.[88] John Cam Hobhouse, on the other hand, had insisted that the birds were not eagles at all, but 'vultures'. Poetic eagles or culture-vultures (Trelawny's Byron mentions both species): the disagreement all too neatly symbolises the distance between the two young men, and the apparent dichotomy between Byron's Romanticism and the constraints of classical scholarship.

In fact Hobhouse and Byron had been far closer than Trelawny's caricature suggests, far more mutually involved than the comical after-portraits would have us believe, and this despite their undeniable differences (it was because, rather than despite of these, that their friendship survived). Trelawny's *Recollections* are written from a mid-Victorian perspective, by which time the career paths of the two men had diverged widely – Byron had become the famous poet, Hobhouse the antiquarian scholar, baronet and Whig member of Parliament – paths which in 1809 had not yet emerged and seemed far from inevitable. If we piece together the visit to Delphi and Parnassus in December 1809 from the various after-accounts written of it by Byron and Hobhouse, something stranger and more complex appears, centred upon the powerful claims of the place itself. In important respects, Parnassus/Delphi is the *first* or primary spot in that series of spots 'it has been our fortune to traverse together' (as the dedication to *Childe Harold* canto four puts it), since the poem stages its beginning in nostalgia for 'Delphi's long-deserted shrine'. The December 1809 visit to this deserted shrine was one of great expectations and equally great disappointments for the English philhellenes, an experience at once grave with significance and self-seriousness, and light-headed with banality and comedy. What exactly did Byron and Hobhouse expect to find at Delphi and Parnassus in 1809? And what, exactly, did they find?

John Cam Hobhouse's *Travels in Albania and Other Provinces in Turkey in 1809–1810*, was first published in 1813, the three-year delay being a result of the pains of verification, fact-checking and double-checking undertaken by Hobhouse who meanwhile had become increasingly anxious that the first two cantos of Byron's *Childe Harold* would steal his thunder. Hobhouse's travelogue has the spontaneity of a diaristic day-by-day account, weighed down with the lumber of scholarly foot-notes, learned disputes, evidences and proofs, which had been added at a later date.[89] On 15 December 1809, Hobhouse's *Travels* recalls the approach to the sacred mountain of the muses, 'a very romantic prospect' opening up as the travellers beheld a 'well-cultivated corn-field, bounded by Parnassus, and interspersed with extensive groves of olives'.[90] From the beginning of his own account of the visit, Hobhouse is acutely aware of the layering of place, the fact that modern Greek towns have grown up on classical sites and that nothing perhaps is quite what (or where) it seemed to be. It was from the modern Crisso, 'a poor Greek town of three hundred houses', that the travellers set out on the following day, 16 December 1809, to view 'the ancient wonders of Delphi'.[91]

Faced with such a famous and well-documented place as Delphi, Hobhouse adopts an approach which is a familiar one in his writing – placing his trust in details, shrinking into minute particulars. 'The writings of well-known travellers, and the accurate though popular work of the Abbé Barthelemy, have rendered even the unlearned reader so familiar with the ancient wonders of Delphi, that I shall do little more in this place than minutely note what I myself saw, when conducted to the spot by a Greek guide from Crisso, on the 16th of December, 1809.'[92] The sense of awe and diminishment in the face of greatness and in the shadow of previous writing became of course the central topos of Byron's lines to Parnassus: he too shrinks before the moun-tain, the summits of which 'were totally invisible' from the foothills, as Hobhouse records.[93] In fact Parnassus is a mountain *range*, and the name is given to the loftiest part of the range, which breaks into twin peaks, one called Lycoreia, Byron's 'Liakura'. Hobhouse himself makes this point, that the mountain is naturally, physically, *not* in one single place but at least two. It is therefore difficult to point to a specific spot or object as 'Parnassus', particularly as its twin peaks are snow- and cloud-capped. Such geographical non-specificity – the sense of being *near* Parnassus/Delphi – is both a matter of fact, and a figure for the way the mountain's symbolic presence defies comprehension. In the face of this Hobhouse refuses to offer the general descriptive accounts expected of travelogues, accounts which are not only over-familiar but in fact untrue to the experience of actually being there. Byron's letters home from the Levant during 1809–10 constantly make the same refusal, for the same reasons. Hobhouse in fact avoids talking about Delphi or Parnassus as if either were single entities to be comprehended 'whole', instead concentrating upon that which is immediately beneath his nose, praising the precisely detailed account of the place in Livy's history of *Rome and the Mediterranean*, 'which answers most exactly to the spot, and might have been written yesterday'.[94]

This textual contract between on-the-spot concentration on the one hand, and what we might call awe-struck evocation on the other, is a curiously potent one, foreshadowing the kind of exchanges that occur between the body of Byron's *Childe Harold's Pilgrimage* and the supplementary system of notes accompanying that text. Hobhouse's account attempts to negotiate the same balance between the perceived reality of such a place (where 'reality' means the humdrum, the merely visible) and all that it represents imaginatively or historically, all that expands invisibly and magically beyond the circumference of the actual spot. The 'small mud town' of Castri (ancient Delphi), is 'situated a little to the east of a circular hollow in the mountain, round which are the rows of seats belonging to the Pythian stadium' (the site of ancient athletic games). Conducted to caves (now cattlesheds) supposed to be the Pythian caves themselves, in which Apollo's priestess performed her rituals, Hobhouse is doubtful: 'That this was the cavern whence the Pythia received the divine subterranean vapour does not seem at all probable; yet the people of the country have fixed upon it for the sacred spot; "for", said our guide, "here the Greeks worshipped, in the days of Apollo, the king of these places."'(pp. 200–1)

The guide's confusion of the sacred and secular meaning of place only compounded Hobhouse's scepticism, as if he was being passed off with something other than the genuine article, or as if this particular guided tour had been mapped around weakly grasped history and visitor expectations. His hesitation is not entirely that of the out-and-out demystifier or rationalizer, however, since he rejects a cattleshed as the authentic site of the Pythian caves only because such a spot does not live up to the place-hunter's highly developed sense of the classical *locus*: this particular locale will not answer to the idea. Such a reaction is one that lurks within the experience of tourism – a reluctance to acknowledge the authenticity of the 'real' because it fails to live up to high imaginative expectations, and it is a mark of Byron's distance from this mentality that he is more ready to accept the authenticity of the cattleshed, while simultaneously recording and relishing its incongruity: 'Though here no more Apollo haunts his grot, / And thou, the

Muses' seat, art now their grave, / Some gentle spirit still pervades the spot, / Sighs in the gale, keeps silence in the cave'(I.62). The succinct-ness of Byron's accompanying note, as so often, places the rumination upon the spot in the context of worldly realism: 'A little above Castri is a cave, supposed the Pythian, of immense depth; the upper part of it is paved, and now a cow-house.'[95] For Byron, unlike Hobhouse, the con-trast between the imagined grandeur of the site of classical antiquity and the present reality of humble cow-shed is precisely what he is seeking, satisfying as it does the poem's desire to brood upon transitory glories, while at the same time allowing Byron to claim an historical continuity: a gentle spirit 'still pervades the spot'.

In this respect, Byron's response to Parnassus is significantly different from his response to the Parthenon, which he would visit a month later. Parnassus is not a site self-evidently caught up in the web of global imperial relations and conflicts. Its remoteness, its decayed grandeur, would appear to exist in a realm that transcends such conflict, offering the possibility of a quite different order of response in which anxieties about belonging to an imperial nation are temporarily allayed. At the same time, Parnassus is undoubtedly a disappointment, but this is a disappointment that accompanies the experience of secular pilgrimage and is certainly not a threat to it; rather, disappoint-ment offers a strange confirmation of authenticity and becomes a central part of those stages of Byron's pilgrimage which seem to take him out of the map of power and into the harmless regions of the 'pure' past. The *genius loci* in these regions inspires a not unpleasing melancholy, since it does not stand as a symbol of current political impotence or incrimination, nor in the Scottish sense as a mock-heroic parody, but as a much grander and mistier symbol of transience. Here the spirit-of-place is diminished, decayed, but, since no one is to claim otherwise by plundering Parnassus, it still 'pervades the spot'. In what sense, however, does it *pervade*?

For Hobhouse authenticity ought to be more solid than this. His atten-tion in the *Travels* is absorbed by the terrain: borders, spatial organisa-tions, numbers, distances, parameters. The landscape is an empty one across which are traced the faintest outlines and coordinates of an earlier place. Wandering around with these different instincts and expectations, what Hobhouse and Byron are next shown by their guide is a spring sup-posed to be the Castalian (thought to confer the powers of poetry upon those who came into contact with it). 'Here,' Hobhouse comments, 'if anywhere, being literally "dipped in dew of Castaly"[96] – for this was the immortal rill, and we were sprinkled with the spray of the falling stream –

here we should have felt the poetic inspiration' (p. 202). Quoting Spenser (who is recalling Horace), Hobhouse is not touched by unmediated poetic rapture in this place – this place which of all places should be *the* place. It is not a spot where he discovers a poetry of his own, but of others before him. Byron's account in the notes to *Childe Harold* is similarly sober:

> The fountain of Dirce turns a mill: at least, my companion (who resolving to be at once cleanly and classical bathed in it) pronounced it to be the fountain of Dirce, and any body who thinks it worthwhile may contradict him. At Castri we drank of half a dozen streamlets, some not of the purest, before we decided to our satisfaction which was the true Castalian, and even that had a villainous twang, probably from the snow, though it did not throw us into an epic fever, like poor Dr. Chandler.[97]

The sixty-seventh chapter of Richard Chandler's *Travels in Greece* (1775) describes falling down with a fever thought to be contracted from bathing in the dews of Castaly. Hobhouse fails to mention himself bathing in the fountain of Dirce, perhaps embarrassed by the enthusiasm of such a gesture, or conscious of it recalling Dr Chandler's misfortune. He, too, relishes Chandler's misfortune, and seizes the opportunity to ironise the notion of Castalian inspiration:

> Perhaps it may increase the interest in perusing this account of the present appearance of Delphi to believe that the basin below the church of St. John is that in which the Pythia bathed before she ascended the sacred tripod; that the cleft in Parnassus is the one which divided the two summits of the poetic hill: and that the monastery stands on the site of the Delphic gymnasium... . Dr Chandler's conjectures as to the first point were somewhat confirmed by washing his hands in the cool water of Castalia, when he was seized with a shivering fit. (p. 204)

What emerges from these separate accounts is a sharp sense of the impossible and comical pursuit of authentic place, the treacherousness of naive acts of geographical faith. Nevertheless, such acts fascinated Hobhouse at least as much as Byron, and would go on fascinating him for many years, including those spent amassing the notes for the later cantos of *Childe Harold*. Hobhouse is always more seriously committed to antiquarian place-hunting than Byron, and is also more seriously committed to the sanctity (the visibility) of the classical originals. Evaluating, sifting evidence, bathing himself in the fountain, authenticity for Hobhouse is to be discovered empirically or not at all. Byron by contrast is quite comfortable here at Parnassus (in contrast to Athens) with the melancholic sensation of an historical gap between then and now, and happy to leave the work of closing that gap to the imagination. Hobhouse, pottering 'with map and compass', was unable quite to relinquish the hope that actually being dipped in the dews of Castaly *might* bring on poetic inspiration, that something tangible would emerge to confirm a sense of authenticity. For Byron this belief in the literal truth of a *genius loci*, as if such a spirit can be excavated and unearthed, exactly located or put in a bottle, is absurd and dilettantish. At the same time, the *materiality* of history-in-place held a deep appeal for Byron too, in particular the authority gained through his physical presence upon the spot – the materiality, we might say, of his own bodily situatedness. The difference is one which centres partly around contesting claims for the 'real' and for authenticity, and partly around the materiality of historical memory, or the kinds of ways a spirit-of-place is taken as manifesting itself. But the different perspectives of poet and antiquarian are absolutely unable to free themselves from existing in relation to each other. Byron's entire poetic career is shaped by the claims for authority he stakes upon the authenticity of historical places.[98] That the self could experience unmediated connection with the spirit-of-place, as for example upon the plains of Troy (when not thinking about Scotland), where Byron stood daily 'for more than a month' in 1810, is a constant claim of his poetry, a claim for 'the truth of *history* (in the material *facts*) and of *place*'.[99] Such a notion exists only as it is consciously differentiated from Hobhouse's empiricism, or from the practical archaeological investigations of those who sought to cast doubt upon the veracity of the Troad. Byron's claim for communing with the spirit-of-place must define itself as *contrary* to that which seeks firstly to ground authenticity in verifiable facts, and later to discover a *genius loci* within those facts.[100] The aura Byron routinely ascribes to historical 'spots' is a guarantee of the facts, and not vice versa, so that his own physical presence is often enough in itself to provide for him an infallible measurement of authenticity. At the same time, Hobhouse's sceptical encounter with the Castalian spring is predicated upon the possibility of intuitive knowledge of the authenticity of place, even as it necessarily fails to discover such inspiration. For Hobhouse the trail of facts and the endless fact-checking leads towards (and is led on by) a ghostly spirit of place which always fails to materialise, but which is there as a commanding idea. In other words, Hobhouse and Byron are negative but vital presences in each other's experience as they react to the sacred mountain and its environs: each relies on an implicit repudiation or reversal in the logic of the other. What they have in common, I would like to suggest, is in their re-working of the disappointment and discomfort they inevitably felt as English philhellenes in this situation, and to surprisingly similar ends.

Hobhouse confesses outright:

> On the whole, any one would, I think, be disappointed with the situation of this place... . We were very much at a loss to guess where a town of nearly two miles in circumference could have been placed, for there are not more than two small spots of level ground anywhere within the circuit of the present remains. In vain we looked for the 'woods that wave', as, except in the little olive-grove surrounding the monastery, there is not a single tree on the rocks either above or below. (p. 205)

To lose or misconceive an entire town and woodland is a disappointment indeed – a sublime disappointment even, and in part belongs to conventions of travel-writing. In particular the anti-climactic sensation upon reaching the long-dreamed-of destination is a familiar topos, particularly when the destination is as grand as Delphi or Parnassus.[101] The ways in which Hobhouse and Byron represent their own disappointment with Parnassus, however, are complex. For Hobhouse, being 'at a loss' was in part a way of preserving classical ideals from the grubbiness of contemporary Greek realities (the mill, the cowshed, the dirty fountain). Furthermore, reluctance to grant authenticity has a political inflection in that it emphasises most strongly the present degradation of the Greeks and their need for political help. Most significantly of all, what he finally discovers in the foothills of Parnassus is not poetic inspiration at all, but proof of the suitability of this locale for concealing treasure from enemies:

> If, however, forgetting the poetic raptures we expected to feel in the bosom of Parnassus, we had considered only the object which the Greeks must have had in view in offering their wealth and the richest productions of art at this favourite shrine, we should at once have allowed that no place could have been selected better adapted for the security of their united treasures than Kastri, which to an open enemy must be perfectly inaccessible. Indeed, though Delphi was often plundered, yet, when a serious resistance was made, the Gauls under Brennus, as well as the Persians of Xerxes army, were repulsed, and did not dare to advance into the fast-nessess of the mountains. (p. 206)

The true significance of this place, as Hobhouse defines it here, is its resistance to discovery. Parnassus is a hiding place; the inaccessibility of the terrain had been exploited by the Greeks in times of danger to conceal and bury their treasures. Forgetting his 'poetic raptures' and ceasing to think of Parnassus as a literary subject at all, Hobhouse was able to understand the true political purpose of the locale. As a symbol of invulnerability and safety, Parnassus is also entirely distinct from the ransacked Parthenon, seeming by contrast to possess a 'natural' immunity built into its landscape which frees it from the power nexus inescapably evident in Athens, and fixes it forever within the landscape of the Greek classical past. Delphi–Parnassus is a sacred place precisely because we do not 'dare advance into the fastnesses of the mountains'. It was this very impregnability that would be exploited by Trelawny after Byron's death when he took refuge with the Greek bandit-chieftain Odysseus Androutzos, an alarmingly Byronic figure, in caves in the precipices of Parnassus that were only accessible by ladders bolted to the rock.[102] Parnassus refused to disclose its *genius loci*, whether that *genius* was the Pythian priestess and her treasures or those fleeing the imperial Ottoman forces. Finally then for Hobhouse, the proof of authenticity is exactly where he had been looking for it all along; that is, in the topography.

What Byron made of his disappointment is of course now famous:

> Oh, thou Parnassus! whom I now survey,
> Not in the phrenzy of a dreamer's eye,
> Not in the fabled landscape of a lay,
> But soaring snow-clad through thy native sky,
> In the wild pomp of mountain majesty!
> What marvel if I thus essay to sing?
> The humblest of thy pilgrims passing by
> Would gladly woo thine echoes with his string,
> Though from thy heights no more one Muse will wave her wing.
>
> Oft have I dream'd of Thee! whose glorious name
> Who knows not, knows not man's divinest lore:
> And now I view thee, 'tis, alas! with shame
> That I in feeblest accents must adore.
> When I recount thy worshippers of yore
> I tremble, and can only bend the knee;
> Nor raise my voice, nor vainly dare to soar,

But gaze beneath thy cloudy canopy
In silent joy to think at last I look on Thee!

Happier in this than mightiest bards have been,
Whose fate to distant homes confined their lot,
Shall I unmov'd behold the hallow'd scene,
Which others rave of, though they know it not?
Though here no more Apollo haunts his grot,
And thou, the Muses' seat, art now their grave,
Some gentle Spirit still pervades the spot,
Sighs in the gale, keeps silence in the cave,
And glides with glassy foot o'er yon melodious Wave.

(I.60–3)

Byron's note tells us that these lines 'were written in Castri (Delphos), at the foot of Parnassus';[103] in other words, composed on the very spot, a fact that wholly determines their meaning. In a crude sense Byron transforms disappointment into conventional (we might even say professional) anxieties of the self as poet. Ostensibly the stanzas record the commonplace of not knowing how to respond to the mountain sacred to Apollo and the muses, a place over-burdened with meaning. They display an awareness that the significance of this place dwarfs the poet and cancels out the possi-bility of a spontaneous, original or entirely authentic response. And of course at the same time the stanzas take just this anxiety about *being here* as their subject. Parnassus, 'classic ground and consecrated most' (II.413), produces anxiety in an English poet going over such ground again, an anxiety which is neither balked nor resolved but is recorded as a fracture between the classic past and the humbled present. This has political meaning for Byron too – symbolising the subjugation of modern Greece to Turkey – but that is less important here than the fact that while the place records difference and decline, it also, faintly, records continuity: 'Some gentle Spirit still pervades the spot, / Sighs in the gale, keeps silence in the cave...'; indeed continuity and decline cannot be separated. The sacred spirit of place is recognised *in* and *through* its diminishment, which corre-lates to the experience of disappointment, and therefore in an important sense the 'gentle spirit' that 'still pervades the spot' repre-sents both the *genius loci* and the poet himself as he listens to his own responses to this sacred place. Byron is discreet about speaking and silence in his apostrophe to Parnassus. Here, as elsewhere in

Childe Harold, there is an etiquette of lowered voices in holy places, of a respectful hush or awe-struck silence as if a spot consecrated by events of historical significance becomes a kind of church.[104] Other poets are singing and raving while Byron is silently gazing and while the spirit (perhaps with a pun on 'still'[105]) is keeping silence in the cave, like the poet. Nevertheless, the poem belies this silence by the very fact that it is addressing Parnassus: it speaks of its inability to speak, paradoxically breaking and enforcing a silence which is both the embarrassed silence of disappointment and the electrical hush of awe. In this way disappointment becomes something quite different from merely conventional anti-climax. Disappointment – the sense of a place as diminished – is offered not as demystificatory, but as the very secret of the place itself. To experience disappointment here is to embody in oneself the invisible and disembodied *genius loci*, sighing in the gale and keeping silence in the cave.

The subject of these lines, then, is Byron's presence upon Parnassus. The same sentiment and rhetoric (being in awe of the famous mountain) in the mouth of Hazlitt's schoolboy, or in the 'phrenzy of a dreamer's eye', or in the bards 'whose fate to distant homes confined their lot', might be open to the charge of cliché or commonplace, but as these lines record an on-the-spot experience they have a literalness which claims its own authorisation and authentication, and returns the commonplace to an originary truth. In some ways Byron's response is similar to Hobhouse's. For both men the experience of visiting Parnassus represented a discovery of the fact that something was hidden; an experience of disappointment, and then a recasting or transformation of disappointment into the proof of authenticity. As such their various accounts of the experience reveal some of the anxieties of the English philhellenic traveller in Greece and the ways in which philhellenism negotiated the peculiar relations of certain 'situations'. Philhellenism is one cultural manifestation of what we might call the deeper ontological strangeness of place, the ability of places we have never visited to inspire us with powerful feelings of nostalgia and belonging, while at the same time representing displaced images of where we ourselves come from, our 'home'. As such, philhellenism is one example of the mysterious collusion between history and geography in that it allows a nostalgic notion of the past to appear as a homeland rooted in a real terrain. The Greek nationalism of non-Greeks was therefore a powerful nationalism, but a nationalism by proxy, entwined around the classical fantasies of home and a sense of British patriotism, and therefore in an oblique relation to British imperialism. This site like so many in Greece was thick with the signs of the travellers' fellow countrymen. Hobhouse in fact expresses his delight at discovering the graffitoed names of 'Aberdeen, 1803, and H.P. Hope, 1799, to which Byron and I added our own names' on the pillars of the Church at Castri.[106] Lord Aberdeen (as has been noted) was an antiquarian named along with Elgin as one of the 'classic thieves' who had ransacked Greece, and had also been listed among the men who might have delivered knowledge of modern Greece to the British public, but who had failed to do so. Signing their names here alongside Aberdeen's reveals the ways in which Hobhouse and Byron felt an allegiance to a British aristocratic network, even as they would elsewhere distance themselves from its collusion with British imperial interests. In 1809, however, the line between British and Greek patriotism, both of which were central to philhellenism, was much more ambiguous than it would become a decade or so later when the Greek uprising began. In 1823 Hobhouse would become an active member of the London Greek Committee, a radical parliamentary organisation established to assist the uprising, and which exploited Byron's name to publicise its activities. The fact that, in the end, Byron would die in Greece, his death a significant event in the struggle for independence, casts a retrospective purity upon the entire course of his relationship with Greece which perhaps disguises some of the ambivalence both he and Hobhouse experienced in being there.

'What would he give? to have seen like me the *real Parnassus*', Byron wrote to Henry Drury on his way home from Greece in 1811, imagining the envy of his classicist friend Francis Hodgson. This notion of the 'real Parnassus' was a powerful one precisely because Parnassus also belonged to a distinctly English imagination. In particular the anglicisation of Parnassus in the eighteenth-century picturesque tradition, the possibility of transposing the mountain to England, or finding an English equivalent, a 'Parnassus-upon-Thames', had mystified any notion of the 'real' sacred mountain.[107] Fame, whether it be of a mountain or of a poet, as Byron would learn, causes strange and unpredictable reactions in those who come into contact with the real thing after long familiarity with its image. More significantly, since in Byron we are confronted with what we might call the cult of the 'real', the authority of contact with the thing itself, emerging from this is a sharp sense of the difference between landscapes which exist only in literature and those directly experienced in life. An often-quoted letter to Leigh Hunt in 1815, for example, takes great pains to correct Wordsworth's description of the Greek climate in *The Excursion*:

> He [i.e. Wordsworth] says of Greece in the body of his book – that it is a land of
>> '*rivers* – *fertile* plains – & *sounding* shores
>> Under a cope of *variegated* sky'
>
> The rivers are dry half the year – the plains are barren – and the shores *still* & *tideless* as the Mediterranean can make them – the Sky is anything but variegated – being for months & months – but 'darkly – deeply – beautifully blue'.[108]

Here Byron is Wordsworth's most searching critic because he is committed to the truth of experience and the ways in which experience polices the imagination, but also because he believes that the fact of having been there on the spot had a profound literary value in itself. *Being there*, for Byron, has its own imaginative authenticity, which is as pre-eminent and as important as its claim to factual accuracy. In the case of Parnassus the symbolic value of the mountain as home of the muses and therefore as the seal of poetic achievement, literary quality or hierarchy, which Byron self-consciously inherited from early eighteenth-century poetics and which is perfectly exemplified in his 1813–14 notebook drawing of a triangle/mountain ranked with the names of contemporary poets, with Walter Scott at its pinnacle ('the Monarch of Parnassus'[109]) – this same symbolic value leant a further disturbance to the notion of the 'real'. The double nature of Parnassus as an historically significant place, and as the sign for historical and literary significance, made visiting the 'real' Parnassus and writing poetry on the spot an experience we would now call over-determined. And this was just the kind of topographical experience around which *Childe Harold* was organised.

In a sense, then, Parnassus embodied English philhellenistic desire and meaning in its literary mode more than any other part of Greece, which is why the problems of such desire became particularly manifest on visiting the mountain for 'real'. The pedantic effort exactly to locate and identify sacred classical sites in fact asks deeper questions of the meaning and durability of the 'classical' and its relation to modern Greece. Is literary inspiration or 'poetic rapture' to be found there or not, and, if not, then what role had literature to play in the wider politics of philhellenism? What is the relation of this place to hostile force, to the encroachments of power and the violations of history? Above all, the question of the ultimate significance and efficacy of English philhellenism in Greece is thrown into sharp relief through the presence of Hobhouse and Byron in *this* place. Was their philhellenism at this moment anything more than an aristocratic leisure activity, like appreciating cameos or writing poetry, two aspects of what was essentially the same antiquarian mentality? Or worse, was there perhaps a sense in which the classical itself stood in a collusive relation to British imperial interests which made it hostile to the interests of modern Greece? This darker possibility seems to be hovering somewhere in Byron's consciousness at this period, and would become more explicit in his later writing. But if the visit to Parnassus in December 1809 was a disappointment for Byron and Hobhouse, it was also paradoxically an affirmation of philhellenistic faith. This is so despite the fact that there is something familiarly *post*-Romantic in their accounts of the experience. As Hobhouse fails to receive inspiration from the dews of Castaly we might even think of it as a peculiarly modern phenomenon – the birth-pang (or twang) of mass tourism with its commodification of the 'authentic' (Byron and Hobhouse bottling-up the Castalian spring as a souvenir). Wandering around ancient ruins with very little sense of connection between then and now may seem to anticipate the kind of experience Clough would document, 'Murray in hand', in the post-Byronic *Amours de Voyage* (1849). Nevertheless, there are significant elements which distinguish this encounter from either Victorian, modern or postmodern tourism. The authentically real is discovered by Hobhouse and Byron within their experience of disappointment, and confirmed *by* this experience, and this remains a distinctly Romantic accommodation of desire to reality even as the comedy of the pottering with map and compass and the ghost-hunting in the cowshed gestures towards a later sensibility in which the *genius loci* is merely a figure of speech. Here at least it is more. At Parnassus (on, near or around Parnassus) Byron and Hobhouse experienced something of the strangeness, even the impossibility of *being there* in the sense in which it is so frequently invoked by both writers, that is, as a seal of authenticity and authority as well as a claim to a particular kind of reality. At the same time they confirmed a sense of direct communion with the historical significance of a place precisely and only through being there themselves. As such, Parnassus offered a positive contrast with those other sites of classical civilisation such as the Acropolis in which the experience of being there merely registered the distance between the historical past and the political present. Parnassus offered its secret refuge for the British aristocratic philhellenic traveller to enjoy the sensation of 'the truth of *history* (in the material *facts*) and of *place*'. And perhaps this might suggest that there is at this period something hidden, something fugitive and secretive about philhellenism itself, centred upon its problematic relation to British imperialism, which becomes secretive and fugitive precisely as the philhellene arrives in Greece. *Being there* radically changes the relation the English traveller has both with home and with Greece, because the bonds which connect Byron and Hobhouse to the British imperial realm, scratched into the pillars of the church at Castri, become more present to their consciousness and more complex when in Athens or Delphi or Parnassus, than when in London.

2
The Spirit and Body of Place: 1812–18

2.1 Having been there: the fantastical and the real

Since the 'Orient' is a 'word merely relative', as Sir William Jones famously observed, Orientalism will always beg the question it pretends to answer, which is where the 'Orient' *actually* is.[1] This particular literary fashion (simultaneously in vogue and deeply over-familiar by 1812) has something to do with geography, while also being a mystification of geographical realities, and this partly explains the uncertainty as to how to label the group of verse narratives Byron produced between 1812 and 1815 – whether they should be known as his Turkish, Eastern, or Oriental tales. However they are labelled, the poems are bound together by strong formulaic homogeneity: the codes of the Eastern 'other' overlap and intersect with those of British aristocratic mores, refracted through literary convention and in oblique relation to British imperial politics, set within narratives of pseudo-chivalry, illicit love, guilt and vengeance, etc. But the nuances of generic label in this case are instructive because Byron's tales seem simultaneously to remember the actual places he had visited between 1809 and 1811 (mainly Turkish, in the sense of contained within the Ottoman empire), and to participate in the literary mode of imagining the East known as Orientalism in which, as a reader, Byron had been deeply absorbed from an early age. And so while they overlay the *real* places of Byron's journey with the heightened colours of a literary tradition, they also take pains to reveal the *fantastical* reality of the places Byron had visited, authenticating the strangeness of the East partly through a dedication to the accuracy of what Byron called 'costume', as if Orientalism could be the most naturalistic of modes in the hands of those with insider knowledge.

Things are further complicated by the example of Greece which, as we have seen, provoked an ambivalent reaction in the Western aristocratic traveller, while itself belonging in different ways both to the East and the West.[2] The philhellenic idea of Greece is not easily accommodated within a system of Orientalism predicated upon the binarism of East–West relations, nor does it ever quite escape that system, but remains a ghostly and anxious presence in all Byron's writing about his travels. And it is the very notion of ghosts or spirits-of-place and their relation to the material reality of Byron's Eastern journey which the tales cannot escape. How ideas of 'spirit' inform the notion of the physical material or body of landscapes and places of historical significance, will be the subject of this chapter.

The Giaour: A Fragment of a Turkish Tale (1813) opens with a description of what was thought to be Themistocles' tomb on the promontory of the Piraeus. In an extended simile of twenty-two lines Byron connects Greece with the appearance of a fresh corpse:

> He who hath bent him o'er the dead,
> Ere the first day of death is fled;
> The first dark day of nothingness,
> The last of danger and distress;
> (Before Decay's effacing fingers
> Have swept the lines where beauty lingers)
> And mark'd the mild angelic air –
> The rapture of repose that's there –
> The fixed yet tender traits that streak
> The langour of the placid cheek,
> And – but for that sad shrouded eye,
>   That fires not – wins not – weeps not – now –
>   And but for that chill changeless brow,
> Where cold Obstruction's apathy
> Appals the gazing mourner's heart,
> As if to him it could impart
> The doom he dreads, yet dwells upon –
> Yes – but for these and these alone,
> Some moments – aye – one treacherous hour,
> He still might doubt the tyrant's power,
> So fair – so calm – so softly seal'd
> The first – last look – by death reveal'd!
> Such is the aspect of this shore –
> 'Tis Greece – but living Greece no more!

So coldly sweet, so deadly fair,
We start – for soul is wanting there.
Hers is the loveliness in death,
That parts not quite with parting breath;
But beauty with that fearful bloom,
That hue which haunts it to the tomb –
Expression's last receding ray,
A gilded halo hovering round decay,
The farewell beam of Feeling past away!
Spark of that flame – perchance of heavenly birth –
Which gleams – but warms no more its cherished earth!

(ll.68–102)

A note to the text provides corroboration:

I trust that few of my readers have ever had an opportunity of witnessing what is here attempted in description, but those who have
will probably retain a painful remembrance of that singular beauty
which pervades, with few exceptions, the features of the dead, a
few hours, and but for a few hours after 'the spirit is not there'. It
is to be remarked in cases of violent death by gun-shot wounds,
the expression is always that of langour, whatever the natural
energy of the sufferer's character; but in death from a stab the
countenance preserves its traits of feeling or ferocity, and the
mind its bias, to the last.[3]

This claim for acquaintance with the aspect and phrenological
patterns of the newly violently dead has a certain matter-of-factness
which is characteristic of Byron's notes, especially when they are supporting moments of textual mystery or supernaturalism. The cross-
authenticating relationship between Byron's texts and their supporting
materials would in fact be a significant element of the poetry written
after 1812, but in this particular case the note itself is about authenticating death, about the signs or the evidence of a recently departed
life, and the possibility of an inhering spirit which may or may not be
read in a newly dead body ('A gilded halo hovering round decay'). The
spirit-of-place here then is equated with the spirit-of-life, and the
power of death with that which robs a place of its spirit or essence.
(The motif recurs later in the poem with the description of Leila's beautiful corpse.) The 'tyrant's power' which might be doubted for 'one

treacherous hour' by gazing on the newly dead, has broad political resonances in the context of Byron's on-going critique of imperial interests in Greece, suggesting that the tyranny of imperialist power might
be suspended for a moment by meditating upon the physical landscape of Greece and its historical associations, and by recognising an
enduring spirit-of-place there. Such a claim – that meditation, or rather
reverie upon a particular landscape and its history may suspend the
relations of contemporary power – is however a consciously insecure
one. The presence of such a spirit remains in doubt, seeming to hover
there (a 'parting breath', a 'beauty' a 'hue', a 'last receding ray', a
'gilded halo', a 'farewell beam', a 'spark of that flame – *perchance* of
heavenly birth' [my italics]). Nevertheless, as the first of the Turkish
tales it is significant that *The Giaour* should begin with this metaphor –
the spirit read upon the physical surface of the body – and that it
should operate, as it were, between the notes and text, because there is
a structural analogy in the Turkish tales between the function of the
supplementary matter of the supporting notes in authenticating the
mysterious or supernatural events of the narrative proper, and
the notion of a spirit-of-place inhering in and in some way authenticating the material reality (or body) of an historical landscape.

Byron's desire to return to the East was strongest between 1813 and
1814 when the 'sight of a *camel*' during a trip to the zoo was enough to
make him 'pine again for Asia Minor. "Oh quando te aspiciam?"'[4] The
writing of the tales was meant to be a cure for such nostalgia, but of
course merely exacerbated his longing, although these moments of
weakness belied a tougher sense of the authority he believed his travels
had given him and which he had turned to his advantage in the first
two cantos of *Childe Harold*. This was authority grounded in direct
factual knowledge of the East and exploited primarily in that respect,
but which also provided Byron with the right in his own mind to
produce Orientalist literature. For Byron, Orientalism was a mode for
the imaginative reproduction of the *reality* of the semi-fantastical
nature of the East, and so its legitimate practice relied upon the fact of
having been there oneself. A letter to Lord Holland of 17 November
1813 explains:

> My head is full of Oriental names & scenes...but it is my story & my
> *East* – (& here I am venturing with no one to contend against – from
> having *seen* what my contemporaries must copy from the drawings
> of others only) that I want to make palpable – and my skull is so
> crammed from having lived much with them & in their own way

(after Hobhouse went home a year before me) with their scenes & manners – that I believe it would lead me to St. Luke's [an asylum] if not disgorged in this manner.[5]

The fact of having been there certainly distinguished Byron from the majority of the purveyors of Orientalism and is undoubtedly one reason for the immense popularity of the Eastern narratives. The repeated thematic motif in these narratives of the 'dark secret', upon which it seems the British public became hooked, relies upon the certain knowledge that the author of the tales *knows* what he is talking about, while the appearance of 'knowing' shared by the heroes of the poems produces a narrative excitement. Thanking the traveller John Galt for his *Letters from the Levant* (1813), in which Galt had recounted his meeting with the poet, Byron wrote that he felt 'much more flattered than I could possibly be by the praise of any one who has not been on the spot'.[6] In another letter to Galt of 11 December 1813, he went further:

> I do not know how other men feel towards those they have met abroad; but to me there seems a kind of tie established between all who have met together in a foreign country, as if we had met in a state of pre-existence, and were talking over a life that has ceased.[7]

Here the Eastern traveller is himself a kind of ghost or spirit surviving a pre-existence and living on to tell the tale, a bearer of secret, even esoteric, knowledge. Byron wrote to Edward Daniel Clarke four days later to thank him for his praise of *The Giaour* and *The Bride of Abydos*, praise which was more agreeable 'because – setting aside talents – judgement – & ye. "laudari a laudato" &c. *you* have been on ye spot'.[8] Although Byron did his best to reassure Tom Moore that Orientalism could be indulged in by anyone – Moore had never been to the East and was anxious lest this deficiency might be conspicuous in his own 'Oriental Romance' *Lalla Rookh*[9] – his own feelings on the matter were quite unambiguous, i.e. that literary Orientalism could only properly be practised by those who had personally witnessed the scenes they pretended to describe. John Hamilton Reynold's poem *Safie, an Eastern Tale* (1814), dedicated to Byron, for example, was 'wild, and more oriental than he would be, had he seen the scenes where he has placed his tale'.[10] Felicia Hemans' *Modern Greece: A Poem* (1817) was dismissed in a letter to Murray as 'good for nothing – written by someone who has never been there'.[11] And although Byron was equally persuaded that 'something more than having been across a Camel's hump is necessary to write a good Oriental tale',[12] his most savage critique of those who dared to write of the East without having been there, was reserved for Wordsworth in the letter to Leigh Hunt correcting the Greek topography of *The Excursion* (discussed in the previous chapter).[13]

The East represented for Byron a realm of experience in which the factual realities themselves could often seem fantastical and therefore would need careful corroboration, but not so much corroboration as to detract from their exotic appeal. The 'advertisement' for *The Giaour* attempts to reassure its home readership that the pivotal event of the narrative (the female slave Leila, who is in love with the Giaour, is punished by her Turkish master Hassan by being put into a sack and thrown into the sea) is 'founded upon circumstances now less common in the East than formerly'. 'Formerly', however, means the recent past (circa 1779), while a later note suggests that the gruesome practice 'was not very uncommon in Turkey' and provides anecdotal examples. If Byron's readers were inclined to disbelieve the circumstances of his narrative (and the opposite would surely be the case) then these notes offer corroborative evidence that such gruesome things actually happened. Later in the narrative the extra-sensory perception of 'stern Taheer' (l.1076) who fore-hears and forewarns Hassan of the 'deathshot', is corroborated in a long note recounting a similar example of soothsaying to have occurred to Byron on his journey in 1811 to Cape Colonna. Moreover, as is well established, the poem was suggested by the 'real circumstances' of an incident which took place while Byron was in the East, the details of which he had sought not to appear to exploit in writing the poem, but which were half-known anyway in London literary circles.[14] In Athens in 1811 Byron had intervened to prevent a young girl found guilty of infidelity from being thrown into the sea, securing the girl's release and arranging for her safe passage away from the city. The story of the episode had circulated in Athens and later in London, and when he received Lord Sligo's account of what had happened (as Sligo had heard it from others shortly after arriving in Athens following Byron's departure), Byron wondered whether to append this description, which he allowed to pass between his friends, to later editions of the poem. A note, not published during Byron's lifetime, reveals his indecision:

> The circumstances related in the following letter [Lord Sligo's account] I have kept back for reasons which will be sufficiently obvious – and <had no other testimony than a> indeed till no very long time ago I

was not aware that the occurrence to which it alludes was obvious to the writer – and when once aware of it – it will not perhaps appear unnatural that I should feel desirous to be informed of 'the tale as it was told to him' on the spot and in a country where oral tradition is the only record – and where in a <few years> short time facts are either forgotten or distorted from the truth…the writer of the letter was the only countryman of mine who arrived on the spot – for sometime after the event to [which] he alludes… .[15]

Byron's sense of honour in not exploiting the real circumstances of his intervention is in a tug-of-war here with the overwhelming authority and significance he accorded just this kind of on-the-spot corroboration. There is indeed something about the fact that Sligo had 'arrived on the spot' and had been told this story 'on the spot' which is itself assumed to be sufficient evidence of its truth. If honour won out in the end, then it did so in circumstances where the direct reality (and not merely the local truth) of the circumstances upon which *The Giaour* was written had gained enough purchase in readers' minds, and yet still tantalisingly remained unauthorised, as to suit his purposes. In short, an element of mystery had woven itself around a factual reality, which is precisely the central effect worked for by all of the Eastern narratives. An exotic or magical spirit (the spirit, as it were, of the Orient) is connected to hard factual matter (Byron's personal knowledge of the East).

The Giaour was quickly followed by *The Bride of Abydos: A Turkish Tale* (1813), in which the possibility of a concealed set of real circumstances seems to be hinted at in the lines from Virgil Byron wrote in his journal in reference to the poem: '"quaeque ipse….vidi, / Et quorum pars magna fui."' ['I myself saw these things in all their horror, and I bore great part in them.']**[16]** In this case Byron not only had direct geographical knowledge of the spot he was writing about, but had re-enacted Leander's legendary feat of swimming the Hellespont – a constant boast in letters home during 1811 and an achievement not wholly concealed by the poem: 'Oh! yet – for there my steps have been, / These feet have press'd the sacred shore, / These limbs that buoyant wave hath borne –' (II.3.ll.28–30).[17] An important note to the poem picks up on the Homeric adjective 'broad' as a conventional description of the Hellespont, and discusses the scholarly controversy over the word:

The wrangling about this epithet, 'the broad Hellespont' or the 'boundless Hellespont', whether it means one or the other, or what it means at all, has been beyond all possibility of detail. I have even

heard it disputed on the spot; and not foreseeing a speedy conclusion to the controversy, amused myself with swimming across it in
the mean time, and probably may again, before the point is settled.
Indeed, the question as to the truth of 'the tale of Troy divine' still
continues, much of it resting upon the talismanic word 'ακειϙοζ':
probably Homer had the same notion of distance that a coquette
has of time, and when he talks of boundless, means half a mile; as
the latter, by a like figure, when she says *eternal* attachment, simply
specifies three weeks. [18]

Again the tenor of the note is one of brisk and unmystified matter-of-
factness, and again it is a corroborative note *about* corroboration and
authenticity, one which both answers and makes redundant the philo-
logical argument about the precise meaning of a word in Homer. What
exactly Homer thought of as the Hellespont, and whether coastal mor-
phology in the intervening centuries had altered its dimensions, had
long been and still remains the kind of detail upon which examina-
tions of the authenticity of the Homeric tales rested. By swimming the
Hellespont himself Byron out-performs textual wrangling (arguments
Byron had even heard conducted 'on the spot'), but in doing so he also
puts the fantastical and legendary feat of Leander to the ultimate
proof. This second authentication is not mentioned (it hardly needs to
be) because Byron is more interested here in the debate about the truth
of the tale of Troy. A textual digression in the poem itself has been
considering the terms of this debate:

> Minstrel! with thee to muse, to mourn –
>   To trace again those fields of yore –
> Believing every hillock green
>   Contains no fabled hero's ashes –
> And that around the undoubted scene
>   Thine own 'broad Hellespont' still dashes –
> Be long my lot – and cold were he
> Who there could gaze denying thee!

(II.3.ll.31–8)

The 'Minstrel' is Homer and Byron's memory here is of his personal
experience of visiting the Troad in 1810 and his certainty of its authenticity. An entry in the Ravenna journal of 1821 looks back upon the
same period in 1810 when Byron had traced 'those fields of yore':

we *do* care about 'the authenticity of the tale of Troy'. I have stood upon that plain *daily*, for more than a month, in 1810; and if anything diminished my pleasure, it was that the blackguard Bryant had impugned its veracity. It is true I read 'Homer Travestied' (the first twelve books), because Hobhouse and others bored me with their learned localities, and I love quizzing. But I still venerated the grand original as the truth of *history* (in the material *facts*) and of *place*. Who will persuade me, when I reclined upon a mighty tomb, that it did not contain a hero? – its very magnitude proved this. Men do not labour over the ignoble and petty dead – and why should not the *dead* be *Homer's* dead?[19]

Jacob Bryant's treatise entitled *Dissertation concerning the war of Troy, and the expedition of the Grecians, as described by Homer; showing that no such expedition was ever undertaken, and that no such city of Phrigia existed* (1796), was part of the late eighteenth-century exegetical debate in Homeric studies which gave close attention to such matters as whether the Hellespont could be described as 'broad'. For Byron, however, the hero's ashes were not 'fabled' but real, and the scene could only be 'undoubted', a rebuke to those antiquarian demystifiers such as Bryant who were 'cold' in their 'denying'. Even though his swim across the Hellespont had proved that it could hardly be called 'boundless', Byron's allegiance, with a possible pun on 'Be long' is firmly with the truth of the Homeric tales, with the imaginative and figurative truth of Homer's 'broad Hellespont' in the face of antiquarian literalism. This sense of authenticity is figured in terms of a lingering spirit-of-place which Byron believed he had perceived in 1810, particularly around the large tumuli ('every hillock green') thought to be the burial tombs of heroes such as Achilles and Patroklos, in fact dating from the later Hellenistic period. In other words the spirit-of-place is again associated with the lingering spirit of life around the dead, the spirit which lingers on in the hero's ashes and which is only denied by those who are 'cold'. Across the notes and text there is a direct chain of authentication working between Byron's feat of swimming the Hellespont and the determined belief that he experienced a direct and unmediated connection with the spirit-of-place upon the Troad. Byron's physical feat authenticates the spirit rather than the letter of the Homeric story (the Hellespont is only figuratively 'broad'), just as his physical presence upon the Troad authenticated to his own satisfaction the tangibility of the spirit of the heroes buried in the tumuli. For Byron, arguments about authenticity could only be settled in this way, where on-the-spot physical intervention supported and authenticated the spirit or imaginative truth of an historical matter. And *The Bride of Abydos* reproduces exactly that structure of proof in the cross-authentication of text and note.

When the longest of the Eastern tales, *The Corsair: A Tale* appeared in 1814, Byron's notes to later editions of the poem took pains to support events in the plot which might have seemed exaggeration or fantasy with historical proof. In this case, lest his readership took a sceptical view of the notion that by killing Seyd in cold blood Gulnare had violated a code of honour passionately adhered to by her lover Conrad, Byron provided long anecdotes illustrating similarly fine (aristocratic) feelings. The first of these anecdotes is taken from the *Boston Weekly Intelligencer* (November, 1814), and describes the gallantry of a superior type of pirate, Monsieur La Fitte (an ex-captain in Buonaparte's army), operating in the Bay of Barrataria, near New Orleans, sparing the life of a bounty-hunter who had come to capture him. The second, taken from the Reverend Mark Noble's *Biographical History of England* (1806), offers a portrait of an archbishop and classical scholar who, it was rumoured, had once been a buccaneer.[20] These distinguished pirates are introduced to make Conrad appear more believable without detracting from his extraordinariness, so that the crucial sense of facticity surrounds the codified tale of rebellion, aristocratic honour, and alienation.

With *Lara: A Tale* (1814) historical anecdotes provided in the notes to the fourth edition of the poem again support events in the plot which may seem improbable. The peasant's testimony of having seen a body dumped in a river 'was suggested by the description of the death or rather burial of the Duke of Gandia', taken from Roscoe's *The Life and Pontificate of Leo Tenth* (1805), and quoted at length.[21] This extract is another piece of historical evidence *about* evidence, about proof and testimony, and centred upon the misrecognition of a corpse – one of the Pope's sons is killed in mysterious circumstances and his body deposited in the Tiber inside a sack (recycling the incident behind *The Giaour*). What may seem fantasy in the tale proper is linked with a specific place, time and context in the corroborative note to the poem, even though Byron had taken pains to insist that the tale itself was placed nowhere. A note, probably written by Hobhouse, appeared in the first three editions of the poem which read: 'The reader is advertised that the name only of Lara being Spanish, and no circumstances of local or national description fixing the scene or hero of the poem to any country or age, the word "*Serf*", which could not be correctly applied to the lower classes in Spain, who were never vassals of the soil, has nevertheless been employed to designate the followers of our fictitious chieftain.'[22] A letter to Murray of 24 July 1814 confirms the unreality of the poem's location: '– the name only is Spanish – the country is not Spain but the Moon'.[23] Nevertheless, the apparent escape to the non-place of the moon fails to disguise the fact that the poem, far from existing in the free spaces of allegory, expresses an acute anxiety about place and location. The setting here is Spain *and* England, a composite place which in turn is haunted by the lingering ghost of the East. Lara's dying speech to his servant/ lover Kaled speaks of another place in another language:

> His dying tones are in that other tongue,
> To which some strange remembrance wildly clung.
> They spake of other scenes, but what – is known
> To Kaled, whom their meaning reach'd alone...
> ...
> And once as Kaled's answering accents ceas'd,
> Rose Lara's hand, and pointed to the East...

> (II.18.ll.444–7;466–7)

The cross-currents of nostalgia, homesickness and alienation are quite disorienting here. Dying, the Byronic hero speaks in an 'other tongue' and points to the East as if possessed by the spirit of his true home, a place enduring in 'strange remembrance' and inspiring his death-bed (once again the spirit of place and the spirit of life are in mysterious communion). Lara's death-tableau speaks for Byron too, pointing to the East with nostalgic longing as a place in which he somehow belongs, an adopted place of secret knowledge, and a place through which his alienation from English society is brought into the sharpest relief. Orientalism seems to have utterly exhausted itself by this point in Byron's writing, as the contemporary reviews had begun to point out, to the extent that the hero (who is a reincarnation of the Giaour and the Corsair) seems homesick and out of place in a tale which is both a recapitulation of the earlier tales, and an anxious bid to escape them (to the moon). Nevertheless, Byron's Oriental tales repeatedly return to these metaphors of hovering between life and death, between spirit and matter. They employ figures of the death-bed and the dying moment, the corpse and the lingering spirit, to suggest a tangible though ambiguous relationship between the spirit of a place and the material or physical 'body' of a landscape or situation. The relation between the poems themselves and their supplementary bodies of notes also functions along a borderline between spirit and matter. The cross-authentication that takes place between notes and poems holds the balance between the real and the fantastical, the reality of the East *as* fantastical, and the improbability of the tales as grounded in actual circumstance.

2.2   Everywhere and somewhere: *Childe Harold's Pilgrimage* III

Contradictory desires for the freedom of spaces unburdened with the material of history (freedom promised by the 'spirit of nature', for example), and at the same time for those consecrated spots offering the 'truth of *history* (in the material *facts*) and of *place*', send Childe Harold out of England in 1816 to follow in the footsteps of his author Lord Byron, himself following in the footsteps of others. The valedictory gestures which were concurrent with the beginnings of Byron's writing career and which continued to the end, nevertheless received their most forceful expression at the beginning of the third canto of *Childe Harold's Pilgrimage*, and are bathed in the poignant light of our knowledge that this really would be the last time Byron saw England and his daughter Ada. But the canto faces both ways as it moves away from English shores, saying farewell *and* turning its back, seeking to substitute the places of human history (indeed of humanity) with the radical freedom of belonging nowhere, or at least with the quasi-religious enthusiasm of belonging everywhere, in 'nature'. The opening stanzas of the third canto of *Childe Harold's Pilgrimage* dedicate the journey to solitudes:

> Where rose the mountains, there to him were friends;
> Where roll'd the ocean, thereon was his home;
> Where a blue sky, and glowing clime, extends,
> He had the passion and the power to roam;
> The desert, forest, cavern, breaker's foam,
> Were unto him companionship; they spake
> A mutual language, clearer than the tome
> Of his land's tongue, which he would oft forsake
> For Nature's pages glass'd by sunbeams on the lake.
>
> (13.ll.109–17)

This is a departure figured as self-exile and self-translation – like the dying Lara, the departing Harold speaks a different natural language to that spoken in 'his land'. The figure of the 'page' in particular (which in nature is blank as the dazzle of sun on the surface of a lake) will begin to recur frequently in the poetry written post-1816. As a metaphor for reading the landscape it is of course complicated by the occasions when nature's pages become history's page, i.e. in the places of significant historical event through which the narrative of *Childe Harold*, partly seeking escape from this kind of inscription, nevertheless inevitably winds its way. Inscription, both 'natural' and man-made, comes to dominate and indeed determine the map of *Childe Harold*, and the material ways in which history has marked the landscape – monuments, epitaphs, ruins, relics, souvenirs – contest the page with the non-material and glassy signature of 'nature'. As a result two quite distinct conceptions of the *genius loci* emerge through their contrasting relation to each other: the spirit of nature purified of humanity (or of purified humanity) on the one hand, and the spirit of history on the other; each with a relation to a different category of 'matter': the former to the actual physical places in which Byron discovers the 'natural'; and the latter to the materiality of historical memory and authenticity with which Byron is fascinated. These contradictory impulses are briefly and strangely united in the figure of Jean-Jaques Rousseau.

'Self-exiled' Harold's wandering cannot be a wandering over nothing for very long. The free places of nature coalesce into the forms of human history. It is as if Harold (or the reader) bumps into Waterloo:

> Stop! – for thy tread is on an Empire's dust!
> An Earthquake's spoil is sepulchred below!
> Is the spot mark'd with no colossal bust?
> Nor column trophied for triumphal show?
> None; but the moral's truth tells simpler so,
> As the ground was before, thus let it be; –
> How that red rain hath made the harvest grow!
> And is this all the world has gained by thee,
> Thou first and last of fields ! king-making Victory?

$$(III.17)[24]$$

The cluster of figures and associations here is familiar: footsteps treading on sacred or sepulchral ground; dust; a particular 'spot'; and, as if the spot were in fact a page and the intensity of place made graphic, there is a moral to read. In this case the field / spot / page tells us that the victory of Waterloo had secured the restoration of the Bourbons in France and confirmed the status quo of the Holy Alliance in Europe; more broadly that History is itself a 'ground' of circular patterns, recurrences and repetitions. But Byron wasn't entirely easy in reading the unmarked field in this way, and these stanzas again have a significant subtext in the accompanying notes. Byron, whose cousin Frederick Howard had died at Waterloo, had visited the battlesite on 4 May 1816:[25]

> My guide from Mont St. Jean over the field seemed intelligent and accurate. The place where Major Howard fell was not far from two tall and solitary trees (there was a third cut down, or shivered in the battle) which stand a few yards from each other at a pathway's side. – Beneath these he died and was buried. The body has since been removed to England. A small hollow for the present marks where it lay, but will probably soon be effaced; the plough has been upon it, and the grain is.
>
>   After pointing out the different spots where Picton and other gallant men had perished; the guide said, 'here Major Howard lay; I was near him when wounded'. I told him my relationship, and he seemed then still more anxious to point out the particular spot and circumstances. The place is one of the most marked in the field from the peculiarity of the two trees above mentioned.
>
>   I went on horseback twice over the field, comparing it with my recollection of similar scenes. As a plain, Waterloo seems marked out for the scene of some great action, though this may be mere imagination: I have viewed with attention those of Platea, Troy, Mantinea, Leuctra, Chaeronea, and Marathon; and the field around Mont St. Jean and Hougoumont appears to want little but a better cause, and that undefinable but impressive halo which the lapse of ages throws around a celebrated spot, to vie in interest with any or all of these, except perhaps the last mentioned.[26]

The ride across the field of Waterloo is an experimental re-enactment which aims to test the historical aura of the place through its material reality, and one in which Byron's own physical presence upon the field would be a kind of barometer of authenticity. It is a bizarre exercise in which the plains of Waterloo are haunted by the authenticity of the battlesites of Greece, against which they are measured and of course found wanting. Byron's reaction (like his reaction to Napoleon's defeat) is deeply equivocal. The 'undefinable but impressive halo which the lapse of ages throws around a celebrated spot' picks up earlier metaphors for the *genius loci*, the 'halo hovering round decay' with which the spirit of place was equated with the spirit of life in the lines on Greece at the beginning of *The Giaour*. Here, similarly, it records a degree of uncertainty and hesitation about whether the historical meaning of a landscape inheres supernaturally and enduringly across the ages or not, but offers no definition of what this 'halo' may in fact be, nor how it is related to the sacred. Does the celebration bring the halo, or the halo bring the celebration to the historical 'spot', and would a better 'cause' have hastened either the celebration or the halo? There is an even more obvious equivocation in Byron's claim that the field of Waterloo seems 'marked out for the scene of some great action, though this may be mere imagination'. If left unqualified, the first part of this sentence would have been an extreme claim to make, i.e. that a field seems 'marked out' (does this mean predestined?) for the historical events that occur there. The odd verb tense ('seems marked out'), and the haste to suggest that such an intuitive response to the field may have been 'mere imagination', both temper the claim. But the possibility at least that a place may be 'marked out for the scene of some great action' is an important part of Byron's topophiliac sensibility. Places may have historical force and significance aside from their written history, even before the monument or the 'colossal bust' is erected (the latter is a joke about the pseudo-Roman imperial image of Napoleon, and also a jibe at the humdrum Wellington). Just as the authenticity of the tale of Troy may be perceived upon the Troad regardless of the historical arguments among Homeric scholars, so the *force* of the field of Waterloo may be experienced as something quite separate from the written accounts of what happened there. This is to suggest that the historical event may have a more powerful claim upon the imagination in its material and lived reality than in its broader political or discursive meanings. The battle of Waterloo – that is, what took place on the fields around Hougoumont and Mont St Jean on 18 June 1815 – has a deep resonance for Byron in its physical reality, which is more immediately powerful than its significance in the realm of European politics, at least for the moment. There is in Byron's stanzas a certain solemn acknowledgement of the tragedy and complexity of the actual event which is quite different, and more subtle, than the haste to glorify or produce national myths in the manner of Southey or Scott.[27] This is of course in part explained by Byron's liberal or Whiggish ideology, his resistance to the pro-government tendency to see the battle as a final confrontation between the forces of good and evil. But the emotional complexity of this response arises not only because Byron had no sympathy with the victors; it is a crucial aspect of Byron's relation to history, to recent European history as much as to ancient history, that contemplation of the reality of the *experience* may produce the most powerful emotional reaction of all, and moreover that contemplation or reverie of this kind upon the battlefield itself may deepen an understanding of the broader meaning of the event in European political terms. This in turn is connected to Byron's belief that the experience of the battle may in some sense be recoverable through relation to the *place*, and particularly, of course, in relation to the 'spot'. (Here it is the 'particular spot and circumstances' of Major Howard's death which seem to represent the centre of the experience, the field-within-the-field of Waterloo, as it were.) In the case of Waterloo this does not mean the same kind of direct communion with the spirit-of-place Byron would later claim to have experienced on the plains of Troy, because the heroic virtues of Homer were not those of Wellington or Napoleon. Nevertheless the possibility that a place may yield the truth of history in the material facts still remains.

A cooler letter to Hobhouse from Carlsruhe dated 16 May 1816, retreats a little:

> The Plain at Waterloo is a fine one – but not much after Marathon & Troy – Cheronea – & Platea. — Perhaps there is something of prejudice in this – but I detest the cause & the victors – & the victory – including Blucher & the Bourbons.[28]

This is for Hobhouse the radical, and so we might expect it to be a little less impressed with Waterloo than with Marathon. But hesitation is still there, this time lest Byron is *under*estimating the power of Waterloo due to 'prejudice' against the victors. As such 'prejudice' stands opposite 'mere imagination' as the two qualifying checks on Byron's response to the battlefield, his curious fascination with the strange emptiness of the place itself, and his wonder at what this might mean. As with Parnassus, Byron offers a reading of the empty space in which the very emptiness has meaning, or tells the moral 'simpler so'. The signs of healthy life on the battlefield, 'the fresh green tree, / Which living waves where thou [Frederick Howard] did cease to live' (III.30), are living signs which refuse memorialisation, which do not speak of the dead. From this Byron forms his famous emblem of the heart 'brokenly' living on, 'Shewing no visible sign, for such things are untold' (33.297). If Waterloo contains a spirit-of-place, then as with the spirit of Parnassus, it is hidden, and as such it is stands for suffering which cannot be physically memorialised, which shows no visible or material sign. This suffering is of course that of Frederick Howard in death as well as those who are mourning that death, in particular Byron, who carries his own secret woes across the battlefield. But it also stands more broadly for the hidden tragedy of the event itself and the fact that this tragedy is not written upon the physical body of the landscape; a fact which is both appalling and of course entirely natural.

The possibility of private communion with historical experience through reverie upon the spot, particularly with the experience of suffering, with the subjectivity of the past, seems available to Byron in places such as Waterloo. But *Childe Harold*'s reading of the 'moral' in the empty fields is a deeply insecure and conflicted one. Riding over the battlefield in the spirit of re-enactment is one way of attempting to counter the indifference of the landscape to the events that occurred there. The letter to Hobhouse reveals that Byron's gallop over the fields of Mont St Jean was on 'a Cossac horse (left by some of the Don gentlemen at Brussels)', as if this brought him even closer to the actual events of June 1815. It is a desire to find signs where none are visibly showing, a desire which continues to defy the knowledge that 'such things are untold' in the opposite belief that the hidden experience of these events may in fact be known through material connection. In a religious sense this kind of impulse to re-enact narratives through the experience of *place* and to establish material contact with history has an obvious relation to the notion of the pilgrimage; but at the same time, there is a curiosity and a desire for comparison and evaluation in Byron's method which, in a secular sense, is closer to that of latter-day tourism. Is Waterloo quite as exciting as Marathon and Troy had been? There is something both of the holy relic and also the souvenir in the 'certain helms & swords' Byron carried away from Waterloo in May 1816.[29] But even before he had visited the battlesite and shortly after hearing news of Napoleon's defeat in June 1815, Byron pretended to have received and translated poems from the French written after the battle itself. Three poems dating from July–September 1815 were written as if 'From the French'. They are: 'Napoleon's Farewell', 'From the French: Must thou go, my glorious Chief...' (as if written by a Polish officer in Napoleon's army), and 'On the Star of "The Legion of Honour"'. These pieces enabled Byron to unbridle his sentimental feelings at the defeat of the Emperor in unambiguous terms, *as if* in another language – and these feelings were unambiguously sentimental only because they were 'translated' – as well as exploring the reality of the battle itself by entering its foreign dimension. The third poem was published in the *Examiner* in April 1816, just before Byron visited Waterloo, and is accompanied by Hunt's editorial note which reveals that the work is an exercise in dramatic monologue rather than an actual translation: 'The friend who favoured us with the following lines, the poetical spirit of which wants no trumpet of ours, is aware that they imply more than an impartial observer of the late period might feel, and are written rather as by Frenchman than Englishman.'[30] In the early spring of 1816 Byron produced an 'Ode: From the French', addressed to the battlesite itself, 'We do not curse thee, Waterloo / Though Freedom's blood thy plain bedew'. This poem was published anonymously in the *Morning Chronicle*, 15 March 1816, accompanied by a note (written by Byron) which claimed to have 'received the following poetical version of a poem, the original of which is circulating in Paris'.[31] In writing fake translations from the French Byron was indulging the fantasy of having swapped his native language for an apparently freer means of expression, momentarily escaping the complexities which would later return in his ride over the fields of Waterloo. Furthermore it was as if these poems were direct communiqués from the battlefield itself, graphic and material connections with the battlesite, like the swords and the helms and the ride on the Cossac horse, which allowed Byron access to hidden aspects of the emotional and experiential truth of the historical event. In fact the idea of exchanging places in this way in order to gain access to an interiority and subjectivity *on the other side*, would become increasingly important in the writing post-1816, and is I would suggest a method that develops partly as a response to Waterloo, where Byron's perspective was already instinctively the reverse of those of the majority of his countrymen.

One impulse of *Childe Harold* is to seek such tangibility and materiality everywhere and to charge it with the aura of history. For this reason the poem is especially drawn to the inscriptions of monument and sepulchre, epitaphs and memorials, where the spirit of the dead was most obviously available as reading matter: the 'small and simple pyramid' of the French General Francois Marceau's tomb at Coblentz, is one example, where Byron had slept in the room in which, as his note tells us, General Marceau was said to have been standing 'when a ball struck immediately below it' during the siege of Ehrenbreitstein.[32] The desire in some sense to re-enact, or to put oneself in another's place like this goes alongside the intense interest and seriousness, and markedly Protestant aesthetic values, with which Byron and Hobhouse examine lapidary inscriptions. Inscriptions should observe a simple decorum of direct, brief and unambiguous expression. The same directness and focus, the same reduction to essence which is figured in the notion of the spot or the halo seems also to have been what Byron and Hobhouse looked for in the epitaph – indeed epitaphs could sometimes be the graphic equivalent of the consecrated historical spot. Those on the monument to Marceau are criticised as 'rather too long, and not required' and are contrasted with that of General Lazare Hoche just outside Andernach:[33]

> The shape and style are different from that of Marceau's, and the inscription more simple and pleasing.
> > 'The Army of the Sambre and Meuse
> > to its Commander in Chief
> > Hoche.'
>
> This is all, and as it should be.[34]

Pausing at a 'spot should not be pass'd in vain'(III.63), the poem commemorates the battlesite of Morat where the Swiss defended themselves against the invading army of Charles the Bold, Duke of Burgundy, in 1476. The ossuary in which the bones of the Burgundian army were collected had been broken up by invading French forces in 1798. Nevertheless, Byron was able to collect 'the leg and wing of a Burgundian'[35] to send home to Murray, and in the notes offered an excuse reminiscent of Lord Elgin: 'Of these relics I ventured to bring away as much as may have made the quarter of a hero, for which the sole excuse is, that if I had not, the next passer by might have perverted them to worse uses than the careful preservation which I intend for them.'[36] As the poem passes through Switzerland Byron's notes quote in its Latin entirety the epitaph supposed to be that of Julia Alpinula, supposed to be the daughter of Julius Alpinus, chief of Aventicum. 'I know of no human composition', Byron writes, 'so affecting as this, nor a history of deeper interest.'[37]

But the third canto has a powerful contrary impulse to escape the materialism of souvenir collecting and lapidary inscription, to escape the inscribed landscapes of human history altogether and to discover a freedom in wandering over 'Eternity', or belonging nowhere. This takes the form of the pseudo-Wordsworthianism for which the canto is famous ('I live not in myself, but I become / Portion of that around me'), which

Byron had supposedly imbibed from Shelley on Lake Geneva. In this mode and indulging in rare metaphysical speculation, Byron wonders whether 'at length', when the mind or spirit is free from the body, there may be an after-life in which the self becomes a universal *genius loci*:

> shall I not
> Feel all I see, less dazzling, but more warm?
> The bodiless thought? The Spirit of each spot?
> Of which, even now, I share at times the immortal lot?

> (III.74).

Everything in this is hesitant and uncertain, including whether the 'immortal lot' of 'each spot' in which Byron claims at times to share, refers to the spots of historical significance where he habitually discovers a transcendental spirit, or the spots of 'nature' where he desires to escape history for a quite different kind of bodilessness. As is frequently noted, the poem is far from comfortable in this mode, which is in fact far from Wordsworthian and which is anxiously set aside ('this is not my theme') (III.76), only to be picked up again later.[38] But one of the ways in which canto three attempts to reconcile the desire for a bodiless diffusion into 'the spirit of each spot' with the historical spirits inscribed into nature's places, is through the figure and landscapes of Rousseau. Rousseau's novel *Julie, ou La Nouvelle Héloïse* (1761) had celebrated a particular spot of earth, Clarens in Switzerland, for which it had claimed a transcendent significance through a universalist and benevolent cult of sensibility. *Childe Harold* canto three, hesitantly moving towards such a philosophy, was also moving towards Clarens:

> Clarens! sweet Clarens, birth-place of deep Love!
> ...
> Clarens! by heavenly feet thy paths are trod, –
> Undying Love's, who here ascends a throne
> To which the steps are mountains; where the god
> Is a pervading life and light...

> (III.99/100)

Byron and Shelley embarked upon their tour of Lake Geneva on 22 June 1816 using Rousseau's *Julie* as a topographical guide. Writing to Hobhouse from Evian on 23 June, Byron announced: 'Tomorrow we go to Meillerei – & Clarens – & Vevey – with Rousseau in hand – to see his scenery – according to his delineation in his Héloïse now before me.'[39] Four days later he wrote to Murray from Ouchy: 'I have traversed all Rousseau's ground – with the Héloïse before me – & am struck to a degree with the force & accuracy of his descriptions – & the beauty of their reality'.[40] The third canto attempted to convey this 'accuracy' and 'reality' in terms of a *genius loci*, not of Rousseau, but of 'Love' inhering in the landscape. The following lines are perhaps among the strangest Byron ever wrote:

> All things are here of *him*; from the black pines,
> Which are his shade on high, and the loud roar
> Of torrents, where he listeneth, to the vines
> Which slope his green path downward to the shore,
> Where the bowed waters meet him, and adore,
> Kissing his feet with murmurs...
>
> (III.101)

Byron's reasons for taking the figure of Rousseau (and the British reviews customarily linked their names together as examples of a certain emotional and political delinquency), are complex. It was partly a desire to rehabilitate Rousseauvian sensibility in a post-Waterloo political context, and partly an urge to escape that very same context through a return to the erotico-sentimental vision of *Julie*.[41] However, the '*him*' of this stanza is not Rousseau, but Love; in fact the historical Rousseau is oddly invisible in Byron's response to Clarens as a landscape. This is not, in other words, the experience of a tourist who clutches his Murray or even his Byron in hand and who visits the scenes associated with a particular literary work in order to be able to discover signs of the author everywhere. Here Byron is claiming to have 'discovered' the same innate, living spirit of place, *in place*, as Rousseau had accurately and forcefully described it, as if this were an extrinsic feature of the landscape to be sketched on the spot. Moreover, it is as if the spirit of the place *itself* actively initiates observation of itself, compelling Rousseau to write *Julie*, and re-compelling Byron who is in a sense re-enacting Rousseau's moment of inspiration:

> 'Twas not for fiction chose Rousseau this spot,
> Peopling it with affections; but he found
> It was the scene which passion must allot
> To the mind's purified beings; 'twas the ground

> Where early Love his Psyche's zone unbound,
> And hallowed it with loveliness...

(III.104)

Spot/zone/hallowed ground: once more we have the image cluster of sacred place; the 'zone' refers to a girdle (Aphrodite's zone conferred upon the wearer the power to attract love), and so is a variant of the 'halo' as both are circular and supernatural figures for a particularly intense experience of the landscape – the 'zone' for the natural ground uninscribed with history and open to the 'mind's purified beings', and the 'halo' for the celebrated or consecrated 'spots' of historical significance.[42] Byron is suggesting that Rousseau *found* rather than invented a place instinct with erotico-sentimental meanings, a place he in turn has found as if it were a distinct feature of the landscape. Byron's note makes the same point:

> In July, 1816, [in fact June] I made a voyage round the Lake of Geneva; and, as far as my own observations have led me in a not uninterested nor inattentive survey of all the scenes most celebrated by Rousseau in his 'Héloïse', I can safely say, that in this there is no exaggeration... . If Rousseau had never written, nor lived, the same associations would not less have belonged to such scenes. He has added to the interest of his works by their adoption; he has shewn his sense of their beauty by the selection; but they have done that for him which no human being could do for them.[43]

As Waterloo seemed to Byron to be 'marked out for the scene of some great action', and as the Troad in defiance of the scholarly doubters offered the truth of history to the observer who stood daily upon its plains and tumuli, so if Rousseau 'had never written, nor lived, the same associations would not less have belonged to such scenes', according to Byron. In other words the spirit of place as delineated by Rousseau in the *Héloïse* inheres in the physical landscape, and is available to the visitor and observer who seeks authentication. Moreover, this spirit was there before Rousseau and is greater than Rousseau ('they have done that for him which no human being could do for them').

Critics have been suspicious of Byron's enthusiasms in the third canto of *Childe Harold*, and have doubted the force of this connection with the spirit of Rousseauvian love-in-nature. Moreover, by taking Rousseau out of Clarens, and by making Clarens and the scenery of

Lake Geneva possess a distinct aura of its own, Byron might be accused of radically misunderstanding Rousseau's sense of the transformative effect individual lives have upon a landscape and context. As Byron proclaims that "Twas not for *fiction* Rousseau chose this spot' (my italics) he seems to want Clarens to conform to his sense of the innate force of historical landscapes such as the field of Waterloo and the plains of Troy, partly in order to be able to claim both for Rousseau and Clarens a significant role in the revisionist history he is offering in a post-Waterloo context. This is to make of Clarens an historical monument to sensibility, and to worship that monument as possessing the historical aura perceived in Waterloo or Troy. When Hazlitt compared Byron and Rousseau in his essay 'On Byron and Wordsworth' he did so precisely to draw a distinction between Rousseauvian sentiment as stimulated by nature, which he believed had a spontaneity and originality, and what he thought of as the false and hackneyed Byronic sentiment for historical monuments:

> When Rousseau called out – 'Ah! voilà de la pervenche!' in a transport of joy at sight of the periwinkle, because he had first seen this little blue flower in company with Madame Warrens thirty years before, I cannot help thinking that any astonishment expressed at the sight of a palm-tree, or even of Pompey's Pillar, is vulgar compared to this.[44]

No doubt Hazlitt would have found the astonishment expressed at Clarens similarly vulgar because it responds to the setting of a romantic novel as if it had an historical significance and aura, and in doing so fails to understand or engage with the individual and private expansions of Rousseauvian sensibility ('Ah! voilà de la pervenche'). What Byron seems to be attempting to do in Clarens, however, is momentarily reconcile the canto's conflicting urges on the one hand to replace the inscriptions of human history with the natural signs of a cult of sensibility; and on the other to read the landscape in terms of spots of historical significance. Byron's own ecstatic exclamations of time regained are for 'Clarens! sweet Clarens', where he believed historical significance and 'natural' sensibility came together. Moreover, Byron was later to discover precisely the kind of personal and material connection with Rousseau and Lake Geneva that was essential to his sense of historical significance and authenticity. A letter to Murray, written the following April, 1817, recounts an odd coincidence which had been brought to Byron's attention by Augusta. John Andre De Luc, a reader to Queen Charlotte, Swiss-born though living in England, had heard recited Byron's *Prisoner of Chillon* (1816):

> I will tell you something about Chillon. – A Mr. *De Luc* ninety years old – a Swiss – had *it* read to him & is pleased with it – so my Sister writes. – He [de Luc] said that he was *with Rousseau* at *Chillon* – & that the description is perfectly correct – but this is not all – I recollected something of the name & find the following passage in 'The Confessions' – vol. 3. Page 247. Liv. 8th –
>> 'De tous ces amusemens celui qui me plut davantage – fut une promenade autour du Lac – que je fis en bateau avec *De Luc* pere – sa bru – ses *deux fils* – et ma Thérèse. – Nous mimes sept jours a cette tournée par le plus beau temps du monde. J'en gardai le vif souvenir des sites qui m'avoient frappé a l'autre extremité du lac, et dont je fis la description quelques années apres, dans la Nouvelle Heloise.
>
> This nonagenarian De Luc must be one of the 'deux fils'. He is in England – infirm but still in faculty.—It is odd that he should have lived so long – & not wanting in oddness that he should have made this voyage with Jean Jacques – & afterwards at such an interval read a poem by an Englishman (who had made precisely the same circumnavigation) upon the same scenery.[45]

The young De Luc had taken a seven day boat-trip around Lake Geneva in the company of Rousseau who had recorded his 'clearest memories of those spots' ('le vif souvenir des sites') which he would later use in *Julie, ou La Nouvelle Héloïse,* and which Byron would retrace (and re-live) in his seven day boat-trip around the lake (23–30 June 1816) with Shelley. During this later trip the two poets visited the Castle of Chillon, where Byron would later set the poem *The Prisoner of Chillon,* which De Luc would hear in England. For De Luc the accuracy of Byron's topographical descriptions would stir memories of Rousseau and the vivid spots on Lake Geneva. But for Byron this odd coincidence confirmed his belief that there was a spirit inherent in the scenery of Lake Geneva that was not merely an imaginative construction of Jean Jaques Rousseau, but could be perceived by visitors, and was authenticated precisely through this direct chain of connection whereby Byron's description of Chillon went back to Rousseau and the scenery of the *Héloïse* through De Luc, who had actually *been there* with Rousseau on the lake. Unconsciously (and a superstitious Byron would have perceived a larger design in this), Rousseau's response to the *genius loci* of Lake Geneva had been re-enacted, and therefore authenticated in the only way that mattered, on the spot.

The link between memory and material connection (there in the translation of the French 'souvenir') keeps drawing the third canto back into the halo of human history and inscription, particularly those inscribed with literary value, even as it seeks the 'desert, forest, cavern, breaker's foam'. In this sense the canto reflects the intense interest in relics and souvenirs displayed by Byron during his travels in Italy at this time. From Ouchy Byron sent Murray a 'sprig of *Gibbon's Acacia* & some rose leaves from his garden', reminding his publisher of the famous passage in Gibbon's autobiography which recalled taking 'several turns in a *berceau*, or covered walk of acacias' (which Byron of course would re-enact) having completed his *Decline and Fall of the Roman Empire* in 1787.[46] Burgundian bones, acacia sprigs, swords and helms: and more. From the Villa Diodati, on 8 September, Byron wrote to Augusta informing her that Scrope Davies would return to England with packets for her 'of seals – necklaces – balls &c. – & I know not what – formed of Chrystals – Agates – and other stones – *all of & from Mont Blanc* bought & brought by me on & from the spot – expressly for you to divide among yourself and the children'.[47] When Byron arrived in Milan in October he wrote to Augusta announcing that what had delighted him most was 'a manuscript collection (preserved in the Ambrosian library), of original loveletters and verses of Lucretia de Borgia & Cardinal Bembo; and a lock of hair – so long – and fair & beautiful', supposed to be that of Lucretia.[48] Byron resolved to obtain copies of the letters and 'some of the hair if I can'.[49] He failed in the former enterprise, but did manage to obtain 'one single hair...as a relic'[50]. An autograph note on a scrap of paper has survived, which reads: '"And Beauty draws us by a single Hair". The Hair contained in this paper belonged to Lucretia Borgia and was obtained by me from a lock of it which is preserved in the Ambrosian Library.'[51]

Relics and souvenirs, inscriptions and epitaphs, proofs and authentications – the poem and its accompanying notes are repeatedly drawn back into the material of the continental journey even as sections of the third canto attempt a flight into the 'free' spaces of nature, or seek a momentary reconciliation of contrary impulses in the sentimental zone of Clarens. Other work of 1816–17 also took up the relationship between 'spirit' and 'matter', or between bodiless thought and the spatio-temporal constrictions determining it, particularly through the notion of interiority and self-sufficiency, or the mind as its own place.

2.3   The mind is its own place: *The Prisoner of Chillon, Manfred, The Lament of Tasso*

Byron's 'Sonnet on Chillon' records the first visit he made to the chateau during the tour of Lake Geneva with Shelley in late June 1816, and offers what was to become a Byronic commonplace of the poetry of 1816–17; that is, that even as the body was confined to chains, the 'chainless mind' remained an emblem of liberty. The dungeons of the chateau at Chillon had been the prison of François Bonnivard, Genevan Republican patriot, between 1530 and 1536:

> Chillon! thy prison is a holy place,
>   And thy sad floor an altar – for 'twas trod,
> Until his very steps have left a trace
>   Worn, as if thy cold pavement were a sod,
> By Bonnivard! – May none those marks efface!
> For they appeal from tyranny to God.

> (ll.9–14)

Here again is the motif of a holy or consecrated place, in this case *marked out* by footsteps – Bonnivard's memory is preserved in the worn stones, retrodden by Byron in 1816. The longer poem to come out of that visit, *The Prisoner of Chillon. A Fable*, is a monologue in couplets, which develops and darkens this meditation upon the relationship between the mind, the place of confinement, and liberty.[52] In the 'fable' Byron's François Bonnivard provides a minute inventory of his prison-cell (supplemented with a fuller description in a note to the poem), in which the couplet form suggests a mind functioning rationally and clearly, its self-rhyming a symptom of self-integration. The prisoner then recounts the slow decline and eventual death of the two brothers confined with him in the cell, until his solitude is absolute:

> *I* only stirr'd in this black spot,
> *I* only lived – *I* only drew
> The accursed breath of dungeon-dew;
> The last – the sole – the dearest link
> Between me and the eternal brink,
> Which bound me to my failing race,
> Was broken in this fatal place.

> (ll.211–18)

Darker than the sonnet (which was written later with a fuller knowledge of the facts of Bonnivard's life, and was intended to celebrate his heroism), *The Prisoner of Chillon* explores the possibility that the republican virtue of free reason ('the mind is its own place') also contains the possibility of a hellish solipsism in which the mind is *alone* in its own place. Bonnivard's total solitude in 'this black spot' leads to a loss of the notion of the mind having a place at all, as the poem slips towards the mindlessness (and placenessness) of insanity:

> It was not night – it was not day,
> It was not even the dungeon-light,
> So hateful to my heavy sight,
> But vacancy absorbing space,
> And fixedness – without a place...

> (ll.240–4)

At the degree-zero of the monologue, in the absence of all other coordinates of the self, the mind is incapable of conceptualising its own existence, sliding instead into a kind of Coleridgean limbo. From this non-place Bonnivard slowly recovers and regains a sense of self, but at just what price exactly is ambiguous. When eventually Bonnivard is set free, his freedom comes with some regret:

> And half I felt as they were come
> To tear me from a second home...
> ...
> My very chains and I grew friends,
> So much a long communion tends
> To make us what we are: – even I
> Regain'd my freedom with a sigh.

> (ll.379–80; 391–4)

Byron's generic subtitle 'a fable' hints at the open-endedness and interpretative challenge posed by the poem. In one sense these lines assert the strength of a human spirit in reconstructing its 'own place' from the limbo-vacancy of the brink of madness, developing the Romantic trope of the 'happy prison' as a means of championing the freedom of the mind over those tyrannical forces which may oppose it. The primary force of Byron's ending with this emphasis is political defiance. But the 'happy prison' is a deeply ambiguous political symbol which may be read quite differently, so that these sentiments might represent the weak assertion of a broken mind that has in fact lost all sense of the meaning of freedom, of a mind grown attached to its prison-cell simply as a means of survival or submission. Given this emphasis the ending of the poem is politically pessimistic, and Bonnivard's 'sigh' on regaining freedom is a sign of the collapse of mental resistance to prolonged oppression. His imprisonment thus becomes an emblem of the way place is crucial in determining us, and may in extreme circumstances wholly assimilate the autonomous self, so that our minds themselves may be reduced, confined, and even reshaped to prison-houses. Bonnivard's observation that 'so much a long communion tends / To make us what we are' plays with the religious connotations of 'communion', a word Byron enjoyed using, to suggest that the mind will instinctively and profoundly interact with *whatever* its location may be. The republican virtue of free reason can easily be made to seem like a politically quietist counsel of despair or resignation, which of course it is, in part, for Milton's Satan. Even worse it may be seen as an act of complicity with the forces that have imprisoned Bonnivard in the first place. Written a year after Waterloo, it is clear that *The Prisoner of Chillon* is deeply troubled by the options open to a republicanism in full retreat, suspicious of the notion of a consolatory self-sufficiency – of the notion that, whatever may be the configurations of the map of Europe, the mind at least remains its own place and as such may claim to have preserved its 'freedom'; while at the same time the poem is clearly anxious to discover historical examples and precedents of absolute political defiance. If the mind is pre-eminently determined by its spatio-temporal condition (and this of course is always fundamentally located in the reality of the material body), then in what sense is the 'spirit' of mental resistance free and self-sufficient?

This question journeyed with Byron on his self-exile from England in 1816, through his travels of 1816–17, and became an obsessive theme in his writing throughout this year. 'Prometheus', for example, is a hymn to the possibility of the mind's 'own concentred recompense' (l.57), in which place no longer acts as a negatively determining element, but is, as it were, overcome. But for Byron this idea of Promethean virtue is always both a political virtue and a private refuge – a form of liberal politics which is also psychologically fatalist. Works such as *The Prisoner of Chillon* were less confident about the possibility of this kind of self-reliance, and more anxious about the slide towards madness. The ambivalence can be perceived in a brace of quotations to which Byron keeps returning during this period. The first is from the closing lines of *Paradise Lost* ('The World was all before them'), which Byron was adopting as 'the world is all before me' in letters outlining his travel-plans post-1814.[53] The separation from Lady Byron overshadows this promise of other worlds with the sorrow of a paradise lost and an exile gained, and in early 1816 Byron begins to quote in letters to friends variations of Shakespeare's *Coriolanus*, III, iii. 1.133: 'There is a world elsewhere'.[54] The two quotations seem to become conflated in a self-consciously exilic letter to Augusta written from the Villa Diodati, 8 September 1816, with the sinister ring that 'I have still a world before me – this – or the next'.[55] The bitterly sorrowful 'Epistle to Augusta' (written in the late summer of 1816, but not published during Byron's lifetime on Augusta's wishes), states that there are two things remaining in Byron's 'destiny': 'A world to roam through – and a home with thee'(l.8), later proclaiming: 'The world is all before me' (l.81). *The Lament of Tasso* (1817) has Tasso draw a comparison between himself in his prison-cell and a ship-wrecked sailor: 'The world is all before him – *mine* is *here*'(l.183). Related to this notion of a world elsewhere, or all before, is a third quotation which seems to be everywhere (though never directly quoted) in Byron's writing of 1816–17, and that of course derives from Milton's Satan: 'A mind not to be changed by place or time. / The mind is its own place, and in itself / Can make a heaven of hell, a hell of heaven' (*Paradise Lost*, I.ll.253–5). Byron was uncertain in 1816 whether having the world all before him represented a heavenly or hellish prospect; and compounded with this uncertainty, came the anxiety that the mind could not always be relied upon to be its own place, but that place would determine the mind, or worse, the mind would slip into the disorder of placelessness. The dangers of the 'Satanic' philosophy (as it is filtered through Miltonic republicanism) were always perfectly obvious to Byron – that the con-centred self would merely descend into solipsism or madness, or that a defeated republicanism would have no other place of refuge but in a form of political quietism and self-consolation – but this was an aware-ness his detractors, from Southey onwards, have failed to notice. To pre-serve the sovereignty of the mind's own concentred space against the determining forces of the spatio-temporal world, meant for example re-processing and interiorising the Alpine landscape through which Byron toured during September 1816 into the psycho-biographical drama of *Manfred* (published 1817).

Byron had left the Villa Diodati in late August 1816 with Hobhouse and Scrope Davies for a tour of Chamouni and Mont Blanc, where he had collected stones and chrystals for his sister, returning to the Villa Diodati at the beginning of September. Later that month he embarked on a more ambitious excursion of the Bernese Oberland with Hobhouse, and during 18–28 September kept an 'Alpine Journal' for Augusta, closely recording the details of their journey, including a return to the chateau at Chillon where a drunken corporal showed the travellers 'all things from the Gallows to the Dungeon (the *Potence* & the *Cachets*)'.[56] In fact it is details such as this, what we might call the less mountainous and anti-sublime aspects of the journal which are the most memorable – the English lady fast asleep in her carriage 'in the most anti-narcotic spot in the world';[57] Byron's description of tumbling down slippery slopes, or attempting to help a bleating goat over a fence, or buying a dog en route. This is all, of course, with his sister in mind, but it is also a mode of seeing which is quite instinctive to Byron, in which the precise evocation of place and circumstance offsets the larger claims of the 'whole', and anecdote and detail replace any general attempt at the 'Alpine'. The sublime aspects of the trip, or what Byron referred to as 'the romantic part' or 'what touches upon the rocks &c.',[58] are experiences of a kind that Byron always insisted defeated prose description, so that the journal focuses on the human culture among the Alps, whether it be the dullness of English tourists, buying dogs or evidence of pastoralism among the Swiss.[59] However, when Byron comes to write *Manfred* 'for the sake of introducing the Alpine scenery in description'[60] he barely touches upon this softer version of pastoral, indeed he does not offer detailed or precise descriptions of Alpine culture at all but rather invokes the mountains abstractly, as if 'the Alps' are in fact a literary mode rather than a place, and as a literary mode (like Orientalism) they readily translate into 'psychological and metaphysical correlatives'.[61] This means not only that the Alps stand for a certain ideal model of the human mind: grand, free, soaring, solitary, etc. – these commonplaces are taken for granted; but that the very process of turning the Alps into a literary and psychological mode is in itself an assertion of the sovereignty of the mind over its determining places. The Alps disappear in *Manfred* into what we might call 'Alpineism', that is, they are not primarily a setting, nor even a metaphor; but a philosophical orientation, which includes the notion that the mind is its own place. In other words, the 'Alps' of *Manfred* represent the overcoming of place, the concentredness of the human mind, while the most vivid evocation of a specific place is not of an Alpine source at all, but Roman,

coming at the beginning of the final scene as Manfred appears alone
inside his tower and remembers the Coliseum in moonlight:

> And thou didst shine, thou rolling moon, upon
> All this, and cast a wide and tender light,
> Which soften'd down the hoar austerity
> Of rugged desolation, and fill'd up,
> As 'twere, anew, the gaps of centuries;
> Leaving that beautiful which still was so,
> And making that which was not, till the place
> Became religion, and the heart ran o'er
> With silent worship of the great of old!

> (III.iv.ll.31–9)

The strange anomalousness of this description has often been commented upon – a memory of Rome returning among the Jungfrau – but
its significance lies in its very specificity of place and the fact that this is
entirely out of place in a drama in which the determinants of the spatio-
temporal world are challenged by the promise of mental self-sufficiency.
Manfred has just rejected the religious counsel of the friar, who will inter-
rupt this meditation to renew his appeal, in vain, in which context
Manfred's claim that 'the place / Became religion' is in part an antitype to
orthodox Christian thinking. The vision Manfred is attempting to recall is
one in which the rays of the moon seemed to reconstruct the architecture
of the Coliseum, filling up 'the gaps of centuries' and returning the great
construction to an original wholeness. (In this sense the arena is a further
example of the zone–halo–spot matrix). Manfred's response to this vision
of restoration was profound and extreme: his heart 'ran o'er' (as if its gaps
too were filled up and made whole) with 'silent worship of the great of
old', an ecstatic experience of history-in-place, and a moment in which
communion with a past that is vividly and tangibly alive seemed possible. Coming as it does at the moment of Manfred's rejection of all
succour to the self except the mind's own sovereignty, this memory of a
place becoming 'religion' stands as a challenge not only to Christianity
but to radical self-sufficiency, so that the Coliseum is, as it were, an antithetical figure to that of the Alps, a place in which Manfred's connection
with the buried subjectivity of history redeems him from the solipsism of
the mind's own place.

   This of course would become one of the most famous of Byron's evo-
cations of the spirit-of-place and would be appended to descriptions of

the Coliseum in John Murray's handbooks. The very fact that the passage was so easily decontextualised demonstrates its odd relationship to a drama ostensibly set in the Alps, since this Roman sense of a place-spirit, or of a place becoming religion, is in sharp contrast to the quite different notion of 'spirits' with which *Manfred* abounds. The 'spirits' of *Manfred* are not religious or historical spirits at all in fact, nor even spirits of particular place – rather the word represents the bodilessness dreamt of in the third canto of *Childe Harold*, and reprised in exclamations such as Manfred's 'Oh, that I were / The viewless spirit of a lovely sound' (I.ii.ll.52–3). Such an emphasis has a Germanic provenance up to a point – the influence of Goethe's *Faust* has been filtered through Madame De Staël's *D'Allemagne*, as well as drawing in part upon more home-grown theories of matter infused with spirit (most often politically inflected) in the science of writers such as Joseph Priestly. It is also, however, a peculiarly Byronic word : 'spirit' in *Manfred* represents the abstract notion of something connecting the human subject to its environment, something bodiless and viewless which has an analogy with the human mind, with which it shares a natural environment. In this sense the metaphysical meditation of *Manfred* is closely related to the political thinking of *The Prisoner of Chillon*, since they are both engaged in a critique of a certain form of materialism (the world as a place empty of spirit), and an exploration of the notion of the mind as its own place. Manfred (having spoken to the ghost of Astarte) finally comes to deny (or defy) the notion of a spirit-world. Instead the vision and condition he embraces is that of the mind as its own place, or a world in which place has no spirit and in which solitude cannot be shared with anything:

> The mind which is immortal makes itself
> Requital for its good or evil thoughts –
> Is its own origin of ill and end –
> And its own place and time – its innate sense,
> When stripp'd of this mortality, derives
> No colour from the fleeting things without,
> But is absorb'd in sufferance or in joy,
> Born from the knowledge of its own desert.

                                                    (III.iv.ll.129–36)

It is impossible to ignore the sabotage of that pun (intentional or unintentional) in which 'desert' is haunted by the sound of 'desart', i.e. that what the mind knows and inherits as its own deserved self-sufficiency may in fact be a wilderness or vacuum. The more positive sense of 'desert' as the mind's 'own concentred recompense' represents the possibility of a triumphant Prometheanism, a mind rising above its place and time, a possibility *The Prisoner of Chillon* had problematised. It represents a renunciation of the notion of the physical world as infused with spirit, a rejection of the analogy between the mind and these natural spirits; and instead constitutes the belief that the mind is *not* determined by place, but is its own place, alone. With this knowledge, or beneath this delusion, Manfred expires.

Byron summarised the plot of *Manfred* for Murray in a letter written from Venice on 15 February 1817, describing it as 'a kind of poem in dialogue (in blank verse) or drama...of a very wild – metaphysical – and inexplicable kind'.[62] Elsewhere he associates it with the third canto of *Childe Harold* and links both works with his unhappiness following the departure from England and the subsequent summer and autumn on the continent. Of the third canto he wrote to Thomas Moore in the new year of 1817: 'I was half mad during the time of its composition, between metaphysics, mountains, lakes, love unextinguishable, thoughts unutterable, and the nightmare of my own delinquencies. I should, many a good day, have blown my brains out, but for the recollection that it would have given pleasure to my mother-in-law; and, even *then*, if I could have been certain to haunt her'.[63] In March 1817, Byron described *Manfred* to Moore as 'a sort of mad Drama, for the sake of introducing the Alpine scenery in description... . Almost all the *dram. pers.* are spirits, ghosts, or magicians, and the scene is in the Alps and the other world, so you may suppose what a Bedlam tragedy it must be.'[64]

Although the drama clearly emerges from a period of psychological torment, taking this as its subject, the relation between mental suffering and the Alps is not a straightforward one, as the mountains offer neither an unequivocal correlative for mental superiority, nor a clear image of mental breakdown. The borderline between the Alps and the 'other world' is an indistinct one, and this very uncertainty represents the frightening prospect of Bedlam or madness. In fact the relation of the Alps to the mind and the mind's sufferings is not straightforwardly metaphorical at all, but is a philosophical and generic relation in which the 'Alpineism' of the drama stands for a freedom from the determining forces of any place. Alongside *The Prisoner of Chillon*, however, it is easy to see that the poem shares an anxiety about the concentred mind and the possibility that mind-without-place represents a loss or collapse of identity. Manfred's visionary insight seems to come in a memory of the Coliseum at midnight, rather than in the soaring wilderness of the Jungfrau. It is possible, as Byron knew, that the Alps might only *fail* to offer 'psychological and metaphysical correlatives', standing in their enormity as particularly large reminders of the absence of any non-material spirit inhering in the physical world. Whether embracing this absence is a manifestation of sanity or madness the drama can never decide. That the Alps, however, were neither distraction, comforting emblem, nor therapeutic symbol for Byron's anguish is attested by the pathetic note with which his 'Alpine Journal' closes:

> But in all this – the recollections of bitterness – & more especially of recent & more home desolation – which must accompany me through life – have preyed upon me here – and neither the music of the Shepherd – the crashing of the Avalanche – nor the torrent – the mountain – the Glacier – the Forest – nor the Cloud – have for one moment – lightened the weight upon my heart – nor enabled me to lose my own wretched identity in the majesty & the power and the Glory – around – above – & beneath me.[65]

This of course is to be like Manfred himself. Nevertheless, in between revisions of the third act of the drama Byron further explored the relationship between the mind and place, between self-sufficiency and madness, and returned to the experience of historical place (the powers Manfred had witnessed in Rome) for the vindicated prophecy of *The Lament of Tasso*.

A short preface to *The Lament of Tasso* records what Byron had seen during his visit to Ferrara in April 1817:

> At Ferrara (in the library) are preserved the original MSS. of Tasso's Gierusalemme and of Guarini's Pastor Fido, with letters of Tasso, one from Titian to Ariosto; and the inkstand and chair, the tomb and the house of the latter. But as misfortune has a greater interest for posterity, and little or none for the cotemporary, the cell where Tasso was confined in the hospital of St. Anna attracts a more fixed attention than the residence or the monument of Ariosto – at least it had this effect on me. There are two inscriptions, one on the outer

gate, the second over the cell itself, inviting, unnecessarily, the wonder and the indignation of the spectator. Ferrara is much decayed, and depopulated; the castle still exists entire; and I saw the court where Parisina and Hugo were beheaded, according to the annal of Gibbon.[66]

Byron had visited Ferrara on his way from Venice to Rome, choosing to travel to Bologna via Ferrara rather than Mantua in order to see 'the cell where they caged Tasso, and where he became mad'.[67] Writing to Hobhouse from Florence on 22 April, Byron described what he had seen in Ferrara, fascinated (as the preface emphasises) by handwriting and manuscripts, 'Tasso's correspondence about his dirty shirts',[68] by places of public execution (Byron had a particular interest in beheadings), by inscriptions, and of course by the *actual place* where Tasso had been imprisoned. Hobhouse's *Historical Illustrations of the Fourth Canto of Childe Harold's Pilgrimage* (1818), quotes the inscription above the cell in full, and scrupulously examines the ways in which it may be flawed. Moreover, Hobhouse gives the exact dimensions of the cell, 'nine paces long, between five and six wide, and about seven feet high',[69] before going on to discuss the reasons for believing that this particular place had dubious claims to authenticity. Hobhouse, like Byron, emphasises the current decay and depopulation of Ferrara, observing that 'when Tasso arrived in Ferrara in 1565, he found the city one brilliant theatre. The largest streets which he saw thronged with all the forms of gaiety and splendour, are now ulmost untrodden, and support a few paupers in the fruitless attempt to eradicate the grass and weeds.'[70] This fact is crucial to the ways in which the poem offers prophecy of future vindication.

Writing the *Lament* on the journey to Rome, Byron adopted a version of the Torquato Tasso legend which he knew had been historically debunked, and to which Hobhouse would himself offer further demystification in the *Historical Illustrations* – that is, the version in which Alphonse III Duke of Ferrara has the poet Tasso imprisoned in the Hospital of Sant' Anna between 1579 and 1586 because of his love for Leonora, Alphonse's sister. This enabled Byron to write a monologue for a poet wrongly imprisoned and persecuted at the hands of a tyrant, for love which offends social convention, and so placed the poem in the on-going sequence of persecution poems dating from Byron's departure from scandalised England in 1816, in which Byron's protagonists are also versions of his troubled self, prophesying their own vindication in posterity. It also of course enabled Byron to return to the subject of imprisonment and madness, and the question of the ability of the mind to be its own place. Tasso had completed his masterwork *Gierusalemme Liberate* in Sant' Anna's, and in doing so had, as it were, travelled in his imagination. But Tasso's description of his own misery is also a testament to the mind's painful dependence upon its immediate spatio-temporal condition:

> Feel I not wroth with those who bade me dwell
> In this vast lazar-house of many woes?
> Where laughter is not mirth, nor thought the mind,
> Nor words a language, nor ev'n men mankind;
> Where cries reply to curses, shrieks to blows,
> And each is tortured in his separate hell –
> For we are crowded in our solitudes –

> (ll.82–8)

The phrase 'crowded in our solitudes' refers to the close grouping of the separate cells in Sant'Anna's, where solitary confinement would not detach a prisoner from the sense of those others around him. But this also suggests a more abstract condition, an allegory indeed of the divided self or the self-in-exile, in which the mind is simultaneously alone (as Bonnivard discovered himself to be), and suffocated by other presences, other strangers. Here there is no possibility of an autonomous space delineating the self, only a hell of crowded solitude, a mind invaded by that which is alien to itself. If Bonnivard's imprisonment had reduced him to a defeated quietism, Tasso's confinement is a more painful reduction of the world to the mind:

> Perchance in such a cell we suffer more
> Than the wrecked sailor on his desart shore;
> The world is all before him – *mine* is *here*,
> Scarce twice the space they must accord my bier.

> (ll.181–4)

Even for a major poet in resistance to a political tyranny, imprisonment might fail to be a source of liberation through which the mind (or spirit) is free to wander over a 'world elsewhere' in the imagination, but instead might represent the *death* of the mind and all possibility of consolation (worse than the '*desart* shore'). The reality of suffering undermines the political motif of the happy prison, or the resistance to tyranny through the independence of the reasoning faculty. Tasso (in Byron's version) has to reflect upon the fact that his confinement had made him go mad. As the mind's 'own place' has proved not to be enough to sustain his sanity, he turns to the place of his confinement, his prison-cell, and predicts a future life of fame for *this* place, and of decline for Ferrara:

> and I make
> A future temple of my present cell,
> Which nations yet shall visit for my sake.
> While thou, Ferrara! when no longer dwell
> The ducal chiefs within thee, shall fall down,
> And crumbling piecemeal view thy hearthless halls,
> A poet's wreath shall be thine only crown,
> A poet's dungeon thy most far renown,
> While strangers wonder o'er thy unpeopled walls!

> (ll.219–27)

Symbolically, Tasso is reclaiming his mind by performing his own act of consecration for the very place (the prison-cell) that took away his sanity, making of it a 'future temple'. And of course such a prophecy is self-enacting as Tasso's 'predicted' future is fulfilled by the poem itself and by the fact that in 1817, as the preface reveals, the decaying and depopulated Ferrara was visited partly due to this very renown and the interest posterity had in the hospital of Sant' Anna's. This is the first of many such 'prophecies' retrospectively enacted in Byron's poetry of post-1816. They rely firstly upon the structure of the dramatic monologue as an act of poetic ventriloquism which enables Byron to make the contemporary moment seem like a future to the deeper past. But they are also in each case connected to Byron's own direct experience of specific spots, and often with some kind of physical re-enactment or exchange in which Byron literally puts himself in the place of his subject – in this case by visiting the cell in Sant'Anna's, the 'spot' which then comes to occupy the centre of the poem's vision. *The Lament of Tasso* again draws upon an imaginative investment in the idea of a material connection with the past which gives access to the subjectivity of the historical person. The authentic physical connection through *place* allows Byron to ventriloquise these subjects in dramatic monologues which offer prophecies of vindication. In this case the prophecy of 'far renown' is re-stated towards the end of the poem as Tasso predicts a future when the tyrant has been forgotten, and the prison-cell in Sant' Anna's has acquired a holy status:

> when the towers
> And battlements which guard his joyous hours
> Of banquet, dance, and revel, are forgot,
> Or left untended in a dull repose,
> This – this shall be a consecrated spot!

(ll.236–240)

As we have seen, the 'consecrated spot' represents Byron's most intense engagement with the meaning of place, his largest claims for a direct connection with historical material, and his strongest invest- ment in the notion of an ecstatic or even mystical communion with the dead. Another way of phrasing this would be Manfred's the 'place / Became religion', and here similarly there is a sense of the interpene- tration of historical subjects. This is undoubtedly an extraordinary his- toriographical method, mixing religious emotion with historical narrative, and it is one that may be obscured by readings of Byron which get stuck on the fact that Tasso's voice is quite obviously the poet's own (so that Byron could be seen as merely 'projecting' himself into a vessel for his own narrow concerns). But this would be to fail to see the complexity in Byron's use of historical exchange, the possibility that an inter-subjective engagement of this kind with history may in fact change the conditions of the present – so that Byron/Tasso's 'prophecy' may not only anticipate the contemporary situation in the decaying and depopulated Ferrara, but may also in fact *create* the con- ditions of Tasso's 'far renown', bringing the work of the poet into the consciousness not just of an English audience, but to an Italian literary public in need of the unifying national myths and figures necessary for a *risorgimento*. The very fact that Tasso's 'far renown' is being celebrated by an English poet, gives Italian literary culture the European dimen- sion Byron and Hobhouse both felt was a necessary element in a nationalist sensibility. At the same time these 'prophetic' dramatic monologues are also more subtle exercises in Byronic self-construction than has been allowed. Crumbling and unpeopled Ferrara, and the towers and battlements of Alphonse's ducal palace 'left untended in a dull repose' are also a transposed version of a decaying Newstead Abbey, which Byron had finally resolved to sell during this same period of early 1817 – a protracted process of legal manoeuvring signalling the final abandonment of his metonymic ancestral identity.[71] Tasso's desire to belong in memory to a specific place derives from Byron's sense of homelessness and wandering, of being out of place, and it is partly in defiant response to this that the poem is prophesying both its own success or afterlife as a poem and Byron's own future vindication when the injustices of which he felt himself to be the victim will be avenged. Decaying Ferrara is not only, then, a version of Newstead Abbey but of the 'brilliant theatre' of regency London left behind in 1816 ('thronged with all the forms of gaiety and splendour'), so that as so often in the verse post-1816, there is a veiled warning against the complacency of British culture, or at least there is the fantasy of a future moment in which London will have been brought to its knees.

This axis of exchanged places (a geographical and historical inter-changeability) is the central component of Byron's writing in exile, most obviously in relation to Italy and Italian politics, but also always obliquely to England. In the case of Ferrara, prophecy and vindication *in place* offer a symbol of redress for the suffering of the historical Tasso, or at least offer a self-enacting prophecy of vindication which contributes to the notion of a liberal and defiant Italian unification movement centred in a national literary canonicity. Such retrospective acts of reclamation of course fall far short of any notion of consolation for the madness of the individual, and *The Lament* firmly belongs to that sequence of works which anxiously examines the notion of the mind as its own place and how this fits into a broader political context. But at the heart of Byron's historiographical method is this notion of the sanctuary, in which the memory of a figure of national historical significance is preserved through association with a specific place, a 'consecrated spot' that offers an intense and inter-subjective relation with the past, experienced and witnessed by Byron, and placed at the centre of his 'prophecies'.

2.4 The spirit and body of place: *Childe Harold's Pilgrimage* IV

The fourth canto of *Childe Harold's Pilgrimage* is dedicated to John Cam Hobhouse whose own life, as the dedication acknowledges, is bound up with the compositional history of the poem, and whose collabora-tive contributions were to be significant in creating the symbiotic rela-tionship of the body of the poem to its supplementary system of notes. Perhaps we should reverse the terms of this metaphor and say that the *body* of the system of notes supports the spirit of the poem, since it is the notion of spirit that seems central to the canto, and because the body of the book of *Childe Harold* soon grew too large to contain Hobhouse's material, giving birth to the separate *Historical Illustrations* (1818). Byron saw the final book of *Childe Harold's Pilgrimage* (poem and notes) as the completion of his monument to experience, and Hobhouse himself as the person who had shared in much of that experience. It is this connectedness which is celebrated by the dedication:

> It has been our fortune to traverse together, at various periods, the countries of chivalry, history, and fable – Spain, Greece, Asia Minor, and Italy; and what Athens and Constantinople were to us a few years ago, Venice and Rome have been more recently. The poem also, or the pilgrim, or both, have accompanied me from first to last; and perhaps it may be a pardonable vanity which induces me to reflect with complacency on a composition which in some degree connects me with the spot where it was produced, and the objects it would fain describe; and however unworthy it may be deemed of those magical and memorable abodes, however short it may fall of our distant conceptions and immediate impressions, yet as a mark of respect for what is venerable, and of feeling for what is glorious, it has been to me a source of pleasure in the production, and I part with it with a kind of regret, which I hardly suspected that events could have left me for imaginary objects.[72]

It is not certain whether 'imaginary objects' refers to the poem itself, or the objects 'it fain would describe', or the 'magical and memorable abodes', or the 'spot where it was produced'. In an important sense the terms are interchangeable; that is, each could be described with the oxymoron 'imaginary objects', because Byron perceives the chain of connection between the spot, the abodes, the objects, and the four cantos of the poem as both a creative process and an *actual* sequence of physical and material connections, and furthermore believes that the imaginative life of the former is embodied in the material reality of the latter. In the case of the fourth canto, the dedicatee John Hobhouse also belongs to this incorporated sequence, as if he were a further 'imaginary object' Byron was giving up with regret. In later years Hobhouse remembered being physically present during the fourth canto's process of composition, (or 'coupleting'), as he and Byron had taken their evening rides at La Mira on the banks of the Brenta near Venice in 1817.[73] More significantly perhaps, Hobhouse claimed to have supplied some of the fourth canto's 'objects' himself:

When I rejoined Lord Byron at La Mira...in the summer of 1817, I found him employed upon the fourth canto of 'Childe Harold', and, later in the autumn, he showed me the first sketch of the poem. It was much shorter than it afterwards became, and it did not remark on several objects which appeared to me particularly worthy of notice. I made a list of those objects, and, in conversation with him, gave him reasons for the selection. The result was the poem as it now appears, and he then engaged me to write notes for the whole canto.[74]

By 'objects', Hobhouse is referring to architectural constructions – he listed, for example, Hadrian's Mole – as well as particular places he deemed worthy of notice, including the Capitol, and historical figures such as Livy and Virgil; but the word 'objects' seems particularly suited to the kind of fleshing-out or objectification he aimed for in his notes to the poem. The final canto of *Childe Harold* is an extended meditation upon these 'objects' and the spots or abodes in which they are encountered, but it is also a meditation upon the very process of bringing creative thought to bear upon the 'things' of the world, how (or whether) the spirit of a poetic work may be rooted in the materiality of historical place, and how (or whether) certain material objects may also become 'imaginary', or charged with an aura or halo. This interaction of spirit and body is then given a specific historical resonance in the canto's Italian context as the relationship between historical place and a regenerative national 'spirit' is closely examined. At the same time, it is always a concurrent part of Byron's writing-as-an-exile, particularly in the last two cantos of *Childe Harold*, to resist the compelling material realities of place and abode, in order to assert the radical freedom of the mind as its own place:

> I've taught me other tongues – and in strange eyes
> Have made me not a stranger; to the mind
> Which is itself, no changes bring surprise;
> Nor is it harsh to make, nor hard to find
> A country with – ay, or without mankind...

> (IV.8)

The hope that belonging nowhere may represent a freedom to belong anywhere and to speak any language, to cease to be a stranger, is a hope that had come under sharp pressures post-1816 for Byron, and yet it is a hope that *Childe Harold* canto four re-asserts. As we have seen, this desire for a concentred self is bound to the notion of a 'world elsewhere' and to the sharp memory of departure from England. In fact the memory of England is always in an acute and troubled relation to the claims in Byron's writing for a limitless cosmopolitanism, citizenship of the world, or the desire to dissolve into the elements. At the beginning of the fourth canto Byron again wonders about the ability of the spirit to travel independently of the body after death, and thinks of England:

> Perhaps I loved it [England] well: and should I lay
> My ashes in a soil which is not mine,
> My spirit shall resume it – if we may
> Unbodied choose a sanctuary. I twine
> My hopes of being remembered in my line
> With my land's language...

> (IV.9)

The notion of the 'sanctuary' – that is, a resting place for the spirit in eternity, an *in-placement* of the kind Byron had imagined for Bonnivard and Tasso, particularly in the context of a national (literary) identity – is another of the central subjects of the fourth canto, as the poem treads its paths through Northern and Central Italy, marking its progress by way of tombstone, home, epitaph and inscription. Byron connects the notion of an 'unbodied' spirit choosing to return to its native soil from exile with the notion of literary remembrance in posterity, and one of the questions the fourth canto repeatedly asks is what kind of physical sanctuary or resting place Italy can offer the spirit of those whose hope is to be remembered with their 'land's language'. In this respect the relationship between the poem and its heavy body of supporting notes is again a vital one, as the notes methodically examine the authenticity of these places of sanctuary and remembrance by recording the fact that Byron and Hobhouse had indeed actually *been there* themselves. But whereas the poem narrates a sequence of charged moments in consecrated places, dwelling upon the mysterious or supernatural force of certain 'spots', the notes follow in the footsteps of the poem with the material supplement of facts and details, and with a sense of a certain distance between the pilgrim and, as it were, the pilgrim's pilgrim, or editor. This sense of shadowing the poem with a secondary act of empirical and clear-headed information-gathering is crucial to the effect of the whole, to the sense of an interaction between a body of knowledge and its 'imaginary objects', but it also means that there is a powerful analogical and structural relationship between the notion of the poem as authenticated by its notes, and the kind of cultural sanctuary both poem and notes bear witness to in Northern and Central Italy. If there is a spirit of national identity which may unify the Italian peninsula in the regeneration of a *risorgimento* then it is nourished by the kind of cultural memorialising and celebration which the notes to the poem take pains to enact and record. Taken together then the poem and its notes represent the kind of recuperative and memorialising project both Byron and Hobhouse believed was necessary for just such a *risorgimento*, the gathering and unifying of a set of literary and historical figures under the transcendent sign of a national 'spirit'. This 'spirit' is recorded by the poet Lord Byron, while the acts of tending and protecting are repeated by the poet's editor, John Hobhouse – many of Hobhouse's notes furnish or *tend* Byron's poem with examples of precisely this kind of cultural and memorial guardianship or sanctuary. Hobhouse records of Petrarch, for example, that 'every footstep of Laura's lover has been anxiously traced and recorded. The house in which he lodged is shewn in Venice. The inhabitants of Arezzo...have designated by a long inscription the spot where their fellow citizen was born';[75] or of Ariosto: 'They possess his bones, they show his arm-chair, and his ink-stand, and his autographs. "Hic illius arma/ Hic currus fuit..."[*Aeneid* I. 16–17] The house where he lived, the room where he died, are designated by his own replaced memorial, and by a recent inscription.'[76]

The fourth canto puts itself in these places and retraces the footsteps of those literary and historical figures it deems centrally important to Italian nationalism. These include the footsteps of Lord Byron himself, as the poem remembers journeys in the East Byron had made in 1810. Stanzas 44 to 46 follow the path described in the 'celebrated letter of Servius Sulpicius to Cicero', which Byron's note to the stanzas quotes in English translation from Conyers Middleton's *History of the Life of M. Tullius Cicero* (1741):

'On my return from Asia, as I was sailing from Aegina towards Megara, I began to contemplate the prospect of the countries around me: Aegina was behind, Megara before me; Piraeus on the right, Corinth on the left; all which towns, once famous and flourishing, now lie overturned and buried in their ruins. Upon this sight, I could not but think presently within myself, Alas! how do we poor mortals fret and vex ourselves if any of our friends happen to die or be killed, whose life is yet so short, when the carcases of so many noble cities lie here exposed before me in one view.'[77]

Byron had 'often traced' this path in 1810, and retraces it in his memory in the fourth canto:

> Wandering in youth, I traced the path of him,
> The Roman friend of Rome's least-mortal mind,
> The friend of Tully: as my bark did skim
> The bright blue waters with a fanning wind,
> Came Megara before me, and behind
> Aegina lay, Piraeus on the right,
> And Corinth on the left; I lay reclined
> Along the prow, and saw all these unite
> In ruin, even as he had seen the desolate sight;
>
> For Time hath not rebuilt them, but uprear'd
> Barbaric dwellings on their shattered site,
> Which only make more mourn'd and more endear'd
> The few last rays of their far-scattered light,
> And the crush'd relics of their vanished might.
> The Roman saw these tombs in his own age,
> These sepulchres of cities, which excite
> Sad wonder, and his yet surviving page
> The moral lesson bears, drawn from such pilgrimage.
>
> That page is now before me, and on mine
> *His* country's ruin added to the mass
> Of perish'd states he mourned in their decline,
> And I in desolation: all that *was*
> Of then destruction *is*; and now, alas !
> Rome – Rome imperial, bows her to the storm,
> In the same dust and blackness, and we pass
> The skeleton of her Titanic form,
> Wrecks of another world, whose ashes still are warm.

(IV.44–6)

The retracings and overlayerings here are complex. Byron's journeys in Greece in 1810 had taken him in the footsteps (or the sailing path) of Servius Sulpicius, whose famous letter of 45 BC to Cicero consoling him on the death of his daughter (her death is coincident with the passing of the Republic – a fact picked up perhaps in Byron's emphasis of 'Rome imperial') described the journey through the gulf of Corinth with its sights of once-great cities in ruins. What Middleton translates and Byron's note reproduces as 'when the carcases of so many noble cities lie here exposed before me in one view', is, in fact, two lines of poetry Sulpicius quotes from an unknown source ('uno loco tot oppidum cadavera / proiecta iaceant'), so that the Sulpicius letter is itself already a rehearsal of a commonplace. Byron himself elsewhere comments that 'we can all feel, or imagine, the regret with which the ruins of cities, once the capital of empires, are beheld; the reflections suggested by such objects are too trite to require recapitulation', and among many examples he may have been remembering Walter Shandy's expansive quotation from Sulpicius' letter on hearing the news of the death of his son.[78] But these stanzas attempt to revive and deepen the commonplace by overlayering it with multiple examples and ironies which have been brought into focus through Byron's own journey over these same common places. The stanzas retrace Byron's paths of 1810, and reflect upon the fact that Sulpicius' and Cicero's Rome can now be added to the list of ruined cities. This fact is figured in terms of the place-page: Sulpicius' 'surviving page' is 'now before' Byron (as Megara was 'before me'), and 'on mine' (i.e. here in the fourth canto) Rome is figured as a further example of the 'cadavera', although in the case of Rome her 'ashes still are warm'. The place-page is then both a palimpsest (layered with Byron's writings upon Middleton's translation of Sulpicius' letter) and, as in the case of Greece in *The Giaour*, a fresh corpse in which there are still perhaps faint traces of life. The notion of interchangeable places underpins this passage in several ways. The lingering warmth in the ashes of Rome derives from the exchange of places or the intermixing of texts between Byron and the Roman, the closing of the gaps of centuries in the re-enactment of Sulpicius' journey, and the re-experience of his 'sad wonder' in 1810 and again now, albeit textually, in 1817; for a moment the temporal gap seems to have closed: 'all that *was* / Of then destruction *is*'. Nevertheless, the possibility of changing places across history also of course points to the destruction of imperial powers – Rome has exchanged her glory for the 'ashes' of her present condition, since exchanging places brings with it both the possibility of connection with the past *and* the certainty of empires falling. This paradox is a recurring one in the fourth canto and always carries with it the unspoken warning that British imperial power occupies a similarly interchangeable place, as well as the unspoken hope that the current oppression of Italy is reversible. The fact that Sulpicius' 'surviving page' was able to deliver a moral lesson, 'drawn from such pilgrimage', but that this did not prevent Roman civilisation from succumbing to the same fate, places Byron's retracing of his journey in a relationship to the commonplace in which the danger and irony of *reversibility* becomes the moral lesson, rather than the fragility of worldly power. This different shading of emphasis – as if to say 'beware of the sentiment of wondering at the passing of worldly power', rather than 'see the passing of worldly power', is characteristic of the ways in which the fourth canto is suspicious of 'History', even as it immerses itself in historical detail and narrative, and fastidiously re-traces historical journeys.

This in fact is the paradox in which the canto is grounded. The possibility that *buried* national history may be remembered and brought back to life and that this is central to the hope of an Italian *risorgimento*, goes alongside the supposition that 'History' itself offers only cautionary lessons or examples of futility. The spirit of 'History' then seems to be radically at odds with the poem's mysterious faith in the aura of historical materials, a faith born out in Hobhouse's untiringly radical and republican notes to the poem, in which Italy's political fortunes, her cultural legacies, her treasures, her prophetic future are read into the lapidary landscape of tomb and epitaph. But the notion of an enduring 'spirit' is a complex one. The spirit-of-place and the national spirit of the *risorgimento* are shadowed not only by the negative spirit of History, but by the spirit of Nemesis, by Byron's meditations upon the wanderings of his own spirit in a country 'with, ay, or without mankind', and by the spirit of free reason 'Our right of thought – our last and only place / Of refuge...(IV.127).[79] There is a deep tension in the canto between the sense of a living historical spirit experienced in the places associated with the names of Italy's glorious dead, particularly the tombs of great men (Michelangelo, Alfieri, Galileo, Machiavelli), and the contrary sense of 'sad wonder' at the absorption of such a spirit into the brutal moral lessons of the place-page, most clearly readable upon the chaos of the Palatine hill:

> There is the moral of all human tales;
> 'Tis but the same rehearsal of the past,
> First Freedom, and then Glory – when that fails,
> Wealth, vice, corruption, – barbarism at last.
> And History, with all her volumes vast,
> Hath but *one* page...
>
>   (IV.108)

It is to precisely the opposite notion of enduring spirit, to the buried strata of the palimpsest rather than the transparency of the '*one* page', that the fourth canto repeatedly returns: to the *genius loci* of the Egerian grotto (pursued with minute obsession in Hobhouse's notes); to the 'spirit's feeling' in the 'things of earth, which time hath bent' (IV.129); and to the 'genius of the spot' of St Peter's, which may expand the mind of the visitor in contemplation. But this spirit-hunting is most alive in the famous stanzas on the Coliseum:

> The seal is set. – Now welcome, thou dread power
> Nameless, yet thus omnipotent, which here
> Walk'st in the shadow of the midnight hour
> With a deep awe, yet all distinct from fear;
> Thy haunts are ever where the dead walls rear
> Their ivy mantles, and the solemn scene
> Derives from thee a sense so deep and clear
> That we become a part of what has been,
> And grow unto the spot, all-seeing but unseen.

> (IV.138)

These lines again recall *Manfred*'s place becoming 'religion', suggesting a sense of 'deep awe', but also a very particular sense of tangible and material connection to the past: 'we become a part of what has been'. Byron's dedication to the fourth canto had claimed that the poem connected him in some sense with the spots where it had been composed, or around which it organised its composition. Quite how real Byron felt these connections to be, readers of his poetry have found it difficult to measure because there has been an orthodoxy in Byron's critical reception which reads the supernaturalism of lines such as these in Hazlitt's terms of forcefully expressed commonplaces. Their famous afterlife, and the shadow retrospectively thrown by the language of tourism over this kind of topographical writing, has also obscured the extent to which they constitute an unorthodox historiographical method. Here, the dread power that inhabits the Coliseum seems to pass into those visiting the ruin in the midnight hour until they 'grow unto the spot', while at the same time becoming disembodied, 'all-seeing but unseen'. 'Grow unto' and 'all-seeing' are particularly extreme claims for a certain kind of heightened awareness and understanding produced by the fact of being present on the spot, where the hidden and buried connections of history become manifest, where the very knowledge of *inter*connection becomes possible through contemplation of one's own presence in a particular place. There is nothing quite like this in early nineteenth-century historiography, nothing to resemble this particular historical method, if indeed we allow it to be a historical method, in which a strict literalism and material reality of place go hand in hand with a supernaturalism centred upon the notion of a 'magic spot', and in which direct and practical experience is raised to the level of visionary insight. The poem remembers the Coliseum's history and the 'bloody Circus' genial laws' (with a pun on 'genial', invoking the *genius loci*); and then taking their inspiration from the famous sculpture believed to be of a dying Gaul, the stanzas raise the historical ghost of a gladiator dying in the Roman circus, out-of-place in the sense of at a distance from his home:

> – his eyes
> Were with his heart, and that was far away;
> He reck'd not of the life he lost nor prize,
> But where his rude hut by the Danube lay
> *There* were his young barbarians all at play,
> *There* was their Dacian mother – he, their sire,
> Butcher'd to make a Roman holiday –
> All this rush'd with his blood – Shall he expire
> And unavenged? – Arise! ye Goths, and glut your ire!
>
> (IV.141)

This too is a famous and much discussed passage, for good reason.[80] Psychoanalytical and psychobiographical readings seize upon the encoded self-description here – Byron is obviously dramatising himself and his perceived condition of suffering-in-exile, his desire for revenge, as well as working through his theories of repetition, catastrophe and decline: the theory or anti-theory of History's single page. But the notion of interchangeability is again crucial to the meaning of the passage. The future invasions and sackings of Rome by barbarian hordes are conceived and made inevitable by this moment of death in the arena. This is how Byron habitually imagined the workings of an historical nemesis, as a direct and unequivocal swapping of places. At the same time the passage makes veiled predictions about contemporary Italian politics, because the promise of a reversal in the balance of power between Rome and the Danube is also of course a prophecy of the current (1817) oppression of Italy by the Austrian Empire. (The same reversal is witnessed by Arnold and Caesar in the second scene of *The Deformed Transformed* (1824).) And if the balance along that historical axis can be reversed once then it can be reversed again, so that this is furthermore a heavily veiled promise of freedom for the Italian states: Rome and the Danube caught in an historical loop, their places and roles interchangeable. In other words, if history is a series of cycles, then those cycles, given the context of the fourth canto, may be liberating rather than merely blindly constraining. Most powerfully of all, the passage attempts to translate this broader symbolic interchange into an imaginative or empathetic act, so that there is a further multiple exchange of places as we enter the consciousness of the dying barbarian, and then imagine the barbarian's own consciousness imagining his wife and children at home. He is dying in *this* place in the Roman circus, but he is also *'There...'*, psychically elsewhere. The deictic *'There'* acquires both a temporal and spatial charge, the furthest place in this sequence of imaginative exchanges and the most demanding for a reader to imagine, the hardest to reach. Those who do not like Byron's writing will find this merely sentimental, even false: the presumption that what is essentially an act of self-pity (Byron is remembering his wife and child *there* in England, his heart is bleeding and he is having thoughts of revenge), may be sufficient to imagine a gladiatorial death. But this passage makes more interesting sense as part of a broader historical method with deep implications for contemporary Italian politics and the hope of a *risorgimento*. Going out of oneself, exchanging places, brings the promise of reversal in political fortune (both a salutary and an encouraging moral lesson), *and* demonstrates the kind of historically recuperative and memorialising act required for the regeneration of a national spirit. In this sense the fourth canto strives to be a lesson not simply in what to remember, but *how* to remember – how to place oneself in an inter-subjective relation with the past. It is perhaps easy to mistake this principle of interchangeability for another version of narcissism, or to fail to engage seriously with its mode of proceeding because it is essentially a visionary or enthusiastic one. But Byron's historiographical method, for all its moments of ecstasy, also contains a hard-nosed pragmatism which understands that the history of the European continent (ancient and recent) is only properly understood in terms of its buried subjectivity, its unseen connections and chains of responsibility, its interpenetration of apparently separate and different interests, and that this very notion of interconnection is best understood *upon the spot*, where the reality of one's own physical presence in a particular place of historical significance makes it more possible to imagine exchanging places. Moreover, the principle of interchangeability always carries with it a specific agenda in the context of British politics. Hobhouse extends the contemplation of role-reversal explicitly to include Britain, in a long passage quoted from Middleton's *History of the Life of M. Tullius Cicero*:

> The author of the *Life of Cicero*, speaking of the opinion entertained of Britain by that orator and his contemporary Romans, has the following eloquent passage: 'From their railleries of this kind, on the barbarity and misery of our island, one cannot help reflecting on the surprising fate and revolutions of kingdoms, how Rome, once the mistress of the world, the seat of arts, empire and glory, now lies sunk in sloth, ignorance and poverty, enslaved to the most cruel as well as to the most contemptible of tyrants, superstition and religious imposture: while this remote country, anciently the jest and contempt of the polite Romans, is become the happy seat of liberty, plenty and letters; flourishing in all the arts and refinements of civil life; yet running perhaps the same course which Rome itself had run before it, from virtuous industry to wealth; from wealth to luxury; from luxury to an impatience of discipline, and corruption of morals: till by a total degeneracy and loss of virtue, being grown ripe for destruction, it fall a prey at last to some hardy oppressor, and, with the loss of liberty, losing every thing that is valuable, sinks gradually again into its original barbarism.'[81]

Hobhouse is clearly responding to and complementing Byron's own fascination with historical interchangeability and is drawing out the moral and political lessons implicit in such imaginative acts. Britain's role as an imperial power stands in relation to an 'original barbarism' which the fourth canto forces a reader to imagine. The complementarity is a subtle one, however, in that Hobhouse's quotation from Middleton figures barbarism as an outer darkness to which British civilisation threatens to return, while Byron's verse attempts to imagine a barbarian interiority, a subjectivity, which will replace Roman civilisation. As such the salutary lessons of the imagination work not merely to undermine imperial power structures from within, but to open space in which to imagine the experience of historical suffering and oppression from outside the immediate context, something potentially even more damaging to the European hegemony.

For both Byron and Hobhouse there is a particular fascination with the space of the Coliseum as one in which this idea of the exchangeability of power is most suggestive and multiple, and in which the past is most tangibly alive. Hobhouse's notes record the story of the statue supposed to be that of Pompey, at the base of which Julius Caesar was said to have died, which was transported under the French to the Coliseum so that during a performance of Voltaire's *Brutus* the actor playing Caesar could fall at the *actual* base of the *actual* statue where the *actual* Caesar fell.[82] The Coliseum seemed to be a place in which authenticity could be stage-managed or re-enacted like this, in which the past might come alive through the aura of the material object. Significantly the *Historical Illustrations* also pays close attention to the history of the arena as a 'consecrated spot', literally consecrated by the Catholic Church at the end of the sixteenth century to honour the Christian martyrs who had died there. It is important to remember that when Byron and Hobhouse visited the Coliseum in May 1817 it was very much a Christian site, 'the picture of Jerusalem and the Crucifixion, still seen within the western entrance',[83] so that Byron's response to the place becoming 'religion', his statement that in 'this magic circle' we may 'raise the dead' and that 'Heroes have trod this spot' (IV.144), must be seen both as representing the counter-claims of a secular pilgrim who wishes to legitimise his own unorthodox enthu-siasm, *and* as drawing upon an existing reservoir of Catholic emotion centred upon this spot. The blood of sacrifice initiates the process of consecration in the case of both heroes and martyrs – indeed the very idea of a direct communion with the heroes/martyrs of the past through the material connection of place has a Catholic inflection. Byron's historical method is, then, one which seeks at least to appro-priate the language and emotion of religion, and even at times to share in it directly.

But as I have been arguing, it is a model of feeling and response that is in tension with a contrary desire in Byron to be radically free of humanity, which means to be free of historical places altogether. The fourth canto of *Childe Harold's Pilgrimage* finally turns away from mys-tical communion with history in place, to the possibility of a dwelling place outside human history, a disembodied abode:

> Oh! that the Desart were my dwelling place,
> With one fair Spirit for my minister,
> That I might all forget the human race,
> And, hating no one, love but only her!
> Ye Elements! – in whose ennobling stir
> I feel myself exalted – Can ye not

Accord me such a being? Do I err
In deeming such inhabit many a spot?
Though with them to converse can rarely be our lot.

(IV.177)

That question – 'Do I err / In deeming such inhabit many a spot ?' is not a question directly asked anywhere else in Byron's writing, because the forceful assertion of not being in error about the *genius loci* is so frequently the prevailing mode. But it is perhaps the question most seriously and secretly posed by his work, especially by *Childe Harold's Pilgrimage*, and for this reason it is an appropriate one for the fourth canto to close with. Here it is addressed to the 'ennobling' elements, and asks, as Manfred had, whether the natural world can offer a sanctuary for the self or whether this is finally a forlorn hope. The same question could be asked of the places of human history with which the fourth canto is equally preoccupied. 'Do I err / In deeming such inhabit many a spot?'. Directed in that way, the question would then constitute a moment of rhetorical self-doubt, since it is obvious that having been in error upon the plains of Troy or Waterloo, in the *bosquets* of Clarens, or in the arena of the Coliseum, would mean an absolute negation of Byron's response to such places, the primary force of which has been to *feel* an innate authenticating quality in the place or landscape itself, a quality he often calls a 'spirit'. In other words, to have pondered the possibility of being in error in these places would have been un-Byronic, and even though our own enlightened scepticism may very well persuade us that the tombs upon the Troad have nothing to do with the Homeric tales, that the field of Waterloo was not marked out for significant events, that Clarens has no unique connection with 'Love', and that communion with the ghosts of history is not possible in the arena of the Coliseum, when we read Byron we are primarily engaged with the assertion of the opposite notion and with the idea of the impossibility of error in such an assertion. Reading him, then, is to enter into a fierce relation with the notion of authenticity and proof, with the notion of a certain kind of value and insight in *being there*, and perhaps above all with the claim to a particular truth in the materiality or body of place. Many readers may find this a difficult relation to sustain. When Byron recalled having stood upon the plain of Troy daily 'for more than a month' in 1810, and observed that 'if anything diminished my pleasure, it was that the blackguard Bryant had impugned its veracity', we might take the person of Jacob Bryant, author of the *Dissertation concerning the war of Troy*, as a figure for the general reader of Byron, who must often feel as if he is in the position of someone who has somehow diminished Byron's personal pleasure by impugning the veracity of his responses. Later readers of Byron, particularly in the Victorian period, found themselves in a secret and sometimes guilty state of doubt in relation to his imaginative claims, and began to measure their intellectual development in terms of growing *out* of a taste for Lord Byron's poetry. It is a commonplace of Byron criticism to observe that modern readers are far more comfortable with the scepticism and demystification of *Don Juan*, than they are with the enthusiasm, even the 'religion', of *Childe Harold's Pilgrimage*. But this is also crucially to do with the shape of Byron's own writing life, his uprooting in 1816 and his subsequent 'translation' in the years following. The commanding precedence of place, the overwhelming claim to authenticity through *being there* on the spot, and the sense of mystery in the historical *locus*, all really belong to the first half of Byron's writing career, and become realigned with his exile on the continent and his gradual absorption into Italian society, particularly in the years after 1818, when *Childe Harold* is completed. This realignment or translation from one place to another, when travel ceases to be travel and becomes acculturation, radically alters Byron's relation to geo-history, reconstituting the notion of *being there* in terms of being *in-between*. This will be the subject of the next chapter.

3
Translation: 1818–21

3.1   'A strange sensation': *Beppo, Mazeppa, Venice: An Ode, Don Juan* I, II

Beppo: A Venetian Story (1818), takes its epigraph from *As You Like It*, IV.i. Rosalind (in disguise) has been reproaching Jaques for his melancholy, which he tells her he has acquired through travelling:

> *Rosalind*: Farewell, Monsieur Traveller: Look you lisp, and wear strange suits; disable all the benefits of your own country; be out of love with your Nativity, and almost chide God for making you that countenance you are; or I will scarce think that you have swam in a gondola.

Byron added Samuel Ayscough's 1807 annotation to these lines, which observed:

> That is, been at *Venice*, which was much visited by the young English gentlemen of those times, and was then what *Paris* is *now* – the seat of dissoluteness.[1]

From 1817 to 1821 Byron would increasingly come to think of Venice (he never visited Paris) as deserving the reputation it had enjoyed in the seventeenth century. His relation to the city, or more particularly to its inhabitants, shifted from carnivalesque celebration, to disgust. But he would also become increasingly aware of the power of the 'Sea-Sodom' to exert what Rosalind identifies as a crisis of national identity in those who had been there: a sense of England and Englishness paling in comparison, so that visitors would be 'out of love with [their] Nativity'. This leads to the desire to change one's national identity, a desire for acculturation or crossing-over ('to wear strange suits'), which of course is bound up with notions of gender and identity – Rosalind herself is wearing a strange suit in her disguise as a young man. The inescapable connections between the 'strange suits' of gender-roles and those of national costume, or between the cultural, the linguistic and the sexual, would come to dominate Byron's life and writing in the period 1818–21. To what extent is identity, whether of gender or nation, a matter of costume and manners which may be changed at will by the traveller, and would any such change be substantial; or is identity determined and controlled by factors outside (or *before*) the self? What is the relation between 'place' and self, in terms of authenticity, even origin? As this is the period in which Byron met and fell in love with a married woman (the Countess Teresa Guiccioli), became her *cavalier servente* and experienced a gradual absorption into Italian society under this new role, the principle of interchangeability and the idea of an authentic knowledge of place take on quite different aspects in his writing. Repeatedly Byron turns over the themes of acculturation and transplantation, of passing from one place and culture to another, and then passing further into the interior of that culture – becoming acclimatized or going native; being translated, both in the figurative *and* in the literal sense. These themes are informed by a set of assumptions about cultural and national identity derived from Enlightenment sources, most especially from Voltaire and Montesquieu, which are ironised in Byron's writing. They are: that the chief determining factor in cultural identity is climate, or how hot the sun is; that this is closely linked to sexual appetite; that marriage customs and institutions control, regulate and disguise these appetites; in doing so, marriage customs and institutions become the centrally defining aspect of cultural identity – the one aspect of a culture which has to be translated in order to be understood by those belonging to a different culture, and which, of course, it is most difficult to translate; and finally that such customs and institutions are best translated and therefore understood through studying the ways in which marriages break down, or are propped up. This is Byron's anthropological field-guide, securely written, as I say, in post-Enlightenment irony, an irony indefatigable and unyielding, which sometimes pretends to be philistinism, and emerges most often (though not always) in comedy. The comedy – or, to put it another way, the *impossibility* – of translation, is the subject of this chapter.

Beppo: A Venetian Story (1818) is the first major piece to bring England and Italy into a sharp and dynamic contrast and definition. The freedom of voice and subject Byron discovered in his Italian poetic models (the *ottava rima* of the semi-comic verse of Berni and Pulci) allows digressive space in which to talk about the weather, to contrast the climates and customs of England and Italy, and to make a link between these factors and the marked difference of sexual mores and cultural codes that determine the behaviour of husbands and wives: 'With all its sinful doings, I must say, / That Italy's a pleasant place to me' (41.ll.321–2). Significantly, Byron here records the true beginning of his love affair with the Italian language:

> I love the language, that soft bastard Latin,
>   Which melts like kisses from a female mouth,
> And sounds as if it should be writ on satin,
>   With syllables which breathe of the sweet South,
> And gentle liquids gliding all so pat in,
>   That not a single accent seems uncouth,
> Like our harsh northern whistling, grunting guttural,
> Which we're oblig'd to hiss, and spit, and sputter all.
>
> (44.ll.345–52)

Sexualizing the Italian language, but also thinking of it in terms of illegitimate birth (this connection will return in a darker form in *Marino Faliero*), Byron juxtaposes this stanza with a stanza on Italian women. Their looks and glances constitute another (unspoken) language:

> I like the women too (forgive my folly),
>   From the rich peasant-cheek of ruddy bronze,
> And large black eyes that flash on you a volley
>   Of rays that say a thousand things at once,
> To the high dama's brow, more melancholy,
>   But clear, and with a wild and liquid glance,
> Heart on her lips, and soul within her eyes,
> Soft as her clime, and sunny as her skies.
>
> (45.ll.353–60)

This nexus of language, sexuality and climate, of an eroticised Italian and of a linguistic-erotics, will develop in multiple directions over the next two years. In *Beppo* its context is Venetian sensuality and excess,

against which Byron recalls with half-serious fondness and a praise faint
enough to be damning, an England of 'cloudy climate', 'chilly women',
'riots', 'bankruptcies' and the 'Tories'. The comedy of being half out of
love with your nativity and half in love with somewhere else frames the
narrative of Laura, her absent Spanish husband Beppo, and her *cavalier
servente* the Count. On Beppo's unexpected and unannounced return to
Venice during the carnival season (many husbands or fathers will return
unexpectedly in Byron's writing over the next two years), it emerges that
a process of acculturation has occurred through which he has, in some
sense, 'become' Turkish. If 'turning Turk' was the source both of fear and
secret knowledge in the Oriental tales, here it is treated as a comic subject
allowing Byron the further contrast of Turkish national 'character' with
Italian and English types, where, again, the central focus of such a
comparison is upon sexual codes and the institution of marriage:

> Although their usage of their wives is sad;
>   'Tis said they use no better than a dog any
>   Poor woman, whom they purchase like a pad:
> They have a number, though they ne'er exhibit 'em,
> Four wives by law, and concubines "ad libitum".

> (70.ll.556–60)

The bondage of Turkish wives to their husbands then allows Byron to
satirise the relative freedoms of the English literary bluestockings, while
the comedy of the usurped husband develops into a multiple clash of
cultural codes: Christian, Islamic, Turkish, Italian, English. 'And are you
really, truly, now a Turk?' asks Laura of her translated husband, and her
question is not merely the crux of this particular text, but of most of
Byron's writing during this period. Is such a process of acculturation
possible ? Can travel, and prolonged absence from home, and sustained
intercourse with an alien culture, change the nature of the self ? Beppo,
in his self-exile, had suffered a desolation compared to that of Robinson
Crusoe. He returned to Venice 'to reclaim/ His wife, religion, house,
and Christian name' (97.ll.775–6). Once at home, however, the process
of re-assimilation is comically accelerated:

> His wife received, the patriarch re-baptized him,
>   (He made the church a present by the way);
> He then threw off the garments which disguised him...

> (98.ll.777–9)

The speediness of his re-absorption into Venetian society, and the ease with which Beppo slots into the triangular arrangement with his wife and the Count, suggests a comic world in which Rosalind's Monsieur Traveller has returned home (this time from Turkey) *completely* changed, but a complete change so dependent upon context that it can be removed in a second (over a stanza) like a disguise. *Beppo* offers a comedy of uprootings, then, which are both wholly disruptive and wholly impotent. An Italian social arrangement prevails merely because it is the cultural norm, and as such *must* prevail; but within this deter-mining context a fantasy of acculturation is allowed realisation, only to be collapsed. In this case the most extreme kind of alienation (turning Turk) is instantly undone and reversed when confronted by cultural institutions and norms which, by accommodating libidinal energies, reign supreme, but which also represent an originating and therefore perhaps 'authentic' context for Beppo. (He is Spanish, rather than Italian, but the poem also tells us that in Spain a *cavalier servente* is known as a '*cortejo*'.) Clearly such an idea of authenticity is a deeply unstable one because it is not the case that Beppo's change has been superficial – on the contrary, it has been complete. Nevertheless, such changes are instantly reversible when confronted with different cultural institutions, particularly ones to which Beppo is able to revert.

This notion of the absolute determination of the self by cultural norms is primarily and essentially comic, but not exclusively so. If placed in the context of Byron's own circumstances of 1818 – separated from Lady Byron and living in 'exile' among the Venetians with a married Venetian mistress, writing a poem on an Italian poetic model which is, in some way, supposed to strike a blow against English social and literary conventions – *Beppo* clearly represents the first serious exploration of self-translation in his writing. Here Byron is beginning to examine the workings of acculturation, his eroticised relation to Italian language and culture, and above all his familiarity with Italian institutions of marriage and marriage-under-pressure.

Byron's letters of 1818–21 to Moore, Murray, Hobhouse and Kinnaird offer descriptions of Italian (or more specifically Venetian, and later, Romagnuole) customs and ways of life, and their contrast with those of England.[2] Many of these letters were intended for a coterie of listeners at Albemarle Street and perhaps an even wider circu-lation in London, but should be read not only as serving the function of conveying information about Italian culture to friends and acquain-tances at home, but, crucially, as *resisting* the notion that another culture could be readily or easily known and understood. Byron writes not as a traveller but as an insider living in Italian society, and an insider whose interiority would deepen ever further. The particular understanding gained from such access, especially during 1818–19 (before he is caught up in political events in Ravenna) is predominantly focused upon matters of sexual conduct, especially in and around marriage, and how these norms relate to broader definitions of national character.[3] At the beginning of August 1818, for example, Byron is sending Murray, at his request, a very long and detailed account of his affair of the previous year with Margarita Cogni, 'La Fornarina' (the wife of a jealous baker).[4] Margarita was in some sense an embodiment for Byron of the Venetian spirit as it survived in the lower classes ('Her face is of the fine Venetian cast of the old Time...a thorough Venetian in her dialect'): fierce, proud, passionate, but also anachronistic, and therefore faintly comical. Her response to his disapproval of her snatching at Madame Contarini's mask at the Cavalchina ball was revealing:

> I represented to her that she was a lady of high birth – "una *dama*" &c. – She answered – '"se Ella e dama *mi io* son' *Veneziana*" – "If she is a lady – I am a Venetian" – this would have been fine – a hundred years ago – the pride of the nation rising up against the pride of Aristocracy – but Alas! Venice – & her people – and her nobles are alike returning fast to the Ocean – and where there is no independence – there can be no real self-respect.[5]

Venetian anachronism was another subject that would later return in a darker version in *Marino Faliero*, but here living portraits and anecdotal despatches are offered in place of the more conventional travelwriting accounts of customs and manners, accounts which, to Byron's annoyance, his publisher insisted on sending him anyway.[6] Byron's mode of directly reported anecdotage was intended to be richly illustrative, but at the same time tersely context-dependent. The poignancy of Margarita's pride, which Byron sees in political terms as connected with Venice's present decline, is not the material of travel literature, but more nuanced, and intractably comic precisely because it is so context-dependent, so *Venetian*. Letters written for the salon at Murray's develop in this distinctive mode – worldly, ironic – as if in fact they were prose supplements to *Beppo*. They are also determinedly unromantic, as if their ironic relation to the 'strange suits' of nationality extended to those of gender role too. As such, the distance between the lived reality of life in Italy and the audience of English literary gentlemen consuming that life through Byron's letters home, grew widest when Byron met and fell in love with the Countess Teresa Guiccioli in April 1818.

Everyone agreed that Lord Byron's last attachment, the Countess Guiccioli, if not an out and out *blue*, was, nevertheless, born with a book in her hand.[7] Emblematically, that book might have been Madame De Staël's *Corinne, or Italy* as in many ways this was a novel she learnt not just how to read (in French) but how to imitate in life, and in the writings of her life. The parallels between *Corinne* and Teresa's own *Vie de Lord Byron en Italie*, the memoir (in French) of her years with the poet, are many and obvious. Teresa Guiccioli's third-person account presents herself as a version of De Staël's heroine locked in a passionate (perhaps doomed) affair with a British peer who, like Byron, seems to conceal dark secrets from a past life about which he is painfully reticent. Teresa would have us believe that her effect upon Byron amounted to a Corinne-like humanising influence, persuading the poet, for example, to introduce an idealised love-theme into his drama *Sardanapalus* (1821) against his original judgement.[8] Like the love between Oswald and Corinne, the attachment between Byron and Teresa was a struggle, as she put it herself, between 'la passion et le devoir'.[9] Such struggles are almost always cast in a comic or ridiculous light by Byron, who was wary of the influence romantic novels might have upon female readers. Teresa herself records his opinion that books like De Staël's *Corinne*, or Rousseau's *Julie*, were more pernicious than his own *Don Juan*, which, nevertheless, she would succeed for a while in persuading him to stop writing.[10] For Byron, a certain kind of female sensibility might easily persuade itself that life could be organised to resemble scenes from Madame De Staël's novel. Despite this suspicion, and indeed in a gesture which seems to echo and imitate the novel even as it is aware of its own seduction in that mode, Byron placed his famous inscription to Teresa in the pages of her copy of *Corinne*, as he sat alone with the book in the most bookish of settings – a garden (of the Palazzo Savioli in Bologna) – thinking of his temporarily absent lover:

> My dearest Teresa – I have read this book in your garden; – my Love – you were absent – or I could not have read it. – It is a favourite book of yours – and the writer was a friend of mine. – You will not

understand these English words – and *others* will not understand them – which is the reason I have not scribbled them in Italian – but you will recognize the hand writing of him who passionately loved you – and you will divine that over a book which was yours – he could only think of love. In *that word* beautiful in all languages – but most so in yours – *Amor* mio – is comprized my existence here and hereafter.—I feel that I exist here – and I fear that I shall exist hereafter – to *what* purpose – you will decide – my destiny rests with you – & you are a woman [nineteen ?] years of age – and two years out of a Convent.—I wish you had staid there with all my heart – or at least that I had never met you in your married state. – but all this is too late – I love you – and you love me – at least you *say* so – and act as if you *did* so – which is a great consolation in all events. – But *I* more than love you – and cannot cease to love you. – Think of me sometimes when the Alps and the Ocean divide us – but they never will – unless you wish it.[11]

This is an anguished and moving inscription, written in English in order to avoid detection by Teresa's husband or family, and yet declaring love in unambiguous Italian: '*Amor* mio'; in fact playing upon the translatability of that word 'love–amor', making its translatability symbolic: a love which translates, and in doing so, declares itself. It is an odd, contradictory expression of perfect clarity *and* subterfuge; an acceptance of one's fate being in the hands of another, delivered to another, as translation delivers love to 'amor'. And yet it is an expression of the loneliness experienced by someone who finds himself in the paradoxical situation of speaking so openly and covertly at the same time. Byron's own love-letters to Teresa written in Italian speedily adopt all the florid and conventional love-language of De Staël's novel – they are embarrassingly fluent in that mode, at least at first.[12] The *Corinne*-inscription is quite different. Discovering her copy of the novel – a novel he in some sense dreaded – Byron wrote this declaration in its pages and then in fact refused to translate what he had written for 'La Guiccioli', either into French or Italian. This refusal reveals an instinct for self-preservation, a sense of the self retaining autonomy inside its native language, even as he delivers himself erotically to another. But the linguistic and the erotic almost always summon each other in Byron's writing, and refuse to be separated. In the summer of 1819 Byron himself is on the threshold of translation (as the note partially acknowledges), about to take up the role of *cavalier servente* in earnest, entering that curious Italian institution of form, convention, pragmatism and infidelity, in which his refusal to be separated from Teresa becomes both an erotic and a linguistic-cultural commitment. And not for the first time in his life it seemed too that social reality was taking on the generic characteristics of kinds of literature: this time the Goldonian comedy of his compromised position as the lover of a married woman, a sex-comedy richer and more extraordinary than any 'fiction' he might care to make up ('such perils – and escapes – Juan's are a child's play in comparison'[13]).

In November 1819 Byron recounts in a letter to John Murray an incident where it seemed his own writing had, for a moment, invaded his life (or his life had invaded his writing):

> Tonight as Countesss G[uiccioli] observed me poring over 'Don Juan' she stumbled by mere chance on the 138th. stanza of the first Canto [*a suspicious Don Alfonso is arriving at his wife Donna Julia's bedroom with torches and servants, while Juan hides beneath the sheets*] – and asked me what it meant – I told her – nothing but 'your husband is coming' as I said this in Italian with some emphasis – she started up in a fright – and said '*Oh My God – is* he *coming?*' thinking it was *her own* who either was or ought to have been at the theatre.—You may suppose we laughed when she found out the mistake.[14] [*my parenthesis*]

Here the betrayals of understanding risked in translation are connected to betrayal and discovery as subject-matter in the poem *Don Juan*. Taking Byron's translation 'your husband is coming' literally, because it is said in Italian and with emphasis, Teresa fails to read it merely as a translation of the meaning of the 138th canto of *Don Juan*, and so, for a moment, becomes Donna Julia. Misunderstanding of this kind, with the consequence of self-betrayal, is precisely what all translation risks: that somehow original meaning will be grotesquely twisted into a literal version of itself, which is not its original meaning. At the same time betrayal always seeks to adopt disguises, and where better than in the bluff which is translation? Byron begins to portray himself in these letters home during 1818–21 as hidden or even lost inside the forms of *serventismo*. This is an institution which, writing again to John Murray who has been asking for accounts of Italian customs and manners, Byron insists cannot easily be translated: 'Their moral is not your moral – their life is not your life – you would not understand it – it is not English nor French – nor German.'[15] *Serventismo* was something that 'no foreigner can understand or really know – without residing

years in the country'.[16] Indeed the affair with Teresa Guiccioli initiated
Byron into Italian society in a way which was unusual for any
foreigner, particularly in the period following December 1819 when
Byron moved to Ravenna as Teresa's *cavalier servente*. But the complex
social custom of *serventismo* had fascinated Byron from his first
prolonged intercourse with Venetian society, when he had sketched an
outline of its forms in *Beppo*:

> Besides, within the Alps, to every woman
>   (Although, God knows, it is a grievous sin)
> 'Tis, I may say, permitted to have *two* men;
>   I can't tell who first brought the custom in,
> But 'Cavalier Serventes' are quite common,
>   And no one notices, nor cares a pin;
> And we may call this (not to say the worst)
> A *second* marriage which corrupts the *first*.
>
> The word was formerly a 'Cicisbeo',
>   But *that* is now grown vulgar and indecent;
> The Spaniards call the person a '*Cortejo*',
>   For the same mode subsists in Spain, though recent;
> In short it reaches from the Po to Teio,
>   And may perhaps at last be o'er the sea sent.
> But Heaven preserve Old England from such courses!
> Or what becomes of damage and divorces?
>
> ......
>
> But 'Cavalier Servente' is the phrase
>   Used in politest circles to express
> This supernumerary slave, who stays
>   Close to the lady as a part of dress,
> Her word the only law which he obeys.
>   His is no sinecure, as you may guess;
> Coach, servants, gondola, he goes to call,
> And carries fan, and tippet, gloves, and shawl.

> (36–7.ll.281–96;40.ll.313–20)

It took time for Byron to come to terms with the rules of *serventismo*,
if he ever did; he found its power-balance and role-playing disorienting
(and would make much of such unconventional dynamics in *Don*

Juan). Writing to Hobhouse from Venice on 3 October 1819 Byron complains: 'I like women – God he knows – but the more their system here develops upon me – the worse it seems – after Turkey too – here the *polygamy* is all on the female side.—I have been an intriguer, a husband, and now I am a Cavalier Servente. – by the holy! it is a strange sensation.'[17] The strangeness increased at Ravenna, where Byron followed Teresa and her husband to take up his duties, and from where he writes to Richard Belgrave Hoppner, the vice-consul at Venice, at the end of January 1820:

> I am drilling very hard to learn how to double a Shawl, and should succeed to admiration – if I did not always double it the wrong side out – and then I sometimes confuse and bring away two – so as to put all the Serventi out – besides keeping their *Servite* in the cold – till everybody can get back their property. – But it is a dreadfully moral place – for you must not look at anybody's wife except your Neighbour's, if you [go] to the next door but one – you are scolded – and presumed to be perfidious.—And then a relazione or an amicizia seems to be a regular affair of from five to fifteen years – at which period if there occur a widowhood – it finishes by a sposalizio; – and in the mean time it has so many rules of it's [sic] own that it is not much better.—A man actually becomes a piece of female property; they won't let their Serventi marry until there is a vacancy for themselves. – I know two instances of this in one family here.[18]

It is noticeable how much of the business of *serventismo* as described by Byron had to do with clothes and their management, the *cavalier servente* himself being someone who 'stays / Close to the lady as a part of dress', and clothes being both the most serviceable metaphor for the notion of changing roles or putting on disguises, while also offering one of the signs of authenticity itself, of national costume. The odd formality of a set of arrangements which were there, after all, to disguise an adulterous affair; the bizarre hypocrisy of its rule-governed toleration, its demands and sincere expectations of fidelity; and the strangeness of the cuckolded husband colluding in his own betrayal – these factors were almost impossible to translate out of the lived Italian experience. But precisely because of this untranslatability, *serventismo* would stand as a synecdoche for 'Italy' in the work of this period. Writing to Murray at the beginning of 1821 during the suspension of the composition of *Don Juan*, Byron told his publisher that he had meant to have made Juan 'a Cavalier Servente in Italy and a cause for divorce in England – and a Sentimental "Werther-faced man" in Germany – so as to show the different ridicules of the society in each of those countries'.[19] This is a comic vision of national identity consciously opposed to the geo-historical schema of more Romantic writings about culture, in particular to Madame De Staël's studies of national 'character', her 'science of nations' in works such as *Corinne*, *D'Allemagne*, and *De l'influence des passions sur le bonheur des individus et des nations* (1796). De Staël is in fact an important negative influence not only upon Byron's thinking about romantic writing, but also (and the two are connected) in his thinking about cultural identity. In particular Byron's notion of comic national stereotypes or 'ridicules' is antithetical to De Staël's idea of a *genius* of place in which that word carries a broad freight of cultural meanings, as well as being centred in an idea of the exceptional (perhaps archetypal) individual (Corinne), whose psycho-sexual identity is closely connected with that of the nation, and is reshaped through sentimental liaison with the psycho-sexual identity of another individual-nation (Oswald-Scotland). Byron considered such a system or science to be an illusion, and ironised its sublimation of sexual urges in his own insistence on the defining tension between regulatory institutions and lawless sexual instinct. But just as it is clear that this emerges from his own direct knowledge of *serventismo*, it is also manifestly the case that the psycho-sexual configurations of *serventismo* have social and political meanings for Byron beyond the synecdochal. Above all it is the strangeness and danger of the *process* of passing into a different culture (the process of translation), which recurs in the work of 1818–21.

Everything Byron writes during this period is at least in part an exploration of the strange process of acculturation and translation. *Mazeppa* (1819) takes its story from Voltaire and reshapes it to make a generic contrast with the comedy of *Beppo*. In the court of King John Casimir V of Poland, a nobleman's wife of sexually dangerous mixed race ('She had the Asiatic eye, / Such as our Turkish neighbourhood / Hath mingled with our Polish blood...' ll.208–10), her wealthy husband's junior by thirty years, falls in love with a young man, Mazeppa, who is punished for his presumption with a particularly ferocious form of banishment – being tied to a wild horse which is then set loose. Though it was meant to be a sentence of death, Mazeppa survives his directionless and chaotic exile to be rescued (revived from the brink of death by a female), and rehabilitated. As Prince of the Ukraine, he tells his story to his defeated comrades after the battle of Pultowa (1709) in which he had fought and distinguished himself on the side of Charles XII of Sweden against Peter the Great of Russia, reflecting on the process whereby he has passed violently out of one culture and into another:

> Thus the vain fool who strove to glut
> His rage, refining on my pain,
>   Sent me forth to the wilderness,
> Bound, naked, bleeding, and alone,
> To pass the desert to a throne, –
> What mortal his own doom may guess? –
> Let none despond, let none despair!

(ll.848–54)

Most of the poem consists of a description of Mazeppa's terrifying journey bound to the 'foaming flank' of the wild horse, unable to control its direction or pace. Rapid headlong journeying figures the terror of not being in control of one's path of exile, and the darker terror of a lawless libidinal energy. *Mazeppa*, however, reverses the comic assumptions of acculturation in *Beppo* (and later in *Don Juan*) by presenting the passage from one culture to another as an irreversible death-sentence. But it is a death-sentence which is then miraculously reversed; for the self not only survives the process of absolute transformation, but thrives in its new place. In other words, while *Beppo's* turning Turk can be undone across a stanza, Mazeppa's turning cossack prince is secured through the most arduous trial ('To pass the desert to a throne'), so that the comedy of acculturation is recast as a quest-Romance (of a particularly breakneck kind).

Mazeppa first appeared in June 1819, in a volume with Byron's celebration-lament *Venice: An Ode*, a further meditation upon the city, giving formal shape and expression to Byron's doubled position as a foreigner living in a place under foreign rule: 'If I, a northern wanderer, / weep for thee, / What should thy sons do? – any thing but weep:' (ll.5–6). The poem turns and counter-turns from exhortation to despair, from political insurgency to historical resignation; from identifying with the 'sons' of Venice, to feeling like a visitor. The central section of the ode concentrates on the movements and counter movements of empire and colonisation, the pendulum-swing of conquest and defeat – Venice subduing Turkey, Austria subduing Venice – along the axis of interchangeability. But like *Childe Harold*, the poem moves out of this apparently inescapable pattern of violation, and turns again to consider possibilities of liberty. Freedom is celebrated as a certain kind of mobility:[20]

> Still, still, for ever
> Better, though each man's life-blood were a river,
> That it should flow, and overflow, than creep
> Through thousand lazy channels in our veins,
> Damm'd like the dull canal with locks and chains,
> And moving, as a sick man in his sleep,
> Three paces, and then faltering...

(ll.148–54)

It is better that blood should overflow its channels (as in dying for the sake of freedom, or perhaps as in cutting one's wrists), than that it should stagnate through its 'thousand lazy channels' (the canals of the malarial-fevered lagoon). Noble suicide and regenerative sacrifice, then, are offered as alternatives to the sickness of Venice's present subjugation, even as the poem ultimately turns to America (Venice-translated) for its realisation of freedom – the river of blood is also figured as a shift in sensibility via the Atlantic ocean. But this ambiguity about life-blood, as if life-blood can flow and overflow like a river or an ocean current and so overcome the apparently fixed channels of nativity and identity, recurs elsewhere in Byron's writing of this period both as a figure for the connection between national identity and the mobility of abstract notions of liberty, but also as an index of his own ambivalent feelings as an 'exile' and as a *cavalier servente*. The servitude which threatens the life-blood of Venice has another face in the condition of *serventismo*. 'To the Po. June 2nd 1819', one of the most intense of the love lyrics addressed to Teresa Guiccioli, takes the mobility of the river as a conventional figure of traffic between absent lovers, but then goes on to worry about the more significant cultural distances that divide an Englishman and an Italian woman, 'various as the climates of our birth!'(l.40). Byron's resolution of this 'various lot' is to imagine his blood as belonging not to the country of his nativity, but elsewhere:

> A Stranger loves a lady of the land,
>   Born far beyond the Mountains, but his blood
> Is all meridian, as if never fanned
>   By the bleak wind that chills the Polar flood.
> My heart is all meridian, were it not

I had not suffered now, nor should I be –
Despite of tortures ne'er to be forgot –
The Slave again, Oh Love ! at least of thee!

(ll.41–8)

Hot-bloodedness proves that Byron belongs to the South rather than
the North, even though he is a 'stranger' in Italy (an epithet Byron will
frequently use of himself in his letters to Teresa, speaking of his previous 'oltramontane' or 'beyond the Mountains' existence[21]). This
hidden mark of nationality is manifested in his servitude ('The Slave
again'), or rather in his *serventismo*, as this is an all-meridian arrangement, although whether such an identity is an authentic one or merely
an adopted role is an insistent question during the first phase of his
love for Teresa. In fact these poems cannot escape the condition and
representation of prolonged exile and acculturation, with various fates
of translation and transplantation shaping the comedy of *Beppo*, the
dark quest of *Mazeppa*, and manifesting themselves in the imagined
blood transfusions of Byron's love affair with Venice, in particular with
one of her fairer inhabitants. The linguistic and the erotic are never
wholly separated in Byron's writing, and the fullest realisation of their
union comes in *Don Juan*.

In the version of the poem we read today we begin with a preface
to the first two cantos (written in 1818, but abandoned and not published until 1901), introducing the work with a joke at Wordsworth's
expense about re-location. The Lake poet's inferiority in Byron's
mind was always best demonstrated by his parochialism and his
untranslatability.[22] In the preface Byron's immediate object of satire
was the note appended to the poem 'The Thorn', in which
Wordsworth had gone into some detail in describing his supposed
speaker:

> The character which I have here introduced speaking is sufficiently
> common. The Reader will perhaps have a general notion of it, if he
> has ever known a man, a Captain of a small trading vessel for
> example, who being past the middle age of life, had retired upon an
> annuity or small independent income to some village or country
> town of which he was not a native, or in which he had not been
> accustomed to live.[23]

Byron's primary objection to this would not be not so much to the
suggestion that such an exact situatedness might contribute to the

meaning of a dramatic monologue, nor to the fact of appealing to the reader to imagine this context; after all this had precisely been the method of poems such as *The Prisoner of Chillon* and *The Lament of Tasso*. Wordsworth's speaker is someone who has undergone a process of uprooting and dislocation and whose new life leaves him with 'having little to do' and so makes him prone to superstition (the subject of the poem). In some sense, then, the poem is about the effects of transplantation, but in the case of 'The Thorn' it is a transplantation entirely bound within the horizons of Wordsworth's England. What Byron thought of as the narrowness and meanness of Wordsworth's imagination is therefore demonstrated here by the scale of his geographical uprootings: 'a captain of a small trading-vessel...retired upon a small annuity to some village or country town of which he was not a native' – it is this *scale* that makes the imaginative effort to think oneself into his situation bathetic. In a parody of this, Byron's reader is requested to make an effort of imagination to suppose that 'the following epic narrative is told by a Spanish gentleman in a village in the Sierra Morena on the road between the Monasterio and Seville, sitting at the door of a *posada* with the Curate of the hamlet on his right hand, a cigar in his mouth, a jug of Malaga or perhaps "right sherris" before him on a small table, containing the relics of an *olla-podrida*', etc. 'The reader is further requested to suppose him (to account for his knowledge of English) either an Englishman settled in Spain, or a Spaniard who had travelled in England, perhaps one of the Liberals who have subsequently been so liberally rewarded by Ferdinand, of grateful memory, for his restoration'. Out-scaling Wordsworth, however, or correcting his errors of topography, was not merely a game of one-up-manship for Byron, but a question of the political and literary value of experience, particularly the experience of travel. Byron did not believe that captains of small trading vessels retired upon annuities in English villages or country towns were subjects for the imagination, and more importantly he suspected that the very nature of retirement or withdrawal as Wordsworth perceived it here was politically insidious. The preface is therefore meant to be a lesson in what transplantation might actually mean in a European context of political exile and persecution, and to exemplify the seriousness of Byron's cosmopolitanism in comparison with Wordsworth's parochialism. There is moreover an implicit connection made between Wordsworth's narrow-mindedness and British policy in the peninsula, as if a certain kind of insularity has consequences beyond Wordsworth's horizons. The joke is also a preparation for the most serious accusation delivered by the preface, which is that of apostasy, or changing one's place:

> It may be presumed to be the production of a present Whig, who after being bred a transubstantial Tory, apostasized in an unguarded moment, and incensed at having got nothing by the exchange, has, in utter envy of the better success of the author of *Walter Tyler*, vented his renegado rancour on that immaculate person, for whose future immortality and present purity we have the best authority in his own repeated assurances.

There was no darker sin and no greater guilt, to Byron's mind, than that of the apostate. Indeed such was the strength of Byron's feelings upon the subject that it is difficult not to draw connections between apostasy and Byron's own fascination with the workings of *mobilité*, as well as with the principle of historical interchangeability.[24] He uses the term to signify changes of political thinking and allegiance, but the appropriated religious significance of the word increases the gravity of the charge (and in doing so attacks the notion of religious principle being at the root of the Lake poets' political change of heart). As such the accusation is a harder-edged critique of Wordsworth and Southey than that they wrote within narrow horizons, since it represents changing one's place as a self-willed act of mercenary intent. And so if translation is represented as a dangerous process in some degree outside the control of the will and therefore a threat to the self, then apostasy is to turn this process against the self, Southey's turning away from the radicalism espoused in *Wat Tyler* being just such an act – his newly adopted reactionary and high-church politics mocked further by the epithet 'transubstantial' (i.e. capable of changing from one substance to another). The preface moves then from situatedness, to transplantation (and its seriousness), to the self-translation of the apostate, marking out a spectrum of mobility which is primarily an assault on the positions of Wordsworth and Southey, but which obviously resonates further. *Don Juan* itself is structured around the uncomfortably close shades of such a spectrum: the close relation of apostasy to *mobilité*, of mobility to hypocrisy, and translation to betrayal. As Byron's friends (and the first readers) immediately recognized, the poem consciously played upon these fine and treacherous distinctions, not least in the transposition of character and setting.

To take the example that was closest to home: despite Byron's protestations to the contrary, Donna Inez is an unmistakable translation of

Annabella Milbanke, Lady Byron. A letter to Augusta claimed ambigu-
ously, that 'there might be something of her [Annabella] in the outline
but the Spaniard was only a silly woman – and the other is a cut and
dry made up character – which is another matter'; (in what sense, and
of whom exactly, is Byron using the phrase 'made up'?)[25] – this
notwithstanding, Donna Inez is unmistakably a Spanish Annabella
Milbanke in the same way Teresa Guiccioli was, according to Byron, an
'Italian Caroline Lamb';[26] that is, in which the translation separates as
much as it brings together the two persons of identification; and in
which the joke relies as much upon the assault upon each of the
persons to be thus yoked together, as upon its appropriateness. Clearly
this has correspondences with apostasy since it relies upon the
grotesqueness of complete transformation, in this case the comic
grotesqueness of translating someone into the Italian or Spanish
version of themselves. *Don Juan*'s half-serious insistence upon climate
as the primary cultural determinant means that all attempts to transpose something from one climate to another must be comic, impossible, ludicrous – Anglicization being as comic as Italianization or
Spanification, or, as *Beppo* had revealed, Turkification. Byron's first
effort at such a translation of the pains of the 1816 scandal had
occurred in 1817, when he produced the short piece (not published in
his lifetime) entitled *Donna Josepha: A Fragment of a Skit on the
Separation*, in which Byron is Don Julian, Annabella is Donna Josepha,
and Byron's father-in-law Sir Ralph Milbanke is Don José di Cardozo;
and 'is' here also suggests 'is not'.[27] It is a complex strategy: at once an
attempt to be perfectly open, candid and accurate about events leading
up to Byron's departure from England, to set the record straight; at the
same time to make the decorous gesture of apparently concealing iden-
tities; and, tentatively and not at all successfully, to begin to attempt
the comic process of translation, only fully achieved in *Don Juan*, in
which making the central characters Spanish means to have escaped
them.

The comedy of *Don Juan* relies, then, upon the paradox of translation: England is translated to Spain, but this is impossible. Readers are
instantly meant to recognise the sexual relations and hypocrisies governing and regulating the domestic arrangements of the poem, but at
the same time to find them entirely Spanish. Culture is embedded in
climate, and both culture and climate within the erotic, and the erotic
within the linguistic. Once Juan has escaped his Spanish context and is
washed up on the shore of a Greek isle, the poem returns briefly to the
erotic visions of the oriental tales in which the comedy of linguistic

difference, in this case between Juan and Haidee (Spaniard and Greek) is conquered by their love, or sexual attraction:

> And then fair Haidee tried her tongue at speaking,
>   But not a word could Juan comprehend,
> Although he listen'd so that the young Greek in
>   Her earnestness would ne'er have made an end;
> And, as he interrupted not, went eking
>   Her speech out to her protégé and friend,
> Till pausing at the last her breath to take,
> She saw he did not understand Romaic.
>
> And then she had recourse to nods, and signs
>   And smiles, and sparkles of the speaking eye,
> And read (the only book she could) the lines
>   Of his fair face, and found, by sympathy,
> The answer eloquent, where the soul shines
>   And darts in one quick glance a long reply;
> And thus in every look she saw exprest
> A world of words, and things at which she guess'd.
>
> And now, by dint of fingers and of eyes,
>   And words repeated after her, he took
> A lesson in her tongue; but by surmise,
>   No doubt, less of her language than her look:
> As he who studies fervently the skies
>   Turns oftener to the stars than to his book,
> Thus Juan learn'd his alpha beta better
> From Haidee's glance than any graven letter.

(II.161–3).

There are moments in Byron's writing where the notion that sexual love might overcome all difference is allowed brief room; moments in which desire transcends its constraining contexts. Juan and Haidee's desire actually manifests itself through overcoming linguistic difference and as such stands in ideal relation to the linguistic-erotic life of Teresa and Byron (the 'graven letter' of the inscription in *Corinne*). But in placing sexual desire *against* language and culture in this way, these short-lived moments of triumph merely reinforce the notion of regulation and control as the rationale of culture. Language is seen as the primary check and control on sexual instinct, and as such it is an obstacle to be overcome in the *ur-sprache* developed by Juan and Haidee. The comedy of *Don Juan*, however, is rooted in the world of linguistic difference, and the account of Juan and Haidee's love-language is followed by a sly reference to the pleasures of learning a new language under more normal circumstances:

> 'Tis pleasing to be school'd in a strange tongue
>   By female lips and eyes – that is, I mean,
> When both the teacher and the taught are young,
>   As was the case, at least, where I have been;
> They smile so when one's right, and when one's wrong
>   They smile still more, and then there intervene
> Pressure of hands, perhaps even a chaste kiss; –
> I learn'd the little that I know by this:
>
> That is, some words of Spanish, Turk, and Greek,
> Italian not at all, having no teachers...

> (II.164–5)

This last disclaimer is, of course, heavy with a personal irony, Byron's schooling in Italian language and erotics being the most intensive course of study he had undertaken in his life.[28] The variant line: 'Italian rather more – having more teachers', is more accurate, but loses the force of the barefaced lie, and the canny acknowledgement that Byron's linguistic-erotic life in Venice was, in every sense, unique among his travels. This association of being schooled in language and in sex, entering a culture through prolonged and vigorous intercourse, in which language itself is charged with an erotic life and erotic life is inescapably linguistic, never leaves the verse of 1818–21. At its most extreme, love-language offers a temporary restitution of prelapsarian (or pre-Babel) happiness, in which the multiplicity of tongues is reversed.[29] At the other extreme, sexual love becomes a comedy of manners in which cultural strangeness, misapprehension, foreignness, centrally impinge upon knowledge of the object of desire. To love in this way (as Byron discovered in his *serventismo*) is to enter a strange rule-governed world in which the self is potentially *changed*. His fear of such a process is visible in his preoccupation with apostasy – absolute self-willed transformation – the unpardonable sin of which Wordsworth and Southey stood accused.

But where does translation end and apostasy begin? And in what sense does any process of acculturation, and in particular a willing conformity to the new conditions of *serventismo*, resemble the self-willed crossings-over of the apostate? Perhaps Byron felt that the answer was in fact quite closely, not least because he habitually sees broader political and social relations in terms of the condition of the individual (psycho-sexual, domestic, private), and vice-versa. The institution of *serventismo* wasn't simply, then, a convenient synecdoche for 'Italy', but was directly connected and implicated with broader political relations, and the ways in which these relations impinge upon the life of the individual. Resisting the notion that the role of *cavalier servente* necessarily represented a form of servitude, Byron would attempt to discover the liberating possibilities of translation and acculturation, and in particular the prophetic possibilities of speaking another language.

3.2   'I dare to build the imitative rhyme': *The Prophecy of Dante*; translations from the Italian

Having visited Dante's tomb at Ravenna in the summer of 1819, and at the request of Teresa Guiccioli, Byron began work on a poem upon Dante's exile. The dedicatory sonnet to Teresa returns to the notion of a Northern wanderer who finds himself possessed by Southern charms, compelled in some sense to speak another language – Teresa's personal request for a poem on the subject is presented within the terms of *serventismo* as a command which can only be obeyed. Byron expresses a diffident awareness of the presumption in writing a poem in *terza rima*, while at the same time advertising the boldness of his experiment:

> LADY! if for the cold and cloudy clime
>   Where I was born, but where I would not die,
>   Of the great Poet-Sire of Italy
> I dare to build the imitative rhyme,
> Harsh Runic copy of the South's sublime,
>   THOU art the cause...

(ll.1–6)

Whether Teresa also suggested (or demanded) that the poem be in *terza rima*, we don't know. But the preface to the poem makes clear that

Byron believed such an experiment was virtually without precedent in English verse:

> The measure adopted is the terza rima of Dante, which I am not aware to have seen hitherto tried in our language, except it may be by Mr. Hayley, of whose translation I never saw but one extract, quoted in the notes to Caliph Vathek; so that – if I do not err – this poem may be considered as a metrical experiment.[30]

There are in fact examples of *terza rima* transplantations into English in Chaucer, Surrey, Wyatt and Milton, to name a few, and of course 1819 was also the year in which Shelley wrote 'Ode to the West Wind' (published in 1820), in which he drew upon his own earlier apprenticeship in the form in such fragments as 'Athanese'.[31] Nevertheless, Byron was correct in his basic sense of the rarity of English attempts at this difficult formal patterning, and the notion of a *daring* imitation is central to the poem's meaning. The preface goes on to consider the activity of superimposing forms and voices from one language upon another, and the presumption, or superimposition, that such an act may entail:

> Amongst the inconveniences of authors in the present day, it is difficult for any who have a name, good or bad, to escape translation. I have had the fortune to see the fourth canto of Childe Harold translated into Italian versi sciolti – that is, a poem written in the *Spenserian stanza* into *blank verse*, without regard to the natural divisions of the stanza, or of the sense. If the present poem, being on a national topic, should chance to undergo the same fate, I would request the Italian reader to remember that when I have failed in the imitation of his great 'Padre Alighier', I have failed in imitating that which all study and few understand, since to this very day it is not yet settled what was the meaning of the allegory in the first canto of the Inferno, unless Count Marchetti's ingenious and probable conjecture may be considered as having decided the question.
>
> He may also pardon my failure the more, as I am not quite sure that he would be pleased with my success, since the Italians, with a pardonable nationality, are particularly jealous of all that is left them as a nation – their literature; and in the present bitterness of the classic and romantic war, are but ill disposed to permit a foreigner ever to approve or imitate them without finding some fault with his ultramontane presumption. I can easily enter into all this,

knowing what would be thought in England of an Italian imitation of Milton, or if a translation of Monti, or Pindemonte, or Arici, should be held up to the rising generation as a model for their future poetical essays. But I perceive that I am deviating into an address to the Italian reader, when my business is with the English one, and be they few or many, I must take my leave of both.

Dissatisfied with Michael Leoni's translation of the fourth canto of *Childe Harold*, Byron imagines the double dissatisfaction of having an English imitation of Dante translated into Italian, and the vulnerability or exposure involved in such a process. In other words Byron's poem would be revealed as being sorrowfully *unlike* Dante if it were to be translated again, as it were, into Italian, as if passing back to an origin which would then be revealed as not its own. This loss of a centre or authentic origin is part of the danger of any translation or imitation, but has particular point when the literature imitated is so closely bound up with notions of Italian national identity. Byron wants to claim an Italian national significance for his own English poem and therefore anticipates *The Prophecy of Dante* being translated *into* Italian, but is aware of the sensitivities involved in such a process, particularly so in the present circumstances of the 'classic–romantic' war which raged in Italy and England, and within which the Foscolo–Hobhouse essay on the current state of Italian literature published with the fourth canto of *Childe Harold* had offended some Italian sensibilities. *The Prophecy of Dante*, however, is also intended as an intervention in the English version of this debate (as was everything Byron wrote after 1818), in that it would introduce a southern poetics unknown in England and not easily accommodated to the binarisms of the 'classic–romantic' war. The slippery nature of this mediation between an Italian and English audience, the former to be placated and the latter to be provoked, is clear enough throughout the passage, but emerges most obviously in the final sentence's uncertainty. Is the reader Italian or English? The same question is begged of and by *The Prophecy of Dante* itself. Where does it come from, and who is it for? Is it an English poem disguised as an Italian poem, or an Italian poem disguised as an English poem? The very nature of imitation and translation is therefore not only a formal but a thematic aspect of the poem, in particular the relation of translation to the place-exchange involved in writing a dramatic monologue for a historical figure who belongs to another nation. Anglo-Italian; Byron–Dante; North–South: the poem *dares* to build one within another and wonders whether these superimpositions might offer a certain kind of liberty, an escape from the comic world of cultural determinism in which we are imprisoned by our context (our climate, our marriage institutions), to a daring freedom, an inter-space opened up by translation. Such a space would deepen and develop the kind of historical interchange Byron had attempted in *The Lament of Tasso*, where history speaks and its 'prophecies' come true, and in which Italian nationalist hopes are made European.

Central to such an imagined possibility is the poem's complex understanding of exile. *The Prophecy of Dante* begins with Dante 'returning' from the imaginary worlds that have occupied his mind during the composition of his *Commedia* (as Tasso had returned from the world of *Gierusalemme Liberate*) to 'man's frail world! which I had left / So long that 'twas forgotten...'(ll.1–2). But man's frail world is also the world in which Dante finds himself an exile in reality, unable to return to his native Florence after 1301, and tormented by that fact throughout the poem. There is then a double order of exile in the poem. The poet lives as a 'natural' exile from the world, as this is the condition of his imaginative life, but the poet–man is a political exile from Florence in historical reality, and it is the relation and tension between these two different understandings of exile which are significant, and which have obvious resonances for Byron himself. *The Prophecy of Dante* traces the conflict between a present sense of injury (exile, homesickness, nostalgia, injustice, anger), and a compensatory promise of future vindication when Dante will be recognised 'not of this people, nor this age...', but in posterity. It asks to what extent the notion of genius as a state of exile from the world, bringing with it the promise of vindication in posterity, may overcome and redress the former sense of injury and injustice in real historical time. As such it belongs to the series of poems in which Byron had examined the limits of self-sufficiency (the mind as its own place), but in this case because the consolations of genius or of posterity finally seem inadequate, the poem focuses upon the mismatching and painful losses incurred in any negotiation between the present and the vindicating future. Byron's Dante moves from the sense of genius as a sign of divine origin and exile:

> Yes, and it must be,
> For, form'd of far too penetrable stuff,
> These birds of Paradise but long to flee
> Back to their native mansion...

> (III.ll.167–70)

to the tougher, more worldly resignation of the unbowed political exile: stoically enduring exile from a *real* place rather than a symbolic 'Paradise'. Byron had borrowed *Hamlet*'s 'penetrable stuff' towards the end of *English Bards and Scots Reviewers* in his promise to make his literary enemies feel that they too were vulnerable, and the phrase is famously picked up in Shelley's eulogy to Keats in the preface to *Adonais* (1821). But what emerges from *The Prophecy* is not primarily the sense of the poet as an especially sensitive human being who longs to return to some celestial 'native mansion', but as a suffering individual who desires to return to his home in Florence. Origins then are finally situated in the present world of actual places rather than in another world, so that Byron's Dante cannot escape or wish away the harder fate of being an exile in historical reality. In this the promise of future vindication is bitterly tainted by the returning sense of pain at the present:

> Florence! when this lone spirit, which so long
>   Yearn'd, as the captive toiling at escape,
> To fly back to thee in despite of wrong,
>   An exile, saddest of all prisoners,
> Who has the whole world for a dungeon strong,
> Seas, mountains, and the horizon's verge for bars,
>   Which shut him from the sole spot of earth
>   Where – whatsoe'er his fate – he still were hers,
> His country's, and might die where he had birth...

> (IV.ll.128–36)

By presenting Dante's fate primarily in terms of the pain of exile, Byron hopes retrospectively to establish a tradition which he has 'inherited', of the European poet speaking from a political wilderness. For this reason Dante's homesickness is represented in familiarly Byronic terms: the 'spirit' yearning to return home, the 'whole world' being a 'dungeon' for the exile (a reversal of Tasso's and Bonivard's notion of their dungeons as the 'whole world'), and above all the idea of a 'sole spot of earth' which has an irresistible claim upon the imagination. In this case, as Dante portrays Florence as the 'sole spot of earth' in which he would wish to die, our awareness that this desire was thwarted recalls the spot not in Florence but in Ravenna where his tomb is situated and which first inspired Byron to write the poem. The relation then between the place or home to which Dante longed to return (his nostalgia for Florence), and the sanctuary in Ravenna visited by Byron, is the crucial relation of *The Prophecy*, firstly because it constitutes the material connection with place that Byron felt was necessary in order to write dramatic monologues for historical figures, and secondly because within the schema of such material connections, a ventriloquism is possible, a double voicing in which Dante's 'prophecies' are already half-fulfilled from Byron's historical perspective – he predicts among other things the triumph of Italian as a literary language – a prediction confirmed by the very act of literary imitation. Moreover, as a retrospective speech-act, Dante's 'prophecy' also belongs to the historical method I have been describing in previous chapters, in which it becomes not merely an exemplary expression of Italian literary strength, but an intervention in the present context of Italian politics. Significant predictions such as that of Italian unification and freedom are unfulfilled; they are prophesies not of Dante, but of Dante translated, where 'translated' suggests transposed and freed from a constraining context to a trans-historical perspective. Dante–Byron predicts Italian unification, and the prediction is all the more daring and, Byron hopes, all the more plausible for having emerged from this double voice, Anglo-Italian, European.

This is Byron's cosmopolitanism in its most ideal form, and evidence of his earnestness as a reader of the intertextual relationships in European literature. *The Prophecy* assumes that translation *gives* rather than takes away, and that dead writers can be made to 'live' again in the process; furthermore, that contemporary political meaning can be wrested from dramatic monologues in which historical figures are ventriloquised, and that such meaning can be gained *across* cultural and linguistic differences. It disguises Byron's fears about presumption, and about the possibilities of betrayal, or that any attempt to transpose voice-on-voice would only produce a 'harsh...copy'. The poem entertains quite the contrary possibility that translation may in fact fulfil the historical potential of the original, drawing out latent forces, working retroactively as if Dante-in-Byron might be able to shape Italian notions of a *risorgimento* which neither Byron, nor Dante, could effect alone. Translation then is a paradigm for a regenerative process of cultural intercourse which escapes the determinism posited by the opposite notion – that cultural interpenetration is not really possible, except as sex-comedy.[32] In fact the comedy of translation and acculturation has been suppressed, and the poem ends with a particularly plangent clairvoyancy:

> I may not overleap the eternal bar
> Built up between us, and will die alone,

Beholding, with the dark eye of a seer,
The evil days to gifted souls foreshown,
Foretelling them to those who will not hear,
As in the old time, till the hour be come
When Truth shall strike their eyes through many a tear,
And make them own the Prophet in his tomb.

(IV.ll.147–54)

That final 'own' is a subtle one. Byron is ending where he began, at Dante's tomb, a pilgrimage which initiates the imaginative exchanges, the ventriloquism of the dramatic monologue. For the Italian people the word 'own' recognises the future moment when they properly acknowledge Dante's genius, and when they 'own' that genius in the sense not only of recognising it as theirs, but themselves as belonging to it, identifying with it in a national sense. The word carries, then, both a sense of owning up to something (admitting they were wrong) and possessing something properly; forgiving, recognising, belonging *with*. Larger notions of a national unity and properly consolidated identity which as yet do not exist, are also suggested by that final sentence; a future moment when Italy will belong to its own people, recognise its own, and be free from foreign domination. Only then, Byron suggests, will the full prophetic and nationally regenerative force of Dante's poetic powers be properly understood and acknowledged. But as this is a poem in English imitating an Italian model, the word 'own' is obviously problematic in further senses. Who 'owns' what in this poem? To what extent is the prophecy Byron's own? In what ways might it be said to belong to Dante? As the poem takes its inspiration from Dante's tomb in Ravenna, and has Dante prophesy from this spot, it is clear that Byron himself is the owner or author of 'the Prophet in his tomb', and that his anticipation of a moment of future vindication is also a fantasy of success for his poem with an Italian audience. The danger of translation or imitation, however, is that the notion of an authentic originating voice (that which is the poem's own) may become lost along the way, so that writing experiments in *terza rima* for the sake of Italian national regeneration may simply invite the dissatisfaction Byron anticipates in his preface. In a sense that final sentence is an attempt to deliver the poem back to the Italians, although the Italians may well think that this is merely 'ultramontane presumption': no one likes to be told what they should own up to, or what is truly their own. And a larger question arises here about the extent to which any foreign writer may intervene in the national struggles of an adopted country. To what extent and with what seriousness may he think of such struggles as his own?

Byron's writing is consistently sensitive to these questions, and to the possibility of the *faux pas*. The particular danger that translation may be a process of falsification or presumption; that the self translated may in fact be the self lost, or misplaced; that the act of acculturation spirals into a kind of freefall – these possibilities haunt the poetry of 1818–21, and it is not a coincidence that these questions become most insistent during the period during which Byron's own work is appearing increasingly in translation. Early in 1818 Byron is complaining to Richard Hoppner about a proposed translation of *Manfred* into Italian, a project Byron suspected had more to do with current Italian literary feuds than the merits of his own work: 'I can conceive no greater absurdity than attempting to make any approach between the English and the Italian poetry of the present day',[33] he writes, although in this case Byron made the would-be translator an offer he couldn't refuse – two hundred francs to abandon the project, followed up with a threat, according to Moore, to horsewhip him when he persisted in his plan – after which he persisted no further.[34] Byron was clearly much more comfortable making his own approaches between English and Italian literary models and to claim for them the foundations of an English literary school (John Frere's *Whistlecraft*, itself modelled on Niccolo Forteguerri's *Ricciardetto*, and J.H Merivale's *Orlando in Roncesvalles* (1814), an adaptation of Pulci), than for the Italians to seek out the Germanic Romanticism of *Manfred* and attempt to southernise it. As Michael Leoni's translations of Byron began to appear in 1818/19, Byron's letters of acknowledgements and thanks are courteous but rather stiff, encouraging Leoni, with some real embarrassment, to stick to translations of the English classics rather than wasting his time on such things as *The Lament of Tasso* or *Childe Harold's Pilgrimage*.[35] Tom Moore was requested to offer a certain Miss Mahoney a few hundred francs to dissuade her from translating Byron into French in the summer of 1820 ('Was there ever such a notion? It seems to me the consummation of despair'),[36] but of course when such translations began to reach him through Murray, Byron's reaction was predictable; to Murray: 'The French translation of us!!! – Oime! Oime!'; and to Moore: 'Only think of being *traduced* into a foreign language in such an abominable travesty! It is useless to rail, but one can't help it.'[37]

This is also precisely the period when Byron embarked upon the first sustained literary translations of his own, work which perhaps deserves more critical attention than it has received and needs to be placed in the broader context both of *being* translated and of the thematic examination of translation and acculturation throughout the writings of the period. In October of 1819 Byron began his 'literal' translation of Luigi Pulci's *Morgante Maggiore* [*Morgante* (1482)] , a semi-comic romance, the precise moral weight and bearing of which had become something of a literary enigma in England and as such was useful to Byron as a foil to recent criticism of *Don Juan*.[38] The translation was of course bound up with the growing row about English poetics and Byron's claims to have identified a new school; but more simply than that, it was a test of his proficiency in Italian, and by that fact alone was a conspicuous mark of his distance from literary Anglo-centrism of any kind. 'Serviley translating, stanza for stanza, and line for line, two octaves every night',[39] Byron went to work. The advertisement to the poem makes a direct link between the rigours of *serventismo* and the discipline of translation (Byron is talking of himself in the third person):

> He was induced to make the experiment partly by his love for, and partial intercourse with, the Italian language, of which it is so easy to acquire a slight knowledge, and with which it is so nearly impossible for a foreigner to become accurately conversant. The Italian language is like a capricious beauty, who accords her smiles to all, her favours to few, and sometimes least to those who have courted her longest.[40]

Byron insisted that his translation should be printed alongside the original Italian, verse-by-verse, so that the reader could 'judge of the fidelity' of this painstaking project.[41] Long letters to John Murray agonised over the correct translation of the little word 'sbergo', which Byron rendered as 'cuirass', but which he suspected might also mean 'helmet':

> It is strange that here nobody understands the real precise meaning of '*Sbergo*' or '*Usbergo*' – an old Tuscan word which I have rendered *Cuirass* (but am not sure it is not *Helmet*). I have asked at least twenty people – learned and ignorant – male and female – including poets and officers civil and military. – The Dictionary says *Cuirass* – but gives no authority – and a female friend of mine says *positively Cuirass* – which makes me doubt the fact still more than before.

Ginguené says 'bonnet de Fer' with the usual superficial decision of a Frenchman – so that I can't believe him – and what between The Dictionary – the Italian woman – and the Frenchman – there is no trusting to a word they say – The Context too which should decide admits of either meaning equally as you will perceive – Ask Rose – Hobhouse – Merivale – and Foscolo – and vote with the Majority – is Frere a good Tuscan ? if he be bother him too – I have tried you see to be as accurate as I well could –[42]

In the Italianists Frere and Merivale, Byron is asking Murray to enlist the help of precisely those figures with whom he was associating what he called 'the new style of poetry very lately sprung up in England' to which *Don Juan* would claim kinship.[43] Moreover, for an English poet to take such careful pains over a local dialect word in Tuscan would represent a counter-example or rebuke to what he thought of as the petty localisms and untranslatability of Wordsworth and Southey.[44] As Murray delayed the publication of the *Morgante* translation Byron became quite vocal in its praise: it was 'the *acme* of putting one language into another'; 'it is superb – you have no such translation – It is the best thing I ever did in my life'; 'my grand performance'; 'the *best* translation that ever was or will be made'.[45]

Alongside the Pulci translation in the same volume Byron hoped to publish both *The Prophecy of Dante* and his second major translation exercise of this period, a version of Dante's *Francesca da Rimini*. Francesca's story of her love for her brother-in-law Paolo as she narrates it in the fifth canto of the *Inferno* is the most famous representation of marriage breakdown or the struggle between passion and duty in the whole of European literature. Byron's near-obsession with the story is well documented, but obtains a sharper urgency during the relationship with Teresa da Ravenna.[46] According to Teresa, she and Byron had been reading Dante's fifth canto together one day (reading together a poem about the erotic dangers of reading together) when she asked him whether it had ever been translated into English. Byron responded with the proverbial Italian expression: 'Non tradotto, ma tradito': 'not translated, but traduced, or betrayed', referring to what he considered to be inferior English translations. The notion of fidelity in translation is of course the great shibboleth of all translation and translation-theory – phantoms of fidelity and betrayal (often gendered phantoms) haunt all translators – but they seem to have been particularly haunting for Byron, who was particularly susceptible to the notion of language as a woman, or a 'capricious beauty'.[47] With the translation of the Francesca episode the strict watchword was fidelity, verse for verse, in *'third rhyme (terza rima)* of which your British Blackguard reader as yet understands nothing'.[48]

Byron's short, closely worked translation takes up Francesca's own narrative at the end of the fifth canto beginning: 'Siede la terra dove nata fui...'. The variant readings sent to John Murray (the publisher was instructed to choose which was best or print all together), reveal most variation at two significant moments.[49] Firstly, when Francesca describes how one day she and her brother-in-law Paolo read the story of Lancelot for pleasure, Dante's Francesca's 'di Lancialotto come amor strinse' ('of Lancelot, how love constrained him')[50] has three variants in Byron's translation: 'Of Lancilot, where forth his Passion breaks'/ 'Of Lancilot, how passion shook his frame'/ 'Of Lancilot, how love enchained him too'. Byron's ambivalence is subtly graded around the activity or passivity of Lancelot in relation to his passion or love; whether he is constrained, or overcome by it; whether this passion breaks forth (from constraint); whether, indeed, Byron wants to call this passion 'love' (Dante's 'amor') or not. This is indecision about the extent to which forbidden desire represents a form of enslavement, and is recognisably the self-interrogation of a *cavalier servente*. A similar kind of hesitation is revealed too in Byron's three variant readings for Dante's line, 'ma solo un punto fu quel che ci vinse' ('but one point alone it was that mastered us'). These are: 'Yet one point only 'twas our ruin wrought'/ 'But one part wholly overcame' / 'But one point wholly us o'erthrew'. The shades of difference between 'part' and 'point', and between having 'ruin wrought', being 'overcome', and being 'overthrown', again reveal an ambivalence about the kind of tragedy Paolo and Francesca's story represents. Byron is responding as a sensitive translator to the nuances of Dante, the tension between 'strinse' and 'vinse' for example, but he is also quite obviously wrestling with his own relation to this tale of infidelity. To what extent is the story of Paolo and Francesca a story of ruin, or defeat? Of passion breaking forth, shaking a frame, or love enchaining? Of being overcome, overthrown, or having ruin wrought? The emphasis a translator chooses will suggest everything about Francesca's own self-judgement, or self-knowledge, as it will also measure and define the crucial gap between the self-representations of a lover and the broader perspective of a moral order. In these respects, Byron is deeply conscious of the inter-relation of Dante's text with his own situation as a *cavalier servente*, and his own situation as *cavalier servente* with his work as a translator – aware of the close analogy between the process of translation itself (with its broader connotations of acculturation and self-transformation) and the interpretative cruxes of Francesca's story, of fidelity, betrayal, servitude, ruin.[51]

As the triangulation of his role as *cavalier servente* became increasingly constraining, Byron began to think seriously of transplanting himself to South America, either eloping in what he called 'the Anglo fashion'[52] with Teresa, or going alone to Venezuela (translation: 'little Venice') where he was sure he 'should not make a bad South-American planter', or land-settler: 'Better be a[n] unskilful planter – an awkward settler – better be a hunter – or anything than a flatterer of fiddlers – and a fan-carrier of a woman'.[53] Here the union of the erotic and the linguistic becomes most closely configured in the word 'plantation', because the other possibility open to Byron, *cavalier servente*, at the end of 1819 is precisely that of 'plantation' in a sexual sense. The OED credits Byron with the first English use of the term 'planted' meaning 'jilted', removed or replaced in someone's affections, i.e. betrayed, from the beginning of the third canto of *Don Juan* written late in 1819:

> I know not if the fault be men's or theirs;
>   But one thing's pretty sure; a woman planted –
> (Unless at once she plunge for life in prayers) –
>   After a decent time must be gallanted...
>
> (II.4)

In 'planted' Byron is translating (literally) two expressions: 'planter là' from the French, and 'piantare' from the Italian – the latter more probably the phrase he has in mind. A letter from Alexander Scott in the summer of 1819 warning against the continuation of the affair with Teresa contained what Byron described as 'prophecies of *plantation*', meaning predictions, not that Byron would flee to Venezuela, but that Teresa would be certain to dump Lord Byron sooner or later for another.[54] Byron ignored the warnings but continued to associate the two meanings of plantation in his own mind as he pondered his future in the uncertain period at the end of 1819: 'I will leave the country reluctantly indeed – but I will do it – for otherwise if I formed a new liason she would cut the figure of a woman *planted* – and I never will willingly hurt her Self-Love.'[55] Amazed at the behaviour of Teresa in apparently showing off her liaison with Byron at a ball in Ravenna (whither he had transplanted himself at the end of 1819) Byron can only guess, in a letter to Richard Hoppner, the British consul at Venice, that 'it seems as if the G[uiccioli] had been presumed to be *planted* and was determined to show that she was not – *plantation* in this hemisphere being the greatest moral misfortune'.[56]

Byron then sexualised the word 'plantation' for the English language by literal translation from the Italian. But it is a literal translation with more than one literal meaning; its meanings in fact multiply: acculturation, translation, transplantation, plantation, betrayal – the erotic, the linguistic and the cultural shift and exchange places, or, for a moment, are centred in a multilingual pun: 'plantation'. The fate of this word demonstrates the ways in which translation, acculturation and the linguistic-erotic life were absolutely interwoven for Byron during 1819–20, and would remain so, though becoming increasingly associated with up-rootings and transplantations of a political kind under the new existence he came to live at Ravenna in 1820.

3.3   Translation, uprooting, radical politics: *Marino Faliero, Don Juan* V

In place in Ravenna as a *cavalier servente*, Byron sensed for the second time in his life that he had travelled further into the interior of a culture than almost any Englishman before him. The first time had been during 1809 in Albania, where the journey had been as physically arduous as it was defamiliarising. Ravenna was quite different in respect of the geographical challenges it presented to a visitor, and even stranger in other respects. Nevertheless, to John Murray's persistent requests for a book upon Italian manners and customs, Byron was consistently robust in his refusals.[57] This was partly due to a sense of honour in not exploiting or betraying the intimacy he had received from those distinguished families which had taken him into their hearts and homes. But more significantly, the refusal to satisfy Murray's hunger for travel narrative arose from the sense of the impossibility of such a task. The untranslatability of Italian culture, as it was known through prolonged intercourse and familiarity, had become increasingly apparent during these years – the greater his knowledge of Italy and its people the less Byron felt able to shape this knowledge into a summary and generalised account for his English friends. Furthermore, the paradox or doubleness of Byron's existence in Italy would occasionally manifest itself around the fracture between his European-wide fame, and the anonymity of being an Englishman in

Italy. In a letter to Richard Hoppner of June 1819 Byron records an incident in Ferrara:

> One of the Ferrarese asked me if I knew 'Lord Byron' an acquaintance of his *now* at Naples – I told him *No* – which was true both ways – for I know not the Impostor – and in the other – no one knows himself. – He stared when told that I was 'the real Simon Pure.' – Another asked me if I had *not translated* 'Tasso'. – You see what *fame* is – how *accurate* – how *boundless*....[58]

Impostors and dopplegängers are a consequence of fame, but there is also a sense, recognised only too well by Byron, in which the exile himself becomes his own double (and doubly so if he is famous) as he slowly metamorphoses from one cultural identity to another. Here Byron's reputation in Italy, at least with one Ferrarese, is mistakenly founded upon his being a translator of Tasso rather than the author of a dramatic monologue spoken *as if* by Tasso – an example of something being lost in the translation. Writing to Augusta in October 1820, Byron quotes the beginning of Sir Walter Scott's *The Abbot*:

> [']every *five* years we find ourselves another and yet the same with a change of views and no less of the light in which we regard them; a change of motives as well as of actions.' This I presume applies still more to those who have past their *five* years in foreign countries – for my part I suppose that I am *two* others – for it seems that some fool has been betting that he saw me in London – the other day – in a *Curricle* – if he said a *Canoe* it would have been much more likely.—[59]

Byron was vulnerable then to multiple alienations as an expatriate and as a famous poet, as well as being subject to the 'ordinary' self-translations wrought by time, each merely compounding the sense of distance from the English Byron of pre-1816.[60] The precipitous events during 1819–21 as England herself became 'another and yet the same' merely exacerbated this sense of distance. The Peterloo massacre and subsequent government crackdown; the Cato Street conspiracy; the death of George III, the impending coronation of the Regent, and the political crisis precipitated by the Queen Caroline affair (Byron as a peer of the realm was expected to attend the trial in the House of Lords, expectations which fuelled sightings of him in London); Hobhouse's imprisonment in Newgate, his increasing involvement in radical politics and election as MP for Westminster – Byron followed all this with the double sense of familiarity and astonishment experienced by the exile. In the case of radical politics Byron's feelings were deeply ambivalent. Although consistently in favour of constitutional reform in England, he remained opposed to the more extreme leaders of the reform movement (particularly Henry Hunt and Arthur Thistlewood) and was horrified by the Cato Street conspiracy. At the same time he seemed to relish the prospect of some kind of political upheaval (or 'row' as he called it), and frequently fantasised about returning to England to participate in what he felt was an impending civil war, although whether to defend his own rights as a landowner or as a champion of liberty, is never quite clear: 'They say in Italy that "Che nasce Patrizio innora Patrizio" and I am not democrat enough to like a tyranny of blackguards – such fellows as Bristol Hunt – are a choice of evils with Castlereagh – except that a Gentleman scoundrel is always preferable to a vulgar one.'[61] The very word 'radical' is unfamiliar to Byron in Italy, and a measure of his own distance from English life:

> Upon reform you have long known my opinion – but *radical* is a new word since my time – it was not in the political vocabulary in 1816 – when I left England – and I don't know what it means – is it uprooting? ...I protest, not against *reform* – but my most thorough contempt and abhorrence – of all that I have seen, heard, or heard of the persons calling themselves *reformers, radicals,* and such other names, – I should look upon being free with such men, as much the same as being in bonds with felons.[62]

The unfamiliarity of the word *radical* is merely a symptom of the greater and more sinister unfamiliarity of those who exist beneath its sign, 'the persons calling themselves *reformers*', whom Byron consistently portrays as a quite alien social grouping (partly but not wholly based upon class). As English political events and political vocabulary seemed to be moving rapidly enough to induce this sense of estrangement, political events in Italy were drawing Byron ever closer and deeper into the inner circles of Romagnuole society.[63] The Neapolitan revolution in the spring of 1820 had raised expectations among liberal circles throughout Italy, Byron himself composing an address to the Neapolitan insurgents in which he offered financial assistance to their cause.[64] His privileged position as a foreigner received into the heart of Ravenna society ('I have been inoculated among the people rather within these last four years'[65]) meant that he found himself close to revolutionary activity and planning. In August 1820 Byron was initiated into the secret revolutionary society of the Carbonari, with its pass-words and signs, and his letters to England during this period (which he feared the Austrian authorities would be opening) are full of predictions of an imminent upheaval.[66] Politics subsequently begin to take a more central role in the writings of 1819–20, but it is a politics very much of a double Anglo-Italian cast, defined by this paradoxical sense of different kinds of insider knowledge and outsider estrangement, a politics of translation, in other words, which remains bound up with the linguistic and the erotic. At the same time Byron is repeatedly urging Murray to hasten the publication of his Italian imitations and translations because the prophetic element in those writings seemed to be potentially most useful at this moment of possible national regeneration.[67]

Between April and July 1820 Byron composed the verse drama *Marino Faliero*, taking as its subject events in fourteenth-century Venice. Although Byron was reluctant to think of his play in terms other than those of faithful historical reconstruction, these events are in some sense transposed to the European political context of 1820, and clearly embrace both the situation Byron was experiencing in Ravenna and the events in England he was following from a distance. In fact Anglo-Italianness and the impossibility of translation is crucial to the play's composition and meaning; moreover, at the heart of *Marino Faliero* is an historical circumstance that Byron manipulates in ways closely influenced by his situation as a *cavalier servente* in Romagnuole society – that is, the relationship of the ageing doge Faliero to his younger wife Angiolina.[68] According to the historical chronicles Byron consulted, the conspiracy of the doge against the Venetian state had been trig-gered by Faliero's outrage at the light sentence meted out to Michael Steno, who had impugned Angiolina's virtue. It is a vital aspect of the work, and a counter-example or antitype to the many instances of cuckolded husbands and marriages-in-crisis which are everywhere in Byron's post-1816 writing, that the marriage of Faliero and Angiolina is absolutely unshakeable, and, moreover, that the sphere of their private union is an unknowable and inviolable space within the drama. This was partly of course to avoid comparison with *Othello* (a husband 'whom mere suspicion could inflame / To suffocate a wife no more than twenty, / Because she had a "cavalier servente"', *Beppo*, ll.133–5); it was also partly to avoid writing another Byronic comedy about the waywardness of young wives; more significantly, it allowed Byron to examine the nature of honour from the complex double perspective of Faliero and his wife, and to place this critique of honour in a revolutionary context which is both of the fourteenth century and of 1820. The exemplariness of the Faliero marriage (although husband and wife strongly disagree about the appropriate reaction to Steno's slander) should be seen then within the context of Byron's own position of *serventismo*. His portrait of the relationship between Faliero and his wife is of a marriage which has no need of such a crutch, and as such is anomalous when placed within a contemporary Italian (especially Venetian) context. This anomalousness is directly connected to the play's sense of a wider Venetian polity and its threatened uprooting, in which Faliero's political vision (like his marriage) represents an older and more honourable order of aristocratic virtue, which had been manifestly diluted (witness the *cavalier servente*) by 1820. Again the institutions of marriage and those of politics are seen not to belong to separate spheres at all, but to be caught up in the same historical crisis, which is prophetic of the degenerate condition of Venice in 1820.

Byron consulted several different sources for the story of Faliero's conspiracy, including Dr John Moore's *View of Society and Manners in Italy* (1781) which had made sport of the age difference between Faliero and his wife: 'This lady [Angiolina]', Moore writes, 'imagined she had been affronted by a young Venetian nobleman at a public ball, and she complained bitterly to her husband. The old Doge, who had all the desire imaginable to please his wife, determined, in this matter at least, to give her ample satisfaction.'[69] Byron described Moore's account as 'false and flippant, full of stale jests about old men and young wives', 'paltry and ignorant', and became determined to represent the relationship of Faliero and his wife quite differently.[70] He was also determined to provide supplementary material in the notes to draw attention to this difference. One of the several lengthy appendices attached to the play, most of which are in Italian with English translations, is an extract in French with an English translation from the *Histoire de la République de Venise* (1819) by Pierre Darù, which details the decay of Venetian society in the late eighteenth century, in particular the decay of the institution of marriage and the ways in which the state conspired to allow marriages to be nullified (divorce not being legal):

> There was a moment in which, doubtless, the destruction of private fortunes, the ruin of youth, the domestic discord occasioned by these abuses, determined the government to depart from its established maxims concerning the freedom of manners allowed the

subject. All the courtesans were banished from Venice; but their absence was not enough to reclaim and bring back good morals to a whole people brought up in the most scandalous licentiousness. Depravity reached the very bosoms of private families, and even into the cloister....Since that time licentiousness has gone on increasing, and we have seen mothers, not only selling the innocence of their daughters, but selling it by a contract, authenticated by the signature of a public officer, and the performance of which was secured by the protection of laws.[71]

This has nothing directly to do with Faliero and fourteenth-century Venice, but it has much to do with the transposition of that moment to the early nineteenth century, and to the degeneracy Byron had witnessed and participated in. Depravity had 'reached the very bosom of private families, and even into the cloister', while the insitutions of the state were either collusive in this process or ineffectual in preventing it. The symbolism of the doge's marriage is even more obvious when framed in this way, while the direct connection between the domestic arrangements of a society (marriage institutions in particular) and broader political upheaval is further underlined in Byron's preface, which lists a series of examples of historical crises precipitated by private or personal insults, or perceived insults:

a basin of water spilt on Mrs. Masham's gown deprived the Duke of Marlborough of his command, and led to the inglorious peace of Utrecht – that Louis XIV. was plunged into the most desolating wars because his minister was nettled at his finding fault with a window, and wished to give him another occupation – that Helen lost Troy – that Lucretia expelled the Tarquins from Rome – and that Cava brought the Moors to Spain – that an insulted husband led the Gauls to Clusium, and thence to Rome – that a single verse of Frederick II. of Prussia on the Abbé de Bernis, and a jest on Madame de Pompadour, led to the battle of Rosbach – that the elopement of Dearbhorgil with Mac Murchad conducted the English to the slavery of Ireland – that a personal pique between Maria Antoinette and the Duke of Orleans precipitated the first expulsion of the Bourbons – and, not to multiply instances, that Commodus, Domitian, and Caligula fell victims not to their public tyranny, but to private vengeance – and that an order to make Cromwell disembark from the ship in which he would have sailed to America destroyed both King and commonwealth.[72]

Marino Faliero is framed, then, by prose passages in which the private and domestic becomes wholly significant both in terms of determining historical events and in revealing the true state of a nation. Though the play itself takes care not to exploit the comic potential of such inter-connection, the underlying assumptions in this are the same as those of *Beppo* and *Don Juan*: that national identity is determined by the forms and institutions which govern and regulate the lawless energies of the libido. Because Faliero has a notion of personal honour in these matters which is out of accord with his fellow Venetians and which finds no proper redress under Venetian law, the catastrophe of his attempted coup unfolds.

The *Italianness* of this is crucial to grasp. Faliero's actions belong to a Venetian context, which is of a double historical perspective – the anachronism which the doge and his wife embody in fourteenth-century Venice becomes prophetic of Venice's condition in 1820. Lengthy appendices in which a reader is directly confronted with his-torical materials in Italian emphasise that this is a partisan text, an Italophile prophecy which flaunts its belonging in Italy and prides itself upon its fidelity to its Venetian setting, its existence as a piece of insider-art. But at the same time the play offers the very notion of insider-knowledge and the untranslatability of that knowledge as an idea with political consequences for both England and Italy. The Doge's powerful speech in the third act as he hesitates on the brink of offering his support to the revolutionaries and remembers his natural patrician ties, is obliquely addressed to the English radicals as much as it is to the Romagnuole conspirators:

> but *you* ne'er spake with them;
> You never broke their bread, nor shared their salt;
> You never had their wine-cup at your lips;
> You grew not up with them, nor laugh'd, nor wept,
> Nor held a revel in their company;
> Ne'er smiled to see them smile, nor claim'd their smile
> In social interchange for yours, nor trusted
> Nor wore them in your heart of hearts, as I have...

(III.ii.ll.458–65)

Here, not belonging is first and foremost a matter of class. Hunt and Thistlewood, like Israel Bertuccio, do not know what it means to have been bred an aristocrat, and no doubt they make no effort to imagine what it might mean either. The lines also suggest something about acculturation, and in particular they draw upon Byron's growing awareness of the untranslatability of insider-knowledge (in fact they echo Byron's letters home warning Murray that, as far as the Italians are concerned, 'their moral is not your moral – their life is not your life – you would not understand it')[73]. Being on the inside of a social-cultural grouping (whether it be a class or a nation) forges certain kinds of bonds and duties, emotional ties rooted in shared experience, which have specific and unavoidable political conse-quences and significance, not least of which is the fact that they cannot be properly understood by those who do not share them. What is made of this fact of unknowability may vary greatly: it may be used as a check on all antagonism between class or nations on the grounds (as Faliero seems to be urging here) of a concealed humanity which must be *imagined* even as it cannot be known. It may be used in quite the opposite way as the justification for aggressive partisan-ship to the groupings of class or nation in which one belongs and only belongs. Either way, the politics of revolution and national regen-eration alike are founded upon the untranslatability of private social experience, as indeed are the politics of reaction. Faliero hesitates at this moment, before pursuing his alliance with the plebeian conspira-tors against his own class. His predicament is a superb realisation of the translation of the self, its alienation and its crossing-over in a political context.

As Byron journeyed further into the interior of radical Romagnuole society, then, he also became more conscious of the untranslatability of his own ties and bonds with the British aristocracy, so that, paradox-ically, he became more distanced from radical activity in England. *Marino Faliero* expresses this doubleness as a piece of insider-art addressed to an Italian *and* an English audience, belonging separately to each, and revealing Anglo-Italianness in a further stylistic matter. Byron was pleased to hear that William Gifford, who acted as a reader for John Murray, had praised the first act of the play in terms of its fidelity to a certain kind of English poetics:

What Gifford says is very consolatory – (of the first act) 'English ster-ling *genuine English*' is a desideratum amongst you – and I am glad that I have got so much left – though heaven knows how I retain it – I *hear* none but from my Valet – and his is *Nottinghamshire* – and I *see* none – but in your new publications – and theirs is no language at all – but jargon.[74]

Byron's gratitude and pleasure here is telling. The fact that this faithful recreation of fourteenth-century Venice also represents a purity of English language, a 'genuine' English (surrounded by prose note appendices in Italian and French), may at first seem paradoxical, but it is crucial to its conception as an Anglo-Italian project in which the Italian and the English elements are each quite distinctly and faithfully rendered, as if indeed the text were a perfect translation. The play's Anglo-Italianness is *not* then primarily about hybridity or mixing (this is precisely what the play dramatises as a dark threat and is the reason why Byron denied having written an allegory), but about different kinds of purities and fidelities that it presents in the process of transformation.

As Faliero's marriage and aristocratic principles represent a 'purity' under threat from the political forces portrayed in the play (and exploited to a degree by the extreme radicalism represented by Israel Bertuccio), so the play offers a generic and linguistic 'purity' or fidelity which is an anti-type to current trends in English poetry and stagecraft. The two elements are not merely analogous, but connected at a root level, firstly because this play about Italy is written by an English nobleman, and as such is an exploration of the possibility or impossibility of speaking *for* another nation; secondly, because its notion of purity/fidelity is simultaneously a political, a sexual and a linguistic one: Faliero speaks perfect English and attempts to preserve a perfect Venetian constitution and has a perfect marriage. The transposition of a pure English diction to fourteenth-century Venice, then, is meant to be the stylistic equivalent of Faliero's political and spousal anachronism – a noble and heroic anachronism with symbolic meaning in 1820. When Foscolo praised the play for its fidelity to its Venetian setting, Byron's gratification was complete. A long letter to Murray of October 1820 threads together the sense of good English, of accurate Venetian detail, of a Southern European dramaturgy, and of the effect of being a *cavalier servente*:

> Foscolo's letter is exactly the thing wanted – 1[st]ly because he is a man of Genius – & next because he is an Italian and therefore the best Judge of Italics...Gifford says it is good "sterling genuine English" and Foscolo says that the Characters are right Venetian...[The Doge's] speeches are long – true – but I wrote for the *Closet* – and on the French and Italian model rather than yours – which I think not very highly of – for all your *old* dramatists – who are long enough too God knows – *look* into any of them. I wish *you* too to recollect one thing which is nothing to the reader.—I never wrote nor copied *an entire Scene of that play* – without being obliged

to *break* off – to *break* a commandment;– to obey a woman's, and to forget God's. – Remember the drain of this upon a Man's heart and brain – to say nothing of his immortal Soul. – *Fact* I assure you – the Lady always apologized for the interruption – but you know the *answer* a man must make when and while he can. – It happened to be the only hour I had in the four and twenty for composition or reading and I was obliged to divide even it, such are the defined duties of a Cavalier Servente, or Cavalier Schiavo.[75]

The guise of the victim who is reluctantly dragged away from more serious activities to perform the sex act (which of course Byron can never exactly refuse), was one he enjoyed putting on for the vicarious pleasure of the Murray coterie, and is grandly reprised in the figure of Don Juan. Nevertheless, this is an unusually revealing letter in that it demonstrates exactly how deeply Byron's life penetrates his writing, and vice versa. Here he interweaves the notion of a linguistic and generic fidelity with the terrible drain upon man's heart, brain and soul in having to perform the erotic duties of the *cavalier servente*. And just as Faliero wonders whether his role serving the Venetian state may in fact have come to represent a debasement of his aristocratic honour, so Byron offers another term for *serventismo* in 'schiavo', or slave. The very composition of the play seems here to have arisen from the struggle between contending passions and duties, and passionate duties. As such the agonising questions of fidelity and betrayal which beset Faliero – when does the duty to serve become a form of enslavement? – are precisely those tormenting Byron as *cavalier servente*. If this would seem to make Byron vulnerable to the charge of over-dramatising aspects of his personal life, then, apart from the fact that this is also to be like Faliero, it should be remembered that the writing of this period is obssessed with the interaction between marriages and politics, and with the political meaning of private experience (psycho-sexual experience in particular). As Faliero faces execution, his prophecies for Venice envisage her fall in terms of erotic betrayal, profligacy and illegitimacy:

> Yes, the hours
> Are silently engendering of the day,
> When she, who built 'gainst Attila a bulwark,
> Shall yield, and bloodlessly and basely yield
> Unto a bastard Attila...

> (V.iii.ll.45–9)

Byron thought of the Italian language (and by implication the Italian nation), as itself a hybrid or bastardized entity (remember *Beppo*'s 'soft bastard Latin'), and often expressed himself in these terms.[76] Here, however, the impurities hidden in the very core of Italian language and culture emerge most darkly as impure libidinal desires. False lineage, corrupted inheritance, inauthenticity: Napoleon as a bastard Attila; Venice over-run by non-Venetians; the adulteress will be 'boastful of her guilt / With some large gondolier or foreign soldier'; those Venetians remaining will 'bear about their bastardy in triumph / To the third spurious generation'; the daughters of Venice will have become 'a wider proverb for worse prostitution'. Political decline and sexual degeneracy go hand in hand:

> Thou den of drunkards with the blood of princes!
> Gehenna of the waters! thou sea Sodom!
> Thus I devote thee to the infernal gods!
> Thee and thy serpent seed!

> (V.iii.ll.98–101)

In Faliero's thundering final speeches the network of the linguistic, the erotic and the political is given its darkest realisation, and it is a realisation which (like the prophecies of Tasso and Dante) is 'true' to the contemporary situation in Italy, specifically here to the dissoluteness of Venice. Faliero sees Venice's decline in terms of extreme sexual licence because this is the exaggerated aspect of his own perceived injustice, as the state he has served has failed to punish Michael Steno in proportion to his crime, and his anger becomes both symbolic and 'prophetic' in the context of 1820. The sexual habits of the city-state (a foreshadowing of the nation) are entirely and minutely bound up with its political fate.

This, of course, brings the play into a revealing relation to the events in England surrounding the trial of Queen Caroline, the narrative of which Byron might have written himself. An unfaithful English wife living in virtual exile with her upwardly mobile young Italian lover; a wrathful husband, and an unlikely alliance between the plebeian mob of London and the Queen herself. Byron, like the Whigs, sympathised with Caroline's cause without believing in her innocence, and saw the occasion as a political opportunity. But the episode also belongs to the sex-comedy of *Don Juan*, the vigorous suppression of which had been central to the meaning of *Marino Faliero*, and as Byron describes the consequences of the actions of Queen Caroline to Teresa in July 1820, he reaches again for that recent coinage ('piantando'/ planting), with its hint of the new English word 'radical', meaning pertaining to the root (planting/uprooting): 'La sua Maestà ha messo il morale del' mio moralisimo paese in gran periglio e scandalo – mia pare già deteriorato, perche leg[g]o nelle gazzette di una dama Irlandese di 37 anni che e scappata con un' giovane Inglese di 24, – piantando un'marito di 50 – e un figlia di 16.' [Her Majesty has put the morals of my very moral country in great danger and scandal. They seem deteriorated already, for I read in the Gazette of an Irish lady of 37 who has run away with a young Englishman of 24 – leaving behind {*planting*} a husband of 50 and a daughter of 16.][77] When it became clear that the Queen would survive the trial, Byron envisaged her political victory again in terms of its moral implications in England, joking to Moore that its 'ultimate effect, the most inevitable one to you and me (if they and we live so long) will be that the Miss Moores and Miss Byrons will present us with a great variety of grandchildren by different fathers'.[78] When Byron received the news of Caroline's acquittal from Count Giuseppe Alborghetti, his response was to see the outcome in terms of the interwoven fate of Italian and English politics:

> You could not have sent me better news – better for England for it will prevent a revolution – though it may *hasten* a *reform*, – or better for Italy for if (as is probable) the Ministry is changed – we shall have a pacific administration, who may perhaps interfere to prevent the 'bel paese' from becoming the prey alike of factious citizens or of foreign armies.[79]

The interdependence of politics and the cultural institutions regulating sexual conduct (in particular the institution of marriage), was almost too perfectly demonstrated by this episode, which overlapped with the composition and revision of *Marino Faliero* and provided further Anglo-Italian ironies. Indeed part of the process of understanding the politics of Italy involved an awareness of what could and what could not be transposed to an English context, so that translation (and its impossibility) becomes a form of perception and a means of comprehension. Political events in England during 1819–21 were better understood through the failure to transpose them to a different context (Caroline's trial was a thoroughly English affair and Byron joked about the ease with which 'witnesses' could be bought in Italy), just as the radical politics of the Romagnuole circles were more sharply appreciated by their unlikeness either to Henry Hunt's or John Cam Hobhouse's radicalism (the failed insurrection in the Northern states was in a sense a purely Italian episode). At the end of 1820 Byron is writing to Tom Moore to suggest jointly setting up a newspaper in England, a project that he hoped would inaugurate a political and cultural regeneration at home. The names Byron suggests for the journal, however, are all Italian:

> We will call it the 'Tenda Rossa', the name Tassoni gave an answer of his in a controversy, in allusion to the delicate hint of Timour the Lame, to his enemies, by a 'Tenda' of that colour, before he gave battle. Or we will call it 'Gli' or 'I Carbonari', if it so please you – or any other name full of 'pastime and prodigality', which you may prefer.[80]

Eventually (1822) the journal was named *The Liberal*. But its subtitle read 'Verse and Prose From the South'.

In its comic aspect of radical acculturation, however, translation-irony is sharpest in the famous harem scene of the fifth canto of *Don Juan*, written at the end of 1820. Here, as is well known, our hero finds himself exposed to the quickest and most brutal form of acculturation – slavery – carrying with it the sexualized threats of circumcision, initiation into the rites of the harem, cross-dressing, and the exchange of gender-roles with Gulbeyaz – the 'strange suits' of Rosalind's Monsieur Traveller are forcibly imposed upon Juan. Finally, too, the episode serves up a staple moment of British Orientalist comedy when a warlike male (the Sultan) shows sexual interest in a dragged-up boy, believing him to be a girl but in his attraction betraying a latent homosexuality hidden from himself, but always suspected by a western public. Acculturation here is life-threatening for Juan, and the canto culminates in yet another meditation upon the politics of marriage customs:

> The Turks do well to shut – at least, sometimes –
>   The women up – because in sad reality,
> Their chastity in these unhappy climes
>   Is not a thing of that astringent quality,
> Which in the north prevents precocious crimes,
>   And makes our snow less pure than our morality;
> The sun, which yearly melts the polar ice,
> Has quite the contrary effect on vice.

Thus in the East they are extremely strict,
  And *Wedlock* and *Padlock* mean the same;
Excepting only when the former's pick'd,
  It ne'er can be replaced in proper frame;
Spoilt, as a pipe of claret is when pricked:
  But then their own Polygamy's to blame;
Why don't they knead two virtuous souls for life
Into that moral centaur, man and wife?

The connections are unambiguous: climate with sexual appetite, and with marriage custom to accommodate and control that appetite, and therefore with marriage breakdown, or as in the case of the East, multiple marriages, and marriage-as-slavery, culminating in the figure of the monogamous man and wife, 'two virtuous souls for life', that 'moral centaur'. Byron sent the second of these stanzas to Murray as an addition to the fifth canto at the beginning of March 1821, but was furious to discover in August 1821 that the lines had been omitted in the first edition, immediately guessing that the offending phrase must have been 'moral centaur'.[81] The phrase was provocative because the mythic nature of the figure is so suggestive; its hybridity, its impossibility: half one thing and half another, neither one thing nor another, inbetween. The British cultural norm of monogamous marriage-for-life represents, then, for Byron, a moral version of that mythical beast, where 'moral' seems perfectly ambiguous (is the mythological beast displaying moral restraint against its nature, or is there something monstrous about British morality?). At the same time, however, the notion of freakish inbetweenness, of impossibility, is being translated back into the Italian cultural form of *serventismo*, so that Byron is thinking too of the institution of the *cavalier servente* as a moral centaur in which the strange otherness of Italian life is configured: half-man/half horse, or horseman, or chevalier, or cavalier.[82] And not merely the particular forms of *serventismo*, but Byron is characteristically grouping English, Italian and Turkish marriage institutions and arrangements together, since finally all such forms and structures represent (for him) monstrousness of one sort or another – the grotesque shapes adopted by sexual instinct as it is regulated by culture. As marriage institutions are the ultimate expressions of cultural difference, as they manifest cultural uniqueness and identity most distinctly, there may in fact always be something monstrous (something comic) at the heart of acculturation and translation. Such a notion is a common and foundational one in translation history and theory in which the monstrous over-reaching of Babel is most frequently taken to represent an unrestrained originary freedom, necessarily broken down into the servitude of multiple translation. George Steiner has written of translation as itself a 'centaur idiom'[83]; Jacques Derrida, thinking about the alienness of one's own language, has described translation as 'another name for the impossible', while translation theorists have increasingly foregrounded the 'problem' of translation as a major epistemological task.[84] But this monstrousness is a prevailing and normative condition for Byron; it goes into the heart of cultural exchange and difference, into the interior of national identity, where it connects the linguistic with the sexual and the political. Most particularly, the 'centaur idiom' of translation is closely related in Byron's writing to the 'moral centaur' of marriage-institution, both embodying that which is impossible, that which breaks down; but also that which is unique and authentic about a culture. Only in the double-voiced nature of work such as *The Prophecy of Dante* or in the Anglo-Italianness of *Marino Faliero*, is this comic monstrousness transformed into miraculous possibility, including the possibility of prophecy. Nevertheless, the *cavalier servente* has no English equivalent, and cannot be translated. This was a significant and disturbing fact for an English lord struggling over the course of these years to learn the correct method of doubling the shawl of an Italian *dama*.

4
Nostalgia: 1821–24

4.1 Having been there/ having seen (part one)

The burning of Byron's *Memoirs* is one of the sharpest reminders we have of the contingency of English literary history, and the scene of its loss in John Murray's drawing-room at Albemarle Street on 17 May 1824 will haunt the minds of Byron scholars forever. Byron, who thought of himself as 'old' when he was in his late teens and felt ancient by the age of thirty-three, was a natural memoirist. The period of 1821–23 in particular was marked by an increasing number of memorial projects of a distinctly nostalgic cast, which also take a critically dispassionate, sometimes ironised view of 'nostalgia' as a subject.[1] In prose we do at least have a series of surviving supplementary memoirs: the Ravenna journal, 4 January–27 February, 1821; 'My Dictionary', a journal taken up on 1 May 1821, but broken off soon after, to be taken up again later as 'Detached Thoughts', 15 October 1821–18 May 1822. This was also the time when Byron was negotiating publishing arrangements for the *Memoirs* and taking steps to organise and collate other memorial materials such as letters – a period described by Donald Reiman as one of 'rapprochement' with England and Byron's English past.[2] This consisted in part of an awareness of having lived in a particular world (that of early Regency London) which had passed into history. A sense of mourning the disappearance of that world is muted, however, by a temperamental and philosophical inclination to assert that *nothing* had essentially changed, and that knowledge of the world (including the *grande monde*) would merely disclose the cyclical nature of history and its 'fruitless page'.[3] Moreover, the possibility slowly takes shape in Byron's mind (emerging most clearly in the later cantos of *Don Juan*) that even the glittering world of

157

the Regency was ultimately insignificant, perhaps not even worth recording, or that it stood in isolation as a strange historical fragment.

Alongside this *sang froid*, however, runs a powerful vein of nostalgia and a strong instinct to memorialise. 'Nostalgia' isn't a word Byron uses in his thinking about the past, but it is a concept firmly at the heart of his later writings – that is, a longing to return, at least imaginatively, to a particular place and time of historical significance, in this case a few short years in London. And although his desire physically to return to England is at best intermittent, the fact of having once been there, and the subsequent perspective gained through having left England, acquire a clarity which they did not have during his first years upon the continent. Nostalgia, however, is a complex phenomenon, and especially so in Byron's case since he was both peculiarly vulnerable to its influence and particularly suspicious of its effects. His exploration of the theme across the writings of 1821–23, not always in direct relation to England, registers a contradiction between a certain kind of emotion or sentimentality (in homesickness and in place-attachment), and an ironic or unsentimental distance from the forms assumed by the past both in memory, and in historiography.

From a very early age Byron had been fascinated and perhaps a little bedazzled by the world of Whig statesmen, orators and wits of the 1780s and 1790s.[4] His first experience of London society in 1806–7 coincided with Grenville's 'ministry of all the talents' – a brief moment of coalition government and rehabilitation for that rump of Whig statesmen and their associates whom Byron referred to as 'the old school'. The excitement of those times and the hopes for Grenville's ministry were captured in *An Inquiry into the State of the Nation* (1806) by Henry Brougham, who would later become Byron's nemesis.[5] It is during this period, and especially in the slightly later period of 1811–16 (having returned from the East), that Byron enjoyed close involvement with the *bon ton*, and direct contact with the survivors and relics of British cultural life of the previous decades – men such as Richard Brinsley Sheridan and John Philpot Curran who seemed to belong to an earlier, higher order of being. An unfinished piece dating from 1821, headed 'Some Recollections of my acquaintance with Madame de Staël', first published in 1887, recalls a dinner-party at Humphry Davy's in 1813:

> On the day after her [i.e. De Staël's] arrival I dined in her company at Sir Humphry Davy's – being the least of one of 'a legion of honour' invited to greet her. – If I mistake not—and can Memory be

treacherous to such men? – there were present – Sheridan – Whitbread – Grattan – the Marquis of Lansdowne – without counting our illustrious host, – the first experimental philosopher of his own (or perhaps any other *preceding* time) was there to receive the most celebrated of women – surrounded by the flower of our wits, the foremost of our remaining orators and Statesmen – and condescending to invite the then youngest and it may be still least of our living poets.—

[...]

Of this 'Symposium' graced by these now Immortals – I recollect less than ought to have been remembered, – but who can carry away the remembrance of his pleasures unimpaired and unmutilated? – the general impression remains – but the tints are faded.- Besides I was then too young – and too passionate to do full justice to those around me. – Time – Absence and death – mellow and sanctify all things. – I then saw around me but the men whom I heard daily in the Senate – and met nightly in the London Assemblies – I revered – I respected them – but I *saw* them – and neither Beauty nor Glory can stand this daily test.[6]

'Having seen' is a recurring and important trope in these later writings, where 'seeing' is both witnessing something of historical significance but also, as here, literally *seeing*, having physically been present. The anecdote reveals the workings of nostalgia, whereby as the past becomes sanctified by memory there emerges the pain of 'realising' that one was not fully conscious of the value of the moment at the time. Byron attributes this to the familiarity he enjoyed with these 'Immortals' in the day-to-day life of 1813, but it is also part of the consciousness of 1821, and part of the way we remember. In this case the relations between past and present are further complicated by the fact that the world of 1807–16 (and in particular the 'year of revelry' of 1814) was itself in important respects a backward-looking world, particularly in the case of the loosely grouped Whigs and their circle who were fond of remembering not only the 1780s and 1790s, but who looked even further back to the 1760s and the days of 'Wilkes and Liberty', and, indeed, to the founding myths of the Glorious Revolution, before their living memory. There was something essentially nostalgic then about the Whiggism Byron encountered at Holland House, something elegiac at its heart, especially in relation to aristocratic culture and manners, although it was a nostalgia quite distinct from the Tory variety and could accompany progressive politics.

Moreover for Byron, political nostalgia could not be separated from a literary nostalgia for what is still sometimes called 'Augustanism', the pre-Adamite giants of the early eighteenth century, the tallest of them all, figuratively speaking, being Alexander Pope.[7] The *Letter to John Murray Esqre* (1821), Byron's vigorous intervention in the Bowles–Pope controversy, helped to clarify and disseminate his notion of the present age as a degenerate one in literary terms, and of the early eighteenth century as a golden age which was somehow in the process of being betrayed. After all, Byron had known men such as Sheridan, who had known Dr Johnson, and whose father Thomas Sheridan had been Swift's godson. With his fascination in material connection with the past and with the aura or 'halo' of history as it manifested itself in such material, these facts were of considerable importance to Byron. The further fact that Augustanism in its 'authentic' eighteenth-century variety was itself already structured around nostalgia for the notion of a cultural legacy created in Rome under Augustus and inherited by England, sharing therein a certain cast of beliefs and emotions with Whiggism, in one sense merely deepened its appeal since Byron could represent his own version of Augustanism as something like a true literary church of direct descent from Rome, with an apostolic succession that included figures like Sheridan, whom Byron had seen, touched and spoken with. The critical cliché of Byron as somehow paradoxically bifurcated around an Augustan and Romantic opposition fails to understand the romanticism and indeed romance of these notions of eighteenth-century tradition and legacy, and the ways in which they are related to the passions of Byronism. One such tradition is that of the satire upon the contemporary age of poetry, which Byron proposed to take up again like an avenging sword during these later years, but perhaps more interestingly there also emerges a series of neo-classical dramatic experiments which in complex ways take nostalgia (including nostalgia for the classical) as their subject, and which explore different aspects of what I will call the *pathology* of nostalgia, particularly in relation to the attachment to place. Here and in other later writings there is a more urgent questioning of that part of the Augustan legacy which prostrated itself before the idea of Roman civilization and power, an imperial shadow (paralleled in Byron's mind by contemporary European imperialism) that darkened Byron's consciousness of the meaning of 'Augustan' or 'classical' cultural values.

Central to the writing of post-1821, then, is the sense of having been in early regency London and having known people who were relics of a glorious age which itself echoed and imitated a glorious age (and so on in the infinite regression of all cultural nostalgias). Within this Russian-doll sequence the idea of an inherited but damaged tradition is an enduring element in Byron's perception and recollection of these years. So too, as we shall see, is the idea of the *genius* of place being connected to the genius of particular individuals, as well as the reverse notion of the pathological or tragic individual who is broken by a longing for the homeland. Moreover, Byron's nostalgia is future-oriented, that is, it imagines the past – and particularly the years 1811–16 – from a far-future perspective, as if this fossilised segment of British history had been unearthed in some Cuvier-inspired dream of lost worlds.[8] In this sense the classical past, and in particular the fragmentation and fossilisation of Rome, becomes a paradigm to be re-played in British history along the axis of interchangeability, so that Byron's writing, especially in the later cantos of *Don Juan*, contributes both to the historical mythologising of the Regency, the consciousness of this as a particular epoch, and participates in what we might call the time-capsule mystique of those years in London, that is, the imaginative foretaste of their life in posterity. The very notion, however, that such a posthumous existence could only take the form of fragmentation and fossilisation, that is, that the regency would inevitably suffer *periodisation* as if it were a separate and self-contained slice of history, freakishly set apart from what went before and what came after, is also a theme of the later writing. In this there is a tension between the nostalgic desire to mark the regency out as brilliant in and of itself, and a fear that such a project merely turns the past into a monstrous relic.

One form Byron's nostalgia takes during this period is that of intoxication with the memory of the 'Immortals' with whom he had mixed in London, in which the idea of the 'classical' is employed as a straightforward measure of historical parallel, denoting glory, nobility, patriotic duty, etc. *The Irish Avatar*, written in angry response to George IV's triumphal visit to Ireland in September 1821, makes a connection between national character and individual personality in the memory of Irish statesmen of an era just gone, 'Thy GRATTAN, thy CURRAN, thy SHERIDAN, all', where genius is simultaneously a place-spirit (Castlereagh is 'Without one single ray of her [i.e. Ireland's] genius...') and the spirit of nobility on a Roman model.[9] Byron described the poem to Moore as 'in the "high Roman fashion", and full of ferocious phantasy',[10] alluding to Shakespeare's *Antony and Cleopatra* and to

Cleopatra discovering her resolve to commit suicide essentially as a form of imitation, 'Let's do't after the high Roman fashion'. Like Cleopatra, the poem imagines through historical parallel and paradigm, predominantly Roman (Castlereagh is Sejanus), while also borrowing something of the Egyptian Queen's sense of the theatricality of imitation. And like Cleopatra, it consciously exaggerates its postures of grief and lament (in 'ferocious phantasy'), memorialising the virtues of the 'patriot band' with deliberate hyperbole.[11] Nevertheless, the strong imaginative hold these men had upon Byron, and the deep pride he felt in having known Curran and Sheridan in London pre–1816, is interwoven with the awareness of a brighter moment in Irish political fortunes which had also passed and which, like Byron's personal memories, had acquired a nostalgic glow from the perspective of 1821. Here the notion of the *Roman* is directly and unproblematically a virtue.

Byron's prose journals of 1821 return repeatedly to these 'Immortals' and memories of the bright world of 1811–16 in which they lived. The names of Curran ('the man who struck me most') and Grattan and Sheridan, and others, are strongly evocative of that particular period, but are so in an oddly slanted way because for the most part these people were admired as survivors or relics from an even earlier age. The Ravenna journal also recalls the Edgeworths (father and daughter) whom Byron met in 1813; General Richard Fitzpatrick (a friend of Charles James Fox); Richard 'Conversation' Sharp (whose very sobriquet was what we might call *retro*); Dr Samuel Parr, the 'Whig Johnson' who had taught Sheridan at Harrow; Sarah Siddons; Samuel Rogers (whom Byron thought was much older than in fact he was): all remembered and relished principally as survivors.[12] 'Detached Thoughts' recalls further living relics and legends such as John Courtenay the orator, the 'portly remains' of whose 'fine figure – and the still acute quickness' of whose conversation impressed the young Byron; Lord Erskine, the great Whig statesman and orator who had successfully defended Thomas Hardy in the treason trials of the 1790s; Matthew 'Monk' Lewis whose gothic novel had been a *succès de scandal* in 1796. In other words, alongside memories of the contemporary pulse of those years (the 'opposition meeting of the peers in 1812'; the occasion when Byron was called away from a ball to vote on Catholic emancipation; the dandies; the pantomime of 1815–16, which had re-staged the famous masquerade of 1814; etc.), there goes an equally strong, if not stronger sense of the dying echoes of the previous century.[13]

In this respect it is the figure of Richard Brinsley Sheridan who recurs most often in the journals and who most thoroughly embodies the notion of a disappearing world central to Byron's experience of England during 1811–16. The mysterious affinity between the two men in fact not only reflects the double perspective in Byron's understanding of Regency London, the facing backwards and forwards in time, but embodies a characteristic of the period in general, that it is one marked by an increased awareness of generational overlap (this in part is the consequence of a 'regency' precisely because it suspends the transition from one generation to the next). Byron had proudly shown visitors to Harrow the name of Sheridan 'as an honour to the walls' many years before their friendship began over dinner at Samuel Rogers' home in 1813. In turn Sheridan (who was sixty-five years old when he died in 1816, shortly after Byron left England), 'had a sort of liking for me...', as Byron put it himself, and may have wished to authorise the young poet as his biographer.[14] Byron in fact held Sheridan in an esteem bordering on hero-worship for his achievements as a comic playwright and manager of Drury Lane Theatre, for his reputation as a Whig statesman and parliamentary orator whose speeches on the Begums of Oudh in 1787–88 had been among the finest ever heard at Westminster, for the brilliance of his wit in company ('always saturnine, and sometimes savage' as Byron recalled), but also for a certain sentimental appeal, an heroic pathos of resistance and independence which Byron clearly imitated in his own life and which was perhaps the most compelling aspect of the older man. Bewitched by Sheridan's character and manners, Byron glutted on anecdotes of the 1780s and 1790s, writing to Lady Melbourne in October 1813 that he 'would give the world to pass a month with Sheridan or any lady or gentleman of the old school – & hear them talk every day & all day of themselves & acquaintance – & all they have heard & seen in their lives'.[15] The symmetry of their relationship is best exemplified in Byron's 'Monody on the Death of the Right Hon. R.B. Sheridan', read by Maria Rebecca Davison from the stage of Drury Lane on 7 September 1816. This was a moment of cultural homage through imitation and repetition, focused upon the notion of an enduring place (the new Drury Lane had been completed in August 1812), and on the idea of historical continuity and legacy. Byron's piece is self-consciously the heir, as it were, to Sheridan's own 'Verses to the Memory of Garrick. Spoken as a Monody, at the Theatre Royal in Drury Lane', which had been delivered from the Drury Lane stage in 1779. It is precisely this notion of historical re-enactment, in place, which most interested Byron, whose 'feelings were never more excited', Lady Blessington records, 'than while writing the Monody on Sheridan, – every word that I wrote came direct from the heart'.[16] The first part of the poem describes a certain *feeling* for the passing of the moment between night and day:

> When the last Sunshine of expiring Day
> In Summer's twilight weeps itself away,
> Who hath not felt the softness of the hour
> Sink on the heart – as Dew along the flower?
> With a pure feeling which absorbs and awes
> While Nature makes that melancholy pause,
> Her breathing moment on the bridge where Time
> Of Light and Darkness forms an Arch sublime; –
> Who hath not shared that calm so still and deep,
> The voiceless thought which would not speak but weep?
> A holy concord – and a bright regret,
> A glorious sympathy with Suns that set?
> 'Tis not harsh Sorrow – but a tenderer woe
> Nameless, but dear to gentle hearts below,
> Felt without bitterness – but full and clear,
> A sweet dejection – a transparent tear
> Unmixed with worldly grief – or selfish stain,
> Shed without shame – and secret without shame.

(ll.1–18)

This is primarily a meditation upon the complexity of the emotion felt at the death of Sheridan; it is not a wild grief, nor an angry or harsh sorrow, but something less easy to describe, 'nameless', 'secret', a 'pure feeling', 'a sweet dejection'. What it also describes is the sensation of a transitional moment, a 'melancholy pause' between one state and another, relayed in the conventional metaphor of a summer sunset. In his heartfelt response to Sheridan's death, then, Byron is beginning to express his feeling for all that Sheridan stood for, and to trace the larger shape of an historical melancholy 'felt without bitterness' for the passing of the eighteenth century, so that the description of a complex grief is also a delineation of a certain nostalgia, a 'glorious sympathy' for the twilight moment of 1816. As we shall see, the writing of 1821–23 returns to the complexity of this same 'nameless' feeling, part bitter part sweet, again and again, seeking an understanding but refusing any constrictive definition, sometimes ironising the feeling, sometimes allowing it full indulgence. In that latter spirit the monody goes on to celebrate Drury Lane as the place in which a 'Halo of the light of other days'(l.57) may be experienced through the continuing performances (or re-enactments) of Sheridan's plays (*The School for Scandal* was performed on the night of the monody), the figure of the halo standing as we have seen for historical places in which direct communion with the past seemed possible. Byron's experience of those early years of the Regency (1811–16) was one of living within that 'halo of the light of other days', surrounded by 'Immortals' such as Sheridan, but this would mean that Byron's later recollection of those years from the perspective of 1821 would inevitably be one of nostalgia for a time that was already in some sense nostalgic, remembering the light of other days in which one experienced the light of other (earlier) days, which in turn would affect the way in which Byron imagined the moment in the far future when these times would be remembered by those who had had no direct experience of them. Nostalgia becomes an historically vicarious and surrogate phenomenon, experienced on others' behalf, as well as for things unknown to the self.

The Regency then stands for quite different things in Byron's memory and memorial writing. On the one hand it is a twilight moment, tinged with the fading colours of the grand eighteenth-century sunset, a London inhabited by relics and survivors of an age of giants. At the same time Byron would contribute to the historical myths of the Regency which have endured and flourished in our own time, that is, of the fashionable, fast, and frivolous society; a time of pantomimes, masquerades, waltzing and revelry, etc. The Janus-faced mythography of course complicates the question of when and how the Regency came to be considered as a quite distinct epoch, and how conscious it was of itself as such. A distinct 'Regency' identity certainly arises retrospectively quite rapidly after George IV's coronation, and is inaugurated in part by Byron's recollective projects of post-1820. *The Blues*, written in 1821 but not published until 1823, offers a satire of the London literary and social scene Byron had known in the years 1811–16 ('Blues, dandies, and dowagers, and second-hand scribes'I.l.158). But from the context of 1821 its social and literary satire seems anachronistic at least, outmoded in its very form and texture, recalling as it does Sheridan's great comic triumphs of the 1770s and 1780s – indeed with its jokes about poems and pastry-cooks, looking even further back in literary time.[17] This is a Regency remembered in other words through the half-light of an even older world; an epoch distinguished partly by its echo and memory of an earlier epoch of which Byron had had no experience. What it reveals is that Byron's immediate experience of those years in London was a sharply mediated one in an historical sense and that he encountered the *grande monde* for the first time through very powerful literary and cultural stereotypes absorbed from his love of early eighteenth-century literature, or in other words, through a veil of nostalgia. When he later came to represent his experience in works such as *The Blues* a double anachronism inevitably emerged. From the perspective of 1821 the world of 1814 had disappeared; but even from the perspective of 1814, this seemed to be a world overshadowed by the eighteenth century.

Nostalgia for an era of which one has not had personal experience is of course a common enough phenomenon, as is that of experiencing the present through fantasies of the past. When Robert Southey wrote 'A Vision of Judgement' looking back upon the reign of George III and suggesting that 'the brightest portion of British history will be that which records the improvements, the works, and the achievements of the Georgian Age', Byron's response was bound to be problematic, particularly as Southey's preface in some sense set Byron and 'the Satanic school' up *against* all 'the improvements, the works, and the achievements of the Georgian age', and envisaged a heavenly trial in which the King triumphs over his historical accusers.[18] But of course the Georgian Age was also the age of Fox, Curran, Grattan, Erskine and Sheridan, and the 1790s – the years of Southey's jacobinism and subsequent apostasy – were precisely the years Byron longed to have experienced in his maturity. Byron's *The Vision of Judgement* is clearly fascinated, then, by the reign of George III, and relishes in particular the battles of Whig-Liberalism of the1760s, but focuses its polemic against Southey and the laureate's apostasy. A manuscript note probably dating from 1821 and first published in Moore's 1830 *Letters and Journals of Lord Byron: with Notices of His Life*, shows Byron wondering why apostasy seemed so terrible:

> The world visits change of politics or change of religion with a more severe censure than a mere difference of opinion would appear to me to deserve. But there must be some reason for this feeling; – and I think it is that these departures from the earliest instilled ideas of our childhood, and from the line of conduct chosen by us when we first enter into public life, have been seen to have more mischievous results for society, and to prove more weakness of mind than other actions, in themselves, more immoral.[19]

Again apostasy seems to represent a peculiar structural antithesis, for if nostalgia for the age of George III (as distinct from the 'achievements' of the monarch) is founded upon the sense of cultural legacy, continuity and succession, then apostasy represents the radical breakdown and alienation of such values, the undoing of something deeper than mere 'opinion'. It also means that Southey's own 'nostalgia' for the Georgian age is one not based in his own experience of the age at the time, but one acquired retrospectively through a change of political heart. That Byron thinks both of his earliest childhood (the 1790s) and the moment of entering public life (1807) in relation to apostasy, suggests not only that his own cultural nostalgias were authentic, but that they were connected to the notion of moral duty, framing the comic vitriol of *The Vision of Judgement* with a certain *gravitas*. Nevertheless this very possibility – the possibility of a radical and total alienation – casts a 'dark shadow' within Byron's thinking about nostalgia just as the possibility of absolute self-transformation shadows Byron's thinking about translation. As Tom Moore pointed out, Byron's own 'natural tendency to yield...to every chance impression, and change with every passing impulse', gave him a particular insight not merely into 'mobility' but into what apostasy might mean to an individual.[20] And in fact the writing of the period 1821–23 takes very seriously the possibility of a disruption and self-alienation within the historical process, the possibility that golden periods in history may signify nothing, or that they would come to appear to be stranded in history, disconnected and fragmented.

The Age of Bronze (1823), for example, is the last poem Byron wrote in the 'high Roman fashion', and measures the significance and durability of recent European history in the context of the most recent post-war agreement of the Congress of Verona (1822). The poem's subtitle, 'Carmen Seculare et Annus Haud Mirabilis' echoes Horace's *Carmen Saeculare* (song of the age) and Dryden's *Annus Mirabilis* (1666), positioning itself within the English Augustan tradition, but also depreciating the present in relation to that tradition (the year is *not* a miraculous year, the age is one of bronze). The strange consequence is a poem at once firmly rooted in imitation of previous models, but which also thematises the present's degeneration from such models, just as it asks what has endured of the seemingly dazzling previous epoch. At once then nostalgic, and sharply critical or suspicious of nostalgia, the poem begins:

I

The 'good old times' – all times when old are good –
Are gone; the present might be if they would;

Great things have been, and are, and greater still
Want little of mere mortals but their will;
A wider space, a greener field is given
To those who play their 'tricks before high heaven.'
I know not if the angels weep, but men
Have wept enough – for what? – to weep again.

II

All is exploded – be it good or bad.
Reader! remember when thou wert a lad,
Then Pitt was all; or, if not all, so much,
His very rival almost deemed him such.
We, we have seen the intellectual race
Of giants stand, like Titans, face to face –
Athos and Ida, with a dashing sea
Of eloquence between, which flowed all free,
As the deep billows of the Aegean roar
Betwixt the Hellenic and the Phrygian shore.
But where are they – the rivals? – a few feet
Of sullen earth divide each winding sheet.

(ll.1–20)

The central trope of 'having seen' and the rhetorical 'where are they now' (*ubi sunt*) reprise the crucial stanzas of the eleventh canto of *Don Juan*, written only a few months earlier ('"Where is the world?" cries Young at eighty'), which I will discuss later in this chapter. The Titans here are of course William Pitt the younger and Charles Fox, the great political rivals of the last decades of the eighteenth century, both of whom had died in 1806, the year of Byron's first acquaintance with the 'Great World'. The reader who is encouraged to remember when he was 'a lad' and Pitt was 'all', is assumed to share Byron's own nostalgia for the 1790s, the 'good old times' Byron loved to hear Sheridan and others talk of, and the glory of which is indicated by the metaphors from Greek topography. Nevertheless, this nostalgia is burdened with an irony ('all times when old are good') that acknowledges the ways in which sentiment works to colour the past, as well as a certain solemnity that arises from the reflection that the 'good old times' have gone and left no trace, and that the present times *could* be good 'if they would'. The passing of seemingly memorable times and figures is then situated within the context of European imperial power as its interests had been arranged at the Congress of Verona, so that nostalgia for the passing of an era is placed in a starkly political light. What mark have these things made upon the European political landscape? And what is the enduring meaning of the turbulent history of the previous quarter-century? 'All is exploded – be it good or bad'.

A certain distrust then both of the notion of the 'good old times', and the efficacy of nostalgia in the face of European *Realpolitik* (*The Age of Bronze* makes much of the political power of transglobal finance in the form of 'Jew Rothschild, and his fellow Christian Baring', *Don Juan* XII.5), is here in tension with a sentimental attachment to the days when 'thou wert a lad' and the 'intellectual race / Of giants' reigned. But the very idea of 'good old times' seems to confirm the notion of historical discontinuity and fragmentation; the 'race of giants' buried and fossilised, while that which endures from the previous epoch is nothing but a certain wistful sentiment at its passing. In fact it is precisely the sentiment, or rather the *emotion* of memory that most interests Byron in the writing of this period and which, potentially, seems most dangerous to him. A longing to return to a lost homeland is after all a fixed constant within human consciousness, *and* something like a disease that may afflict the individual. Sensitive to both possibilities, Byron's own writing about England in the period after 1820, and in particular the English stanzas of *Don Juan*, emerges from a broader project in which the pathology of nostalgia is explored in depth.

4.2   The pathology of nostalgia: *Sardanapalus, The Two Foscari, Cain, Heaven and Earth*

The plays of 1821 – *Sardanapalus, The Two Foscari, Cain* and *Heaven and Earth* – treat exile, homesickness and nostalgia as various examples of tragic afflictions to befall individuals. In the case of *Sardanapalus*, Myrrha, the 'Ionian female slave' and lover of Sardanapalus, both expresses and embodies a nostalgia for classical Greece mirrored formally and thematically by the neo-classical fidelities of the drama. Her strong pride in her sex and nationality comes straight from the ancient dramatists, as Sardanapalus recognises:

> *Sardanapalus*: My eloquent Ionian! thou speak'st music,
>   The very chorus of the tragic song
>   I have heard thee talk of as the favourite pastime
>   Of thy far father-land.

(I.ii.ll.516–519)

Loving the master who has enslaved her, and longing at the same time for her 'far fatherland', Myrrha's nostalgia for Greece contrasts with the effeminate pastoral longings of Sardanapalus who indulges in a languid theatre upon his imperial galley as if he were one of 'The shepherd kings of patriarchal times, / Who knew no brighter gems than summer wreaths, / And none but tearless triumphs' (I.ii.ll.560–2). Myrrha, however, is conscious of the schizophrenic nature of her situation, asking (when alone) 'Why do I love this man? My country's daughters / Love none but heroes. But I have no country! / The slave hath lost all save her bonds.' (I.ii.ll.641–3). As such her self-divided nature emerges in part from Byron's continuing meditation upon the condition of love and the nature of *serventismo*, examined in the previous chapter, but her paradoxical and impossible 'love' also reveals something about the nature of exile, homesickness, and nostalgia.[21] Myrrha's sense of the slave losing 'all save her bonds' suggests both the bondage of slavery and the bonds or ties to home, as well as the new bonds of love for Sardanapalus. Longing for home metamorphoses into love for an enslaver, homesickness into love-sickness, so that Myrrha's attachment to Sardanapalus becomes a larger figure for the self-divided nature of longing for the impossible return, or desiring the lost homeland.

The paradox and danger of such self-division are explored in greater detail in *The Two Foscari* (written immediately after *Sardanapalus*), in which Jacopo Foscari's attachment to Venice has developed into a pathological condition. Exiled for complicity in murder, the Doge's son incriminates himself again through a treasonable correspondence in order to be transported back to the city. As a Venetian senator expresses it, 'all earth, except his native land, / To him is one wide prison, and each breath / Of foreign air he draws seems a slow poison, / Consuming but not killing.' (I.i.ll.290–3). Such intense place-attachment takes a different form in his father's extreme repression of personal feeling in duty and devotion to the Venetian state, which comes to resemble a form of state terror. As such the neo-classical presentation of 'character' in terms of historical example (usually Roman) becomes warped. Here classical history is a mirror in which Venice attempts to identify herself, but in which the reflection is distorted. So Doge Foscari is more extreme than the Spartans, worse than Draco ('such laws as make old Draco's / A code of mercy by comparison.' II.i.ll.393–4); above all he is burdened with the stifling notion of Venice as the natural heir to classical Rome. To be trapped within a perceived inheritance in this way (and Byron will develop this theme in *Cain*) produces an unnatural polity in which justification for action is found in classical precedent rather than moral reasoning, and in which Loredano's 'hereditary hate' for the Foscari naturally flourishes. Jacopo, on the other hand, who languishes in a Venetian dungeon where he scratches his name upon the wall, clings to the hope of being allowed to remain in Venice, preferring imprisonment there to liberty anywhere else. His wife Marina encourages him to be strong, 'The mind should make its own' liberty, she insists, to which Jacopo replies:

> That has a noble sound; but 'tis a sound,
> A music most impressive, but too transient:
> The mind is much, but is not all.

(III.i.ll.85–7)

Byron had been turning over the question of Miltonic–Satanic self-sufficiency in almost all of his writing since his own 'exile' of 1816, and Jacopo Foscari's answer summarises his thinking during that time. 'The mind is much, but is not all', and what counts for most in the conditioning of the mind is *place* (the absent word is provided by the echo of the line from Milton – 'the mind is its own place'). For Marina, her husband's love for Venice is pathological: 'passion, and not patriotism' (III.i.1.143). Nevertheless, Jacopo's speeches about exile, about homesickness as a life-threatening malady, and nostalgia, are among the fullest treatments of these subjects in Byron's work. Thinking about the exile of the Jews from Zion, and the Roman communities who fled into the Venetian lagoon to escape Attila, Jacopo wonders about those who did not survive:

> Ay – we but hear
> Of the survivors' toil in their new lands,
> Their numbers and success; but who can number
> The hearts which broke in silence of that parting;
> Or after their departure; of that malady
> Which calls up green and native fields to view
> From the rough deep, with such identity
> To the poor exile's fever'd eye, that he
> Can scarcely be restrain'd from treading them?
> That melody, which out of tones and tunes
> Collects such pasture for the longing sorrow
> Of the sad mountaineer, when far away
> From his snow canopy of cliffs and clouds,

That he feeds on the sweet, but poisonous thought,
And dies. You call this *weakness*! It is strength,
I say, – the parent of all honest feeling.
He who loves not his country, can love nothing.

(III.i.ll.168–84)

Here the melody of nostalgia is at the same time a deadly malady. The calenture, a delirium suffered by sailors in which the sea appears to be green fields, is linked with the deadly sweet air known as the 'Ranz des Vaches', which Byron had described in his Alpine journal of 1816:[22]

> The music of the Cows' bells (for their wealth like the Patriarchs is cattle) in the pastures (which reach to a height far above any mountains in Britain –) and the Shepherds' shouting to us from crag to crag & playing on their reeds where the steeps appeared almost inaccessible, with the surrounding scenery – realized all that I have ever heard or imagined of a pastoral existence – much more so than Greece or Asia Minor – for there we are a little too much of the sabre & musquet order – and if there is a Crook in one hand, you are sure to see a gun in the other – but this was pure and unmixed – solitary – savage and patriarchal – the effect I cannot describe – as we went they played the "Ranz des Vaches" and other airs by way of farewell. –

For Byron, there is a connection between a certain kind of nostalgia, and a certain kind of patriarchal social arrangement (as Sardanapalus acts the part of the 'shepherd kings' upon his galley). Jacopo Foscari compares his passion for Venice to the malady of delirious sailors, and to the exquisite emotions of the Alpine 'mountaineer' who, far from home, hears a melody which seems able to take his life away, but which is also the sign of a 'pure and unmixed – solitary – savage and patriarchal' order, more perfectly classical than Greece itself. Lady Blessington recorded Byron's susceptibility to the nostalgia aroused by music, that 'the notes of a well-known air could transport him to distant scenes and events, presenting objects before him with a vividness that quite banished the present'.[23] She also records a summer evening spent with Byron in Genoa, looking down upon the city's harbour:

> While he [Byron] was yet speaking, sounds of vocal music arose; national hymns and baracoles were sung in turn by the different

crews, and when they had ceased, 'God save the King' was sung by the crews of some English merchantmen lying close to the pier. This was a surprise to us all, and its effect on our feelings was magnetic. Byron was no less touched than the rest; each felt at that moment the tie of country which unites all when they meet on a far distant shore. When the song ceased, Byron, with a melancholy smile, observed, 'Why, positively, we are all quite sentimental this evening, and *I – I* who have sworn against sentimentality, find the old leaven still in my nature, and quite ready to make a fool of me. · "Tell it not in Gath", that is to say, breathe it not in London, or to English ears polite, or never again shall I be able to *enact* the stoic philosopher. Come, come, this will never do, we must foreswear moonlight, fine views, and above all, hearing a national air sung. Little does his gracious Majesty Big Ben, as Moore calls him, imagine what loyal subjects he has at Genoa, and least of all that I am among their number.'[24]

The anecdote illustrates Byron's susceptibility to exactly the kind of transports of feeling Jacopo Foscari is describing, and which Byron had described in a different national context in the Alpine journal, as well as illustrating his quick suspicion of such feeling, his distrust of the sentimentality of nostalgia particularly when it takes the form of patriotic (and indeed patriarchal) feeling: the melody of longing for home might so easily become the malady of loyalty to George IV. Jacopo Foscari takes the effect of the 'Ranz des Vaches' as an analogy for his own feeling for Venice, and so draws upon a subtle inlayering of different places and their associations: Greece, the Alps and Venice. But of course Jacopo's identification with the Alpine shepherd has deeper implications in terms of the patriarchal order with which he is confronted in Venice (with its own apeing of the 'pure and unmixed' order of classical civilisation). There is an irony in his description of such intense passion as 'the parent of all honest feeling' in that the love of country which is its consequence has stifled any assistance the Doge may have been expected to offer his son. This kind of love is, indeed, intense enough to kill.

And indeed through these attachments, the Foscari perish. Jacopo, whose life is spared but who is exiled (again), prays to the 'tutelar saints of my own city' to cause a sea-storm that will wreck his ship and wash his 'broken corse upon the barren Lido' (IV.i.l.131). Marina describes this again as 'useless passion', but even so, Jacopo dies before he leaves the shore, and we are meant to understand that he dies *because* he is leaving Venice. Moreover, his death (at least in the eyes of Marina) is a form of martyrdom, the place where he perished 'holy ground' (IV.i.l.219). And even as Marina expresses feminine counter-principles to Jacopo's pathological place-attachment: 'I am a woman: / To me my husband and my children were / Country and home' (V.i.ll.95–7), in doing so she merely confirms the connection between patriotism and patriarchy. The Council of Ten force the abdication of the Doge, who insists on leaving publicly by the Giant's Staircase, but dies before he gets there.[25] Finally then both Foscari and his son seem to suffer from pathological states of devotion to Venice, the one in manic desire for the city as a place, the other in an excessive zeal for the notion of an ideal city-state. The destructive nature of their devotion is mirrored in their own patriarchal relationship, and in the patriarchal legacy of Venice as heir to Rome.

This notion of a patriarchal legacy that binds the individual to a particular place is one Byron explores further in *Cain: A Mystery* (1821). Inheritance, exile and homesickness are treated not as historical but as existential problems in the mystery play, as Cain mourns for Eden as a lost homeland, lingering before its gates 'In twilight's hour, to catch a glimpse of those / Gardens which are my just inheritance' (I.i.ll.86–7).[26] As exile is his inherited condition, something that has always already happened to Cain, it is absolute and irrevocable, and so is experienced as an acute malady exacerbated by the fact that he lives within sight of the 'inhibited walls'. Once again there is a reflection upon Miltonic–Satanic self-sufficiency. This time Lucifer is offering Cain the comfort of the mind as its own place:

> Nothing can
> Quench the mind, if the mind will be itself
> And centre of surrounding things – 'tis made
> To sway.

> (I.i.ll.213–16)

The possibility that the mind may fail to sustain itself, and that *place* may be able to overcome or invade the self, is most darkly realised in the figure of Cain whose very condition of being (the exile who has inherited his punishment) stands as a challenge to the notion of mental triumph. It is part of the subtlety of Byron's 'mystery' to have Lucifer recycle Miltonic–Satanic resistance as a possibility not open to Cain, or worse still, as a condition also inherited – *all* Cain has is the

mind as the 'centre of surrounding things' – and therefore not entered
into freely. Although *Cain* shares with *Sardanapalus* and *The Two
Foscari* the sense of disappearing worlds, the 'neo-classical' plays situate
such loss in terms of the historical individual who may or may not
comfort himself with the thought that there are worlds elsewhere.
Cain, however, is taken by Lucifer into the abyss of space so that he
might see 'The worlds beyond thy little world' (II.i.l.14), 'Worlds
greater than thine own, inhabited / By greater things', (II.i.ll.44–5),
worlds which have been lost or which are doomed to be lost, of which
Cain has no knowledge or experience. The loss of worlds is de-histori-
cized then in the mystery play, so that what is a direct experience for
Sardanapalus or the Doge Foscari, and therefore one bound up with
personal agency and responsibility, becomes a generalised metaphysical law revealed to Cain, and one that confirms the apparent necessity
of his own condition. As such of course it is an argument against God,
and a challenge to the religious and moral cant that Byron believed
had taken a grip on English culture during the previous quarter-
century. The play's exploration of nostalgia-as-suffering in fact darkens
the entire retrospective and memorial project of Byron's post-1820
writing, precisely because it represents longing-for-home as a curse.
Here the dream of a patriarchal and pastoral idyll that had enfeebled
Sardanapalus, and haunted Jacopo Foscari, is represented as the nightmare of human pre-history. As Enoch sleeps his father watches over
him and agonises:

> He must dream –
> Of what? Of Paradise! – Ay! dream of it,
> My disinherited boy! 'Tis but a dream;
> For never more thyself, thy sons, nor fathers,
> Shall walk in that forbidden place of joy !
>
> (III.i.ll.30–4).

Adah (who offers Cain the kind of comfort Marina offered Jacopo
Foscari) responds:

> Dear Cain! Nay, do not whisper o'er our son
> Such melancholy yearnings o'er the past:
> Why wilt thou always mourn for Paradise?
>
> (III.i.ll.35–7)

'Melancholy yearnings o'er the past' lie at the centre of Cain's pain, and at the centre of his consciousness of that pain. The 'frame of mind – that leads to the Catastrophe'[27] (and Byron's phrasing is deliberately open, because it is part of the play's brilliance to have the murder of Abel occur suddenly and without premeditation) is, then, a form of nostalgia, arising out of the longing to return to a 'home' that Cain has never directly experienced but which is inherited by successive generations as a 'dream'. The consequence of murdering Abel is that the man who had inherited exile as a precondition of existence, now hears the angel deliver his fate: 'a fugitive shalt thou / Be from this day, and vagabond on earth !'(III.i.ll.475–6).

Byron was drawn to the story of Cain partly because it allowed him to think further about the question of the self-fulfilling prophecy. The individual who in some sense *enacts* himself is an analogue of the speech-act or prophetic poem that fulfils its own predictions (*The Lament of Tasso*, *The Prophecy of Dante*). In this sense the mystery play is concerned with the ways in which Cain becomes 'Cain', fulfilling the sign or mark by which he is known, and revealing the tensions between free will and providence with a characteristically Romantic emphasis upon psychological compulsion. Nostalgia is an inherited condition (a congenital disease, a malady) which then grows into itself during a lifetime and inherits its own condition – any autonomous action merely confirming its predetermined course. It would seem in fact to contain a violent and destructive momentum of its own, and the offence caused in England by *Cain's* unorthodox theology was merely compounded by the play's suggestion of a dark irony in the notion of 'melancholy yearnings o'er the past', and a longing to return to a lost Eden. The author, with his 'Satanic' reputation, lived in exile in Italy, east of England's paradisal gardens.

Acute homesickness, however, may afflict not only those who feel they have lost their home, but those who live beneath the threat of losing it. Byron had hoped that the first part of his lyrical drama *Heaven and Earth: A Mystery* would appear in the same volume as *Sardanapalus*, *The Two Foscari* and *Cain*. John Murray's delays with the proofs and Byron's later renegotiation of his publishing arrangements, however, meant that it did not appear until the second edition of *The Liberal* in 1823. When placed alongside the other dramatic works of 1821, however, *Heaven and Earth* suggests a certain symmetry and complementarity. Like *Cain* it is a drama about the overlapping of a greater world with a lesser world (a higher order of angelic beings are in love with the 'daughters of men'); like the neo-classical plays it is concerned with the attachment to place in crisis, and the impending disappearance of a

world, though as with *Cain* its apocalypse is, as it were, pre-historical.
Here, however, the Cuvier-inspired catastrophism is approached not, as
in *Cain*, retrospectively, but in anticipation.

Anah is loved by Japhet and by the angel Azaziel; Aholibamah, who
once loved Irad, is loved by the angel Samiasa. The drama takes place
on the eve of the Deluge. As Japhet the son of Noah wanders through
the Caucasus mountains he anticipates a future moment (almost upon
him) when the earth and all its natural beauty, which 'look eternal', will
no longer be there; and when the memories associated with specific
places will have been utterly effaced, along with the landscape: 'And
can those words *"no more"* / Be meant for thee, for all things, save for
us' (I.iii.ll.32–3), Japhet wonders. A global homesickness, or a longing
for the world, is produced through contemplation of its impending loss,
so that the future pain of nostalgia is experienced here and now:

> All beauteous world!
> So young, so mark'd out for destruction, I
> With a cleft heart look on thee day by day,
> And night by night, thy numbered days and nights.

> (I.iii.ll.47–50)

The poem imagines with 'cleft heart' this posthumous moment in
which the present has acquired the glory of a lost world, a future-retro-
spection which is bound up with sexual and romantic desire in the
poem – for Japhet his association of love and place, his desire to die
with this world (as Jacopo Foscari yearned for death in Venice), while
Azaziel and Samiasa linger in the world-about-to-perish for the love of
mortal women, offering them an escape from destruction. The impending disappearance of the world rather urgently raises the question of
whether annihilation could be a price willingly paid for romantic love.
The angels wonder whether to stay with their lovers on earth, while
the women are tempted to abandon the world to its fate in order to
escape to a world elsewhere:

> A brighter world than this, where thou shalt breathe
> Ethereal life, will we explore:
> These darken'd clouds are not the only skies.

> (I.iii.ll.820–2)

[AZAZIEL *and* SAMIASA *fly off, and disappear with* ANAH *and*
AHOLIBAMAH]

Weighing up the relative merits of staying and going in a context within which *everything* is at stake, emerges from the ongoing rumination upon the condition of exile and the meaning of homesickness throughout the work of 1821, particularly in relation to the question of what endures. At the moment of eschatological crisis, place-attachment is in direct opposition to romantic love, and the balance is weighed. Thomas Medwin recorded that Byron had intended to finish the drama by 'conveying the lovers to the moon, or one of the planets; but it is not easy for the imagination to make any unknown world more beautiful than this...'.[28] Byron's 'mystery' had nowhere to go; the only possibility for a further act would have been in mourning the lost world, a mourning which in any case had been done in advance. Nevertheless, part of the process of evaluating the present moment is the imaginative experience of what it would be like to mourn its passing in some future moment; to look back as if from the future. This becomes a central element of the English stanzas of *Don Juan*, where it is the key mode in which Byron remembers and evaluates English culture of seven years previously. In *Heaven and Earth* the question of evaluation is absolute. Is the world worth sacrificing for romantic love? In the face of impending loss, what is most deserving of being saved? What will last? Again according to Medwin, Byron had intended to separate the 'daughters of men' from their angel lovers and return them to a drowning world. Clinging to the rocks as the waters rise, Adah would entreat Noah to allow her on board the ark, while Aholibamah would disdain either to ask for Noah's or God's assistance. Such Cuvier-moments recur in Byron's imagination throughout the year 1821, and are closely bound up with his relation to English culture, particularly his sense of a world having passed into history. Usually these relations are oblique or half-hidden; but sometimes the connection between the kind of 'no more' explored in *Heaven and Earth*, and the idea of the passing of English culture is explicitly made, as in this passage from the *Letter to John Murray Esqre*:

If any great national or natural Convulsion could or should overwhelm your Country in such sort as to sweep Great Britain from the kingdoms of the Earth – and leave only that – after all the most living of human things, – a *dead language*, to be studied and read and imitated by the wise of future and far generations – upon foreign shores, – if your literature should become the learning of Mankind, divested of party cabals – temporary fashions – and national pride and prejudice – an Englishman anxious that the

Posterity of Strangers should know that there had been such a thing
as a British Epic and Tragedy – might wish for the preservation of
Shakespeare and Milton – but the surviving World would snatch
Pope from the Wreck – and let the rest sink with the People.[29]

The proleptic shape of nostalgia is evident here. A future moment of
'national or natural Convulsion' is imagined and vicariously experienced in the present, allowing clear evaluation of the enduring legacies
of a culture, of what will last and what will perish. But the scenario of
Great Britain's passing out of existence was easily imagined, not least
because Byron believed that the *grande monde* of 1816 had suffered precisely this fate, its *'dead language'* snatched from the wreck by Byron
himself in the English cantos of *Don Juan*. Here the fact that Pope is
rescued by 'the surviving World' rather than Shakespeare or Milton
(who would have illustrated the *'British* Epic and Tragedy' [my italics]),
is a further mark of Byron's self-distancing from what he perceived to
be the apostasy in contemporary British literary fashion, even as such
self-distancing inevitably takes on a larger and broader national dimension. But this is the point: Byron's sense of distance and alienation
from contemporary Britain and British culture is absolute by 1821, to
the extent that it emerges in fantasies of Britain disappearing from the
world, and it is *this* fact rather than any process of *rapprochement* that
enables Byron to take the English *grande monde* of an earlier period as
his subject in the latter cantos of *Don Juan*. Only when the English
cantos are situated within the context of the other writing of 1821,
particularly in its obsession with disappearing worlds and with various
morbid or dangerous attachments to place, is this sense of distance and
alienation properly grasped. A sense that the world of the early regency
had completely disappeared allowed Byron to make his imaginative
return.

4.3   Having been there/ having seen [part two]: *Don Juan* XI

Although the plays of 1821 are rarely read in terms of their relation to
a remembered England, it is a commonplace of Byron criticism to note
that *Don Juan* is unremittingly about England even when most energet-
ically cosmopolitan.[30] Indeed a tension with English culture and
Englishness is precisely what shapes and defines this cosmopolitanism,
and distinguishes Byron not only from poets such as Wordsworth and
Southey, but from other European figures of Romanticism with whom
he is often categorised, such as Goethe, whose relationship with their

native culture is not a dramatic *agon*. The notion of England as representing an anomaly within a broader European (or specifically merid-
ian) culture, while being the pre-eminent power within the European
imperialist project, is a crucial anchorage for the poem, a constant
against which it defines itself. Even so, England is equally the embodiment of inconstancy or hypocrisy; that is, England is not what she pretends or claims to be, and it is part of the poem's intention to reveal
this fact, increasingly explicitly.[31]

Almost everyone who has written about *Don Juan* has also noted and
attended to the overlapping or layered chronologies of the poem.[32] It
was composed in 1818–23; its narrative is set in the 1780s and 1790s,
but its English material is drawn from the years 1811–16, sometimes
earlier (so that times are remembered in the poem which belong to the
narrative's future). These three chronologies merge, overlap and inflect
each other throughout the poem, as the best criticism of *Don Juan* has
demonstrated. However, the notion of the poem's *context* is even more
complicated than is commonly observed, because even though there is
a contemporary (i.e. 1818–23) English context for the poem – that is,
current English affairs also intrude upon the narrative – this is constructed around the fact of Byron's exile, his *not* being in England
during this time. The English context of 1818–23 is therefore a highly
mediated one, gleaned from newspapers and letters, picked up by
word-of-mouth, reviews, books, or simply imagined. In fact in his
letters post-1820 Byron increasingly comments (occasionally defiantly,
sometimes wistfully) upon his growing distance from English affairs
and his gradual translation into an Italian. In addition to his much
publicised 'rule' of not meeting the travelling English, his gradual if
troubled sense of acclimatisation to Italian society, and a growing
belief that his reputation as a poet had sunk to low levels at home,
there is the simple fact that he has been away from his country long
enough to be out of touch with what was happening there.[33]
Moreover, in September 1821 Byron writes to John Murray specifically
to ask to be protected in future from literary gossip and reviews, listing
those few living authors from whom he is prepared to receive newly
published work.[34] This amounts to a conscious severing of his links
with the London literary world, a further separation from English
affairs and a further diminution of his ability to write about contemporary England in *Don Juan* with anything like insider knowledge. It
means that the contemporary English 'context' for *Don Juan* is insecure
even before we take into account the fact that it is overshadowed by
the earlier context of 1811–16, often called 'the years of fame' (dating

from 1812). This frequently produces an anachronistic effect in the poem, as if Byron has slipped out of time somewhere around 1814, so that even when the poem *appears* to be speaking in an immediate English context about current English affairs, to its original readership it may have seemed marginally out-of-sync.

To take one example: the long passage on 'the late Marquis of Londonderry' (Castlereagh) in the preface to cantos six to eight, which purports to justify the poem's vilification of the late minister despite his recent suicide, is dwelling on a theme which had its true currency some time before 1818, perhaps around the Congress of Vienna of 1815 (or even earlier during Castlereagh's notorious term as Chief Secretary to Ireland during the rebellion of 1798, or as War Secretary in the administrations of Pitt and Portland during the 1800s). Castlereagh's record as a minister, and particularly his ineloquence as a parliamentary speaker, met with Byron's strong disdain over a period of years unabated. Of course the nagging endurance of this theme is part of the point: Castlereagh won't go away even in death, but lingers unpleasantly in the memory and in the legacy of the European post-war settlements. There may also be a sense in which we are meant to enjoy the narrator's obsession with certain *bêtes noires* in the poem – Wellington, with his government pension, being another. But we can imagine a reader such as Hobhouse, closely involved as MP for Westminster with the actual business of British politics, reading the following passage when it came to be published by John Hunt in 1823 (it was composed a year earlier), with a faint sense of its inconse-quence, its datedness: 'Of the manner of his [i.e.Castlereagh's] death little need be said, except that if a poor radical, such as Waddington or Watson, had cut his throat, he would have been buried in a cross-road, with the usual appurtenances of the stake and mallet.' Samuel Waddington was a radical politician who had opposed the war with France back in 1795. James Watson was a Spencean involved in mob violence of 1816, who had emigrated to America in 1817. These were yesterday's (and the day-before-yesterday's) radicals.

These oddly anachronistic notes (distinct from Byron's conscious attempt to recover the context of 1811–16, which I will discuss later), are struck throughout the poem, moments when the contemporary English world is invoked as *contemporary*, but which seem to lag behind by about six or seven years.[35] If this complicates the sense of an 'imme-diate context' for the poem, or at least of one that is English, the poem's fictional time-frame (the 1790s) complicates things still further since this is the period with which Byron is (as it were) emotionally involved, the time for which he experienced a longing to return even though he had never been there as an adult. The years 1811–16 which *are* then remembered by the poem, both directly and indirectly, and from which the poem in a sense never escapes, are themselves overlayered with 1790s experience, with backward-gazing, with the relics and reminders of an earlier 'glorious' age. In other words there is no stable and distinct English context for *Don Juan*, no singular 'England' to which the poem speaks, but instead a series of overlapping and intersecting memories and what we might call nostalgic-involutes, perceived at a distance, around which the poem is loosely oriented. It is precisely this insecurity of context, this emotional formlessness and fluctuation, that defines Byron's relation to England and English culture, but it is precisely in order to resist that fluidity that the English cantos portray the early Regency as a distinct and unique epoch.

One significant factor in this criss-crossing of memory and nostalgia is the sense in Byron's writing of 1815 (and more specifically the battle of Waterloo) as a year-zero date.[36] The near convergence of that moment with the timing of Byron's flight from England in 1816 produces the effect of an absolute cut-off point or watershed in his thinking, a 'posthistorical' or aftermath-consciousness. The fact that the Regency constitutionally begins in 1811, i.e. the date of Byron's return to England from the East, adds to this sense of a distinct time-frame extending from 1811 to 1816. For Byron historical events and eventfulness seem to end with the fall of Napoleon in 1815/16, inaugurating a period of reflection upon a narrative that is closed, and opening a space in which an author is living, as it were, post-history, or in posterity, and therefore from that privileged vantage-point of retrospection that nostalgia enables us to imagine. Such a sense of the post-historical does not preclude the possibility of *change* after 1815; quite the opposite, in fact – 1815 is seen as a pivotal date after which there can only be change, as the period immediately after that date constitutes the seven or eight short years during which for Byron the whole 'world' of pre–1815 is swept away: 'In seven / I have seen more changes, down from monarchs to / The humblest individual under heaven, / Than might suffice a moderate century through' (XI.82). Although this would seem to bear witness to having lived through extreme eventfulness, it is doing so only in a negative way, as it is the unravelling of the pre–1815 world that Byron 'sees' during these seven or eight years. History begins to disappear in 1815.

This general shift in orientation between the sense of *being there* to the sense of *having been there* is perhaps the single most important development in Byron's life-writing. The authority and authenticity Byron discovered in direct experience of specific geo-historical sites reconfigures itself in the later writing in terms of the authority and authenticity of memory, and produces a vivid sense of the years 1811/12–1815/16 as a unique time-slice in English history, while registering an anxiety that they may be only that: a fragment or shard of history stranded in time, and absurd to posterity. The English stanzas of *Don Juan* therefore participate in the mythologising of the early years of the Regency precisely by seeing them as a self-contained epoch (glittering and unique) that had passed away abruptly, but which Byron had directly witnessed or *seen*, while questioning what this uniqueness might mean in terms of a larger historical perspective. Cuvier's theory of catastrophism and the fashionable new science of geology which shaped the cosmic and existential scenarios in the dramas of 1821 are domesticated in *Don Juan* so that 1811–16 is represented (often with irony) as a buried stratum of history, rich in the strange fossilised remains and shapes of an era somehow larger and more alive than the contemporary world of circa 1822. The future moment in which these remains are discovered, seen again and marvelled at becomes central to the imaginative shape of the later cantos, and to the way in which the recent past is remembered. For Byron early Regency London will be revealed to the eyes of posterity as a strange monstrosity.

The first explicit moment of discovering the present as if it were the past occurs in canto eight during the Siege of Ismail episode when the narrator breaks off to imagine his millenium readership wondering at the existence of monarchies:

> And when you hear historians talk of thrones
>   And those that sate upon them, let it be
> As now we gaze upon the Mammoth's bones
>   And wonder what old world such things could see,
> Or hieroglyphics on Egyptian stones,
>   The pleasant riddles of Futurity –
> Guessing at what shall happily be hid
> As the real purpose of a Pyramid.

(VIII.137)

The joke about the mammoth's bones is at the expense of an obese George IV, but more significantly Byron posits here the notion of the present becoming indecipherable to futurity. Although it is impossible to imagine the ways in which that process will occur, nevertheless, the fact that it will inevitably happen allows radical and provocative speculation as to how. By confidently asserting the historical contingency of an institution like the monarchy that claims for itself a transhistorical (and even transcendent) meaning, the narrator appears to be working through a pure reasoning that must be obvious to anyone. But the narrator's confidence merely disguises the fact that the defamiliarisation of the present is an impossible thing to imagine or realise, that the future strangeness of the contemporary world, when its errors and absurdities are revealed, is not something the contemporary world can experience, so that there is of necessity an historical blindness in the way we see our present condition. Byron returns to this subject in canto IX, imagining his own obsolescence:

> But let it go:– it will one day be found
>   With other relics of 'a former world',
> When this world shall be *former*, underground,
>   Thrown topsy-turvy, twisted, crisped, and curled,
> Baked, fried, or burnt, turned inside out, or drowned,
>   Like all the worlds before, which have been hurled
> First out of and then back again to Chaos,
> The Superstratum which will overlay us.
>
> So Cuvier says; – and then shall come again
>   Unto the new Creation, rising out
> From our old crash, some mystic, ancient strain
>   Of things destroyed and left in airy doubt:
> Like to the notions *we* now entertain
>   Of Titans, Giants, fellows of about
> Some hundred feet in height, *not* to say *miles*,
> And Mammoths, and your winged Crocodiles.
>
> Think if then George the Fourth should be dug up!
>   How the new worldlings of the then new East
> Will wonder where such animals could sup!
>   (For they themselves will be but of the least:
> Even worlds miscarry, when too oft they pup,
>   And every new Creation hath decreased
> In size, from overworking the material –
> Men are but maggots of some huge Earth's burial.)

How will – to these young people, just thrust out
  From some fresh Paradise, and set to plough
And dig, and sweat, and turn themselves about,
  And plant, and reap, and spin, and grind, and sow,
Till all the Arts at length are brought about,
  Especially of war and taxing, – how,
I say, will these great relics, when they see 'em,
Look like the monsters of a new Museum?

(IX.37–40)

Again primarily the joke is upon the King whose obesity will apear monstrous when he is dug up and displayed like a dinosaur in the 'new museum' of the future. And the forms of contemporary English culture will share that monstrosity in the eyes of a future race who, as history repeats itself, will have been recently expelled from Paradise. Byron is superimposing geological science upon Biblical narrative here, as he often did, so that the 'young people, just thrust out' are also themselves 'decreased / In size' according to Cuvier's model of successive degeneration, and are imagined digging up the fossilized remains of an earlier lost world. Nostalgia for Eden is mixed up with the wonder over 'great relics', and a longing for the past tempered by a sense of its monstrous alterity. The yoking of Cuvier upon the Biblical narrative is intended to be provocative, and succeeded in that intention, but it is also a means of ironising the sense of historical uncertainty and insecurity as to exactly how the present age will be perceived in posterity. The irony disguises a tension that nevertheless emerges across the course of canto XI of *Don Juan*, the canto in which the England of 1811–16 is most directly recalled, a tension between a sentimental impulse to remember the Regency in nostalgic terms, and a deep distrust not merely of the sentimentality in such an impulse, but of the delusions it may produce: delusions, for example, of historical significance. Because if a period of English history is to acquire a sense of uniqueness through the sentiment of nostalgia, then such a process of periodisation will both secure its preservation and ensure its posthumous life as a fossilised curiosity, while the very nostalgia in which it is preserved also represents the historical blind spot which prevents its true comprehension or evaluation, particularly by the contemporary. Although the *ubi sunt* stanzas 76–85 are well known, I will quote the lines in full:

'Where is the world,' cries Young, 'at *eighty*? Where
  The world in which a man was born?' Alas!

Where is the world of *eight* years past? *'Twas there* –
  I look for it – 'tis gone, a Globe of Glass!
Cracked, shivered, vanished, scarcely gazed on, ere
  A silent change dissolves the glittering mass.
Statesmen, chiefs, orators, queens, patriots, kings,
And dandies, all are gone on the wind's wings.

Where is Napoleon the Grand? God knows:
  Where little Castlereagh? The devil can tell:
Where Grattan, Curran, Sheridan, all those
  Who bound the bar or senate in their spell?
Where is the unhappy Queen, with all her woes?
  And where the Daughter, whom the Isles loved well?
Where are those martyred Saints the Five per Cents?
And where – oh where the devil are the Rents!

Where's Brummell? Dished. Where's Long Pole Wellesley? Diddled.
  Where's Whitbread? Romilly? Where's George the Third?
Where is his will? (That's not so soon unriddled.)
  And where is 'Fum' the Fourth, our 'royal bird'?
Gone down it seems to Scotland, to be fiddled
  Unto by Sawney's violin, we have heard:
'Caw me, caw thee' – for six months hath been hatching
This scene of royal itch and loyal scratching.

Where is Lord This? And where my Lady That?
  The Honourable Mistresses and Misses?
Some laid aside like an old opera hat,
  Married, unmarried, and remarried: (this is
An evolution oft performed of late).
  Where are the Dublin shouts – and London hisses?
Where are the Grenvilles? Turned as usual. Where
My friends the Whigs? Exactly where they were.

Where are the Lady Carolines and Franceses?
  Divorced or doing thereanent.Ye annals
So brilliant, where the list of routs and dances is, –
  Thou Morning Post, sole record of the panels
Broken in carriages, and all the phantasies
  Of fashion, – say what streams now fill those channels?
Some die, some fly, some languish on the Continent,
Because the times have hardly left them *one* tenant.

Some who once set their caps at cautious Dukes,
   Have taken up at length with younger brothers:
Some heiresses have bit at sharpers' hooks;
   Some maids have been made wives, some merely mothers;
Others have lost their fresh and fairy looks:
   In short, the list of alterations bothers:
There's little strange in this, but something strange is
The unusual quickness of these common changes.

Talk not of seventy years as age! in seven
   I have seen more changes, down from monarchs to
The humblest individual under heaven,
   Than might suffice a moderate century through.
I knew that nought was lasting, but now even
   Change grows too changeable, without being new:
Nought's permanent among the human race,
Except the Whigs *not* getting into place.

I have seen Napoleon, who seemed quite a Jupiter,
   Shrink to a Saturn. I have seen a Duke
(No matter which) turn politician stupider,
   If that can well be, than his wooden look.
But it is time that I should hoist my 'blue Peter',
   And sail for a new theme: – I have seen – and shook
To see it – the King hissed, and then carest;
And don't pretend to settle which was best.

I have seen the landholders without a rap –
   I have seen Johanna Southcote – I have seen
The House of Commons turned to a tax-trap –
   I have seen that sad affair of the late Queen –
I have seen crowns worn instead of a fool's-cap –
   I have seen a Congress doing all that's mean –
I have seen some nations like o'er loaded asses
Kick off their burthens – meaning the high classes.

I have seen small poets, and great prosers, and
   Interminable – *not eternal* - speakers –
I have seen the Funds at war with house and land –
   I've seen the Country Gentlemen turn squeakers –
I've seen the people ridden o'er like sand
   By slaves on horseback – I have seen malt liquors

> Exchanged for 'thin potations' by John Bull –
> I have seen John half detect himself a fool. –

This is arguably the most significant surviving example we have of Byron's own life-writing, and hints at what we have lost in the burning of the *Memoirs*. It also represents the culmination of the nostalgia-project of the years 1821–23, with its sustained meditation upon the very meaning of 'memoir' and its anxiety about the pathologies of memory. 'I have seen John half detect himself a fool' might indeed stand as an epigraph to *Don Juan*, since this is the text in which the absurdities of English culture are detected or found out to most brilliant effect, a discovery the poem offers its (half)-comprehending contemporary English audience. The passage roughly divides into two sections: the first asking *ubi sunt* (i.e. where is the world of Regency London now?); and the second pursuing the unravelling of history after the 1815/16 watershed, through the important trope of having *seen* ('*Twas there-* / I look for it – 'tis gone, a Globe of Glass! / Cracked, shivered, vanished, scarcely gazed on, ere / A silent change dissolves the glittering mass'). The world of Regency London is evoked essentially through personality, as the stanzas pursue a downward trajectory from significant European figures (Napoleon, Castlereagh, Curran, Grattan and Sheridan, Queen Caroline and Princess Charlotte), to more transient figures of the nation's fashion and politics (Beau Brummell, 'Long Pole' Wellesley, Samuel Whitbread, Sir Samuel Romilly), and down further to the personalities of the *grande monde* with whom Byron was intimately acquainted (Lady Caroline Lamb and Lady Frances Webster) – his ex-girlfriends. Byron was also acquainted with Curran and Sheridan, Brummel and Romilly, so that the public world of the Regency overlaps with the private experience of Lord Byron – the history of one caught up with the history of the other: here a private nostalgia stands for the mourning of an epoch in English history, and vice versa. Moreover, the stanzas are rich with the details of English political and social life of that era: economics, Royal events (and George IV's 1821 tour of Scotland), Regency slang, theatricals, and jokes at the expense of the Whigs. In the unravelling of history post-1815, Byron includes the fall of Napoleon and the glorification of Wellington, George IV's tour of Ireland, fiscal and economic matters, the Queen Caroline affair, the Congress of Verona, the revolutionary movements in Europe, Peterloo, etc. This is the *material*, the detail of history, or what Byron described in earlier cantos as 'the *life...the thing*'. But in its very materiality there is a crucial paradox. The ephemera recorded in these stanzas, particularly in the *ubi sunt* section, are by that fact historically preserved, while at the same time remaining obscurely dependent upon a lost context.[37] Byron's stanzas rescue historical material from obscurity but consciously do nothing to prevent such material becoming strange. The details and names are not contextualised, nor fleshed out, but merely suspended in the long interrogative list of 'where?' One consequence is that the lines represent the moment in Byron's writing when the claim of 'I was there' (XIV.21: *'Haud ignara loquor'*, these are *Nugae, 'quarum / Pars* parva *fui'*),[38] becomes most urgent and complex.

At one level the stanzas develop a deceptively straightforward and open sense of personal nostalgia. Byron's life in London during 1811–16 *was* an extraordinary life to have led, and did famously intersect with the major public life – particularly the public personalities – of that time. If 'ordinary' nostalgia seeks to elevate and privilege personal experience above the commonplace, then here for once such a move seems to be justified: this is nostalgia of a certain quality and historical validity, commanding to be noticed – 'Where are the Lady Carolines and Franceses', is also asking 'where are the women *like that* now'. At the same time, there is a faux-nostalgia and a level of irony at work here too, a distrust of the emotion of memory which manifests itself in the conscious exercise of rhetoric: the *ubi sunt*, in other words, is also self-parodic. Many of the examples Byron chooses are obviously examples of false historical significance, so that the stanzas mock those whose fame had quickly passed into obscurity, and who are contrasted with those figures glowing in the authentic rays of posterity. Brummell, Wellesley, Whitbread and Romilly, are among those whose glory turned out either to be the glory of an hour, or whose fame had turned to ignominy, in which case the *ubi sunt* has something of the knowing sting of a cautionary tale. Lady Caroline Lamb and Lady Frances Webster, if they could be said to be famous at all, were so only through having been connected with Lord Byron, so that apart from being a sly confession of personal history, the lines lay bare the blurred and overlapping relations between ephemera on the one hand, and the historically significant on the other. In the life of a nation the two are bound up with each other, just as they are in the individual, and just as what we might call a 'sincere' nostalgia may very well be infected with a mock-nostalgia at the same time; indeed it may be difficult to distinguish between the two.

The very inclusiveness of these stanzas then, their determination to name the historical *and* the ephemeral together, their apparent inability to discriminate between the two, belongs to the time-capsule mystique of *Don Juan*, that is, they prepare for a future moment in which they themselves will be recovered, pored over and deciphered. Seeking to intervene in and accelerate the process of fossilising the recent past, they look towards Cuvier's paradigm in which the contemporary is first entombed and then exhumed, and in which a monstrous alterity is certain to emerge. Indeed it is part of the point in burying signs of the contemporary that such signs will not only illuminate the past but will also remain obscure and unknowable as the 'riddles of futurity'. In other words, these stanzas are written for a posterity in which the recent past-ness of 1811–16 will have become deeply and unmistakeably *past*, even as that *pastness* has already arrived in the short space of seven years.

Byron's ambivalence about nostalgia and memory is central to these stanzas. It is difficult to say where a 'sincere' nostalgia ends and irony begins, difficult to distinguish between a manner of mourning and a manner of pretending to mourn. Irony protects the former from the charge of taking itself too seriously and over-valuing the significance of personal memory, but even so the mocked ephemerality of the Regency from the perspective of 1822 is even more sharply perceived in posterity as the meaning drains out of these newspaper scraps and fragments ('the Five per Cents...the Rents...the Dublin shouts and London hisses'). Strangely, however, these lines are among the most exuberantly comic Byron ever wrote, and at the same time the most moving. Byron's distrust of sentimentality and his ironising of nostal-gia preserve the passage both from the mawkishness of personal memory, and the false evaluation of historical significance. Paradoxically, the result is that the lines have a powerful emotional resonance precisely because the mock-sadness of a seven year *ubi sunt* achieves a deeper pathos in our own reading across the dividing cen-turies. The promiscuous detail, the mixing of ephemera with more durable stuff, the listing of names without explanatory contexts, all acquire a poignancy and authenticity precisely because Byron distrusts the workings of memory and is conscious of the way in which nostal-gia distorts the value of historical material. These fragments are snatched without discrimination from the wreck of national convul-sion, but as such they seem to be a more vivid and authentic record of the Regency and the manner of its passing than any other. Not being certain what remains, wondering where the Regency is now, is the mark of their historical authenticity.

Of all the places of historical significance Byron wrote about, a few square miles of London 1811–16 commands precedence in his memory and imagination, but for this reason the relations of *being there, having been there, having seen*, are at their most complex there. If Byron made much of the fact of having actually *seen* men such as Curran and Sheridan in his daily life pre–1816, and attributed his lack of consciousness of the significance of those times to the very fact of literally having them in his sight on a mundane level, then the repeated trope in the second part of these stanzas of having seen the things that had taken place since his departure from England draws with it an obvious but nevertheless telling irony, as these were the things Byron had not in fact 'seen'. As such perhaps the force of such changes is felt more powerfully, their effect undiminished by familiarity, but at the same time the record of having witnessed history changing is entirely dependent upon the sense of geographical distance from England. In other words it is the fact of Byron's exile in 1816, his new life upon the continent and his gradual distancing from English affairs, which result in this sense of the defamiliarisation of English culture. Shadowing the series of *ubi sunt*s then is one very obvious unspoken question, which is: 'where is Lord Byron now?'; the answer of course being, 'in Italy', and it is because he is in Italy that he is asking 'where are they now?' So if there is an anxiety in the English cantos, and particularly in these stanzas, concerning the nature of historical significance, an anxiety that the early Regency will survive as a monstrous fragment or fossil disconnected from an historical continuum, then that possibility not only has an exact analogy in Byron's own geographical distance from England, but it is the fact of this distance that produces the sense of historical uniqueness and time-slice periodisation. Byron's exile and the 'lost' world of the Regency are therefore wholly connected and interdependent. At the same time the stanzas prepare for a future moment in which Byron's own presence will have disappeared from the world and left these words to posterity. As the *ubi sunt*s multiply, they summon the further ghostly self-questioning a modern reader is forced to hear: 'where is Lord Byron *now*?' Where is the figure whose memory (whose asking 'where') unifies these scraps and fragments of the Regency? Where, oh where, are the *Memoirs*?

If the London of 1811–16 has an authentic spirit of time and place which these stanzas hope to recover, then it is obvious where it might be found. The *genius loci* – that figure which is always in some sense there, and not there, the figure Byron both believes in and does not believe in – is unmistakably *here*, in the pages of *Don Juan*. Byron's own experience of London during the years 1811–16 may have been one shaped and determined by powerful literary and cultural associations centred in nostalgia for ideas of the eighteenth century, but as the Regency is remembered now Byron himself seems central to its historical significance. The question, 'where is the Regency now?' is therefore answered by itself. The Regency is nowhere else but in such a question, nor for Byron was it anywhere else than in the writing he produced during 1821–23, attempting both to recover and bury again a lost world.

Afterword: Dying in Greece

Byron's death in Greece in 1824 presented Europe with precisely the kind of powerful historical event-in-place that had shaped and commanded Byron's own imagination. But such a death, in such a place, also offered a compelling paradox. In many senses this was a moment representing Romantic individualism and heroic self-sacrifice in the least problematic of ways. Byron died at Missolonghi on 19 April 1824, a little over eight months after arriving in Greece to assist with what he described as the 'Cause' of independence. His untiring efforts to obtain and make sense of information concerning the true state of affairs in Greece, his significant and various financial contributions, his patience and courage, were beyond question and remain impressive to this day. His death immediately entered into the mythography of the revolution and became important as a galvanising factor among the disunited Greeks, and especially within philhellenic circles. In France in particular, the response to Byron's death was passionate. When Delacroix came to paint his famous scene of 'Greece Expiring on the Ruins of Missolonghi' in 1826, in many people's minds the fall of the city and Byron's death two years earlier were one and the same event.[1] Byron of course remains to this day a hero to the Greeks, his death a form of symbolic martyrdom which refuses to be interrogated through an ironising or contextualising of its sacrifice.

But there is also a sense of the anti-climactic and unheroic 'reality' of this death, which has also become bound up with mythography and cliché, albeit a mythography more palatable to non-Greek observers of those events, or to those who are drawn, like Byron himself, to the complexity of history-in-place. In this version of Byron's death the mixture of farce and tragedy is soberly emphasised; the factionalism he had to contend with, the attempts at extortion and manipulation; the unruly Suliote bands; his disillusionment and hesitation; the rather absurd figures surrounding him in Cephalonia, and later, in Missolonghi; the rain, the mud, the fever, and the sense of a death accelerated by confused and panicking doctors. Perhaps the outstanding cliché of this way of telling the story is the disparagement of Missolonghi itself, as if the town has become a synecdoche for the most untimely of endings: 'a squalid town, utterly charmless', 'far from heroic, far from Hellenic, merely dirty', 'the absolute dung-hill of the world', etc.[2]

'Two stories', writes Stephen Minta, 'apparently irreconcilable; one of drab decline, the other of unforgettable sacrifice'.[3] Nevertheless, the differences in the kinds of narrative told of Byron's death finally seem less important than the simple *fact* that Byron died in Greece during the War of Independence. It is the most potent fact of his life, connected as it is with history-in-place in a poet whose investment in the meaning of place, and in his own physical presence upon certain *spots*, had been so unremitting and intense. Moreover, this single fact seems to have a retrospective power to organise the narrative of Byron's life, so that his death in Greece tempts us to think in terms of a plot, or of a fated narrative. 'In retrospect', writes William St Clair, for example, Byron's death 'seems to have a certain inevitability'.[4] This I would suggest is partly a result of the extraordinary quality of Byron's own life-writing in his letters and journals, which of course conclude in Missolonghi, and which represent one of the great literary achievements of the period. Reading the twelve volumes edited by Leslie Marchand in consecutive order is like (and unlike) embarking upon a vast interlocking sequence of epistolary novels, a grand historical realisation, but one in which the reader knows the ending in advance. As we approach that ending, half-hoping that Byron will choose not to leave Genoa for Greece, the sense of a plotted narrative is irresistible. Byron's 'fate' seems retrospectively to make poignant sense of, rather than to cancel or undo, what came before.

From his arrival in Greece (and perhaps indeed as part of his conscious motivation in choosing to go to Greece), Byron was himself aware of the doubleness of the enterprise, the possibility that what he was doing was paradoxical, self-divided. His superb common sense meant that he had no illusions about philhellenism, and took some pleasure in de-mystifying those who came to Greece burdened with such feeling. 'He came up (as they all do who have not been in the country before) with some high-flown notions of the sixth form at Harrow and Eton, &c.; but Col. Napier and I set him to rights on those points, which is absolutely necessary to prevent disgust, or perhaps return.'[5] This was Byron reporting the arrival of Colonel Leicester Stanhope back to John Bowring of the London Greek Committee in October 1823, and reveals the ways in which a fine pragmatism had become not merely useful but absolutely expedient in order to survive daily life in such circumstances. Byron was conscious both of the possibility that he was on a 'fool's errand', and that it was a fool's errand that carried with it the distinct possibility of death.[6] He was also acutely aware that there can be different kinds of death in such circumstances, as a letter to the banker Charles Hancock of February 1824 makes clear:

> I take it that a man is on the whole as safe in one place as another – and after all he had better end with a bullet than bark in his body; – if we are not taken off with the sword – we are like to march off with an ague in this mud-basket – and to conclude with a very bad pun – to the ear rather than to the eye – better – *mart*ially – than *marsh*-ally....[7]

In a sequence of epistolary novels, forty pages before the hero died, this would have been crude sign-posting and feeble irony. As it is we can only wonder.

Above all, Byron's sense of place, of the historical aura or halo of place, and of the authority derived from *being there*, was most severely tested and put to the proof in Greece. Where, exactly, was the revolution taking place? Where, exactly, was the Greek government? Writing to Hobhouse in September 1823 Byron describes himself as 'waiting what Napoleon calls "The March of Events"', but in this case 'these Events... keep their march somewhat secret'.[8] The brief Journal Byron kept in Cephalonia between September and October 1823 attempted to make sense of the geographically elusive nature of the uprising in Greece, and to explain why he had remained for so long in Cephalonia. In writing to the Greek Government Byron explains that his 'object was not only to obtain some accurate information so as to enable me to proceed to the Spot where I might be if not most safe at least more serviceable but to have an opportunity of forming a judgement on the real state of their affairs'.[9] That no such 'Spot' unequivocally presented itself, or that there was no sense of a specific place from which the revolution might best be co-ordinated, or even observed, revealed most clearly the chaos of the 'real state' of Greek affairs. Eventually, Missolonghi would become the spot.

And yet, the overwhelming sense of the *here* and *now* which pressed upon Byron's consciousness is obvious from what is among the last pieces of poetry he ever wrote, and his last entry in his journal: 'On This Day I Complete My Thirty-Sixth Year'. This is a famous poem and much anthologised, and has been read as a complex meditation upon the situation in which the poet found himself at this moment of his life, suffering with an unrequited passion for the fifteen year-old boy Loukas Chalanditsanos. In the toils of such a feeling Byron has to remind himself where he is:

> But 'tis not *thus* – and 'tis not *here*
>   Such thoughts should shake my Soul, nor *now*
> Where Glory decks the hero's bier
>   Or binds his brow.

> (ll.17–20)

Byron's sense of speaking from a certain situatedness, with an authority vividly embodied or enabled by that situatedness, had always drawn him to the deictic expression (the dying gladiator's '*There... There*'). In this poem that situatedness and that authority threaten to be eclipsed by an infatuation for a boy. The poem, then, is a self-exhortation not merely to remember where he is and what is happening, but to return to the most enriching sources of his imaginative power, the belief in the significance of being on the spot:

> If thou regret'st thy Youth, *why live*?
>   The land of honourable Death
> Is here: – up to the field, and give
>   Away thy Breath!

> Seek out – less often sought than found –
>   A Soldier's Grave, for thee the best;
> Then look around, and choose thy Ground,
>   And take thy Rest!

> (ll.33–40)

The Miltonic shadow falling over those last lines (from the end of *Paradise Lost*: 'The World was all before them, where to choose / Their place of rest, and Providence their guide...'),[10] signals Byron's aware-ness of the narrative closure promised by dying in Greece, and how such a death would inevitably come to be regarded as in some sense fated or plotted, certainly foreseen, and perhaps even providential. Byron is also thinking of posterity and anticipating a future moment when the advice he gives himself here, to choose a soldier's death *here* and *now,* will have been heeded, and therefore when the full significance of the *here* and *now* (Greece, the War of Independence), will have been realised. The poem is strangely moving because it seems to have an awareness of a duty not merely to Greece at this moment, but more broadly to the notions of historical significance and emotional truth in *being there* which had been so central to Byron's writing life. These are truths not easily possessed, but which require an effort of will and choice in order to recollect them. 'Choose thy Ground / And take thy Rest' is then a self-exhortation of the most profoundly searching kind, as this is not merely to choose a place to lay down a life, but to prove that such places and such imperatives exist; that sacred historical places (the central subject of his writing) are able to elicit such a sacrifice. If Greece has not offered an unmistakable *here*, then Byron's writing must provide it for Greece. The 'land of honourable death' is *here* in the poem, as the poem is choosing its ground (making a subject of dying-in-place) and taking its rest (coming to an end), and therefore producing an epitaph for Byron himself. Here then, in Greece, on the last page of his Journal, Byron meets the *genius loci* with his life and his life's writing.

Notes

Introduction

1. Letter to F.T. Palgrave, Rome 21 June, 1849. *The Correspondence of Arthur Hugh Clough*, ed. by Frederick L. Mulhauser, 2 vols (Oxford: Clarendon Press, 1957), I, p. 260. [Hereafter *CAHC*.] Clough went in person to Mazzini to obtain permission to view certain collections that had been closed during the siege. Palgrave's father had written the *Handbook for Travellers in Northern Italy* (1842), published by John Murray.
2. *CAHC*, I, pp. 253–4.
3. *CAHC*, I, p. 256.
4. *CAHC*, I, pp. 262–3.
5. *Handbook for Travellers in Central Italy, including the Papal States, Rome, and the Cities of Etruria* (London: John Murray, 1843), p. 296. See James Buzard, *The Beaten Track: European Tourism, Literature, and the Ways to 'Culture' 1800–1918* (Oxford: Oxford University Press, 1993), pp. 119–25. The preface to Murray's third edition, which included poetic extracts, promised increased enjoyment 'knowing how much the perusal of [such extracts] on the spot, where the works themselves are not to be procured, will enhance the interest of seeing the objects described', *A Handbook for Travellers on the Continent* (London: Murray, 1942), no page number. I discuss the notion of being 'on the spot' at length in my first chapter.
6. William Hazlitt, 'Byron and Wordsworth', *The Complete Works of William Hazlitt* ed. by P.P. Howe (London and Toronto: J.M. Dent, 1932), vol. 20, p. 156. I discuss this further in Chapter 1. The notion of treading historically overburdened or haunted places is itself a classical commonplace, so that in Byron there is an anxiety about responding authentically to places which recall earlier writers who have already worried about the ghosts of history. See, for example, Cicero's description of Athens in *De finibus*, V, ii: 'quacumque enim ingredimur, in aliqua historia vestigium ponimus' ['wherever we go we tread historic ground'], *Cicero: De finibus Bonorum et Malorum*, translated by H. Rackham (London: Heinemann, 1914), pp. 396–7. I am indebted to Andrew Nicholson for drawing my attention to this passage.
7. 'In asserting that "travel" acquires its special value by virtue of its differential relationship with "tourism", I intend to suggest that the two together make up a binary opposition fundamental to and characteristic of modern culture', Buzard, p. 18.
8. 'An Italian Carnival' (1823), *Lord Byron: The Complete Miscellaneous Prose*, ed. by Andrew Nicholson (Oxford: Clarendon Press, 1991), pp. 190–1.
9. The literature of this encounter is vast, but important summarising collections of essays begin with William E. Mallory and Paul Simpson Housley (eds), *Geography and Literature: A Meeting of the Disciplines* (Syracuse, NY: Syracuse University Press, 1987), and two significant Routledge collections

of the early 1990s: Trevor J. Barnes and James Duncan (eds), *Writing Worlds: Discourse, Text and Metaphor in the Representation of Landscape* (London and New York: Routledge, 1992); and James Duncan and David Ley (eds), *Place/Culture/Representation* (London and New York: Routledge, 1993). See also Kenneth E. Foote and Kent Mathewson (eds), *Re-Reading Cultural Geography* (Austin: University of Texas Press, 1994), and Sara Blair, 'Cultural Geography and the Place of the Literary', in *American Literary History*, 10, 3 (1998) 544–67.

10. Gaston Bachelard, *The Poetics of Space*, translated by M. Jolas (Boston: Orion, 1964). See also Ti-Fu Tuan, *Topophilia* (Englewood Cliffs, NJ; Prentice Hall, 1974); Robert Harbinson, *Eccentric Spaces* (Cambridge Mass.; MIT Press, 1977); Gilles Deleuze and Felix Guattari, *A Thousand Plateaus*, translated by B. Massumi (Minneapolis: University of Minnesota Press, 1987); and more recently Patricia Yaeger's call for a 'new poetics of geography' in *The Geography of Identity* (Ann Arbor: University of Michigan Press, 1996), p. 18.

11. Sara Blair's article (cited above) offers the best summary of the 'new geography' as it has emerged from the thinking of Edward Soja, Saskia Sassen, David Harvey and above all, Henri Lefebvre's *The Production of Space*, translated by Donald Nicholson-Smith (Oxford: Blackwell, 1991). Levebvre's influential notion of *l'espace vécu* Blair summarises as: 'the simultaneously abstract and material lineaments of our social emplacement, a locatedness and relationality at once lived and socially constitutive' (557).

12. 'Place is... that within and with respect to which subjectivity is itself established... place is not founded *on* subjectivity, but is rather that *on which* subjectivity is founded. Thus one does not first have a subject that apprehends certain features of the world in terms of the idea of place; instead, the structure of subjectivity is given in and through the structure of place', J.E. Malpas, *Place and Experience: A Philosophical Topography* (Cambridge: Cambridge University Press, 1999), p. 35. See also Edward S. Casey, *Getting Back Into Place: Toward a Renewed Understanding of the Place-World* (Bloomington and Indianapolis: Indiana University Press, 1993); and *The Fate of Place: A Philosophical History* (Berkeley and Los Angeles: University of California Press, 1997); Stephen Pile and Nigel Thrift (eds), *Mapping the Subject: Geographies of Cultural Transformation* (London and New York: Routledge, 1995); Mike Crang and Nigel Thrift (eds), *Thinking Space* (London and New York: Routledge, 2000); Jon May and Nigel Thrift (eds), *Timespace: Geographies of Temporality* (London and New York: Routledge, 2001).

13. Sigmund Freud, *Civilization and its Discontents* (1930 [1929]) vol. 12 of *The Penguin Freud Library* (Harmondsworth: Penguin, 1991), pp. 256–9. J.E. Malpas summarises the Greek and Roman memory system known as the 'method of *loci*' which operated through 'the association of particular memories with particular "places" or "loci" within a system of such places', Malpas, p. 106. For 'a dialogue between and within' the discourses of psychoanalysis and geography, see in particular the work of Steve Pile, *The Body and the City: Psychoanalysis, Space and Subjectivity* (London: Routledge, 1996), p. 8.

14. See, for example, David Simpson's chapters on 'Localism, Local Knowledge and Literary Criticism', and 'Romanticism and Localism' in *The Academic*

Postmodern and the Rule of Literature: A Report on Half-Knowledge (Chicago: Chicago University Press, 1995), and Alan Liu's important essay, 'Local Transcendence: Cultural Criticism, Postmodernism, and the Romanticism of Detail', *Representations*, 32 (Fall, 1990) 75–113. Thinking about Romanticism and place has been renewed with especial vigour in the last decade in the field of travel-writing and colonial studies. For a recent example, see Amanda Gilroy (ed.), *Romantic Geographies: Discourses of Travel 1775–1844* (Manchester: Manchester University Press, 2000). Jonathan Bate has discussed Wordsworth's 'sacramental' notions of place (including his use of that key-word 'spot') in *Romantic Ecology: Wordsworth and the Environmental Tradition* (London: Routledge, 1991), pp. 85–115. See also Ralph Pite, 'How Green Were the Romantics', *Studies in Romanticism*, 35 (1996) 357–73.

15. See Malcolm Kelsall, 'The Sense of Place and the Romantic Cosmopolite', *Literaria Pragensia*, 3:5 (1993) 28–41; Kirsten Daly, 'Worlds Beyond England: *Don Juan* and the Legacy of Enlightenment Cosmopolitanism', *Romanticism*, 4:2 (1998) 189–201.

16. *BLJ*, VIII, p. 108.

17. Stephen Bann has argued that an increase in a consciousness of history at the beginning of the nineteenth century was 'one of the most potent causes, and one of the most widespread effects of Romanticism. An irreversible shift had occurred, and history – from being a localized and specific practice within the cultural typology – became a flood that overrode all disciplinary barriers and, finally, when the barriers were no longer easy to perceive, became a substratum to almost every type of cultural activity', *Romanticism and the Rise of History* (New York: Twayne Publishers, 1995), pp. 6–7. See also Richard J. Quinones, 'Byron's Cain: Between History and Theology', in *Byron, the Bible, and Religion: Essays from the Twelfth International Byron Seminar*, ed. by Wolf Z. Hirst (Newark: University of Delaware Press, 1991): 'More than any other prior generation, Byron's represents a generation that has been thrown into history. And Byron is the most perspicacious spokesman for this fact. In the turmoil of his intellect he showed the true consequences of the dawning of the age of history. He saw and reacted desperately against the scepticism that was the natural product of this "historicism".' (p. 55).

18. 'Byron's early Calvinism, though rejected, left him with the idea of a remote and terrible God, and this is blended with Lucretian atomism, and Fontenelle's plurality of worlds; with the deism of the *Essay on Man* and the cosmology of *Night Thoughts*; with the pre-Adamites of Vathek and with Buffon's giants and "organic degeneration"; with the spontaneous generation of Erasmus Darwin; and finally with the catastrophism of Cuvier', M.K. Joseph, *Byron the Poet* (London: Victor Gollancz, 1964), p. 121. For Byron's 'manic depression', see Kay Redfield Jamison, *Touched with Fire: Manic Depressive Illness and the Artistic Temperament* (New York: Free Press, 1993), pp. 150–90.

19. See especially Chapter 3, 'Harold in Italy: The Politics of Classical History', in Malcolm Kelsall, *Byron's Politics* (Brighton: Harvester, 1987).

20. Frederick Garber offers an extended reading of the significance of the epigraph, in *Byron: Self, Text, and Romantic Irony* (Princeton: Princeton University Press, 1988), pp. 3–6.

21. J.J. McGann, *Fiery Dust: Byron's Poetic Development* (Chicago: Chicago University Press, 1968), p. 249.

22. '[H]e fought shy of all optimistic, evolutionary theories of history, and his sceptical mind naturally found Cuvier's ideas most congenial. In the mystery plays [*Cain* and *Heaven and Earth*] Byron chose to use Cuvier as a guide to more ancient patterns of historical thought, and he sets out a regressive theory of history to usher in the necessary millennial event. Cuvier's theories appealed to Byron because they asserted a series of cata-clysms in which the earth proceeded from her Golden Age, her youth, to her less and less splendid periods', McGann, *Fiery Dust*, p. 265.

23. 'Secular Calvinism' is J. Drummond Bone's phrase, in 'Byron, Scott, and Nostalgia', *Byron and Scotland: Radical or Dandy*, ed. by Angus Calder (Edinburgh: Edinburgh University Press, 1989), p. 134.

24. For Vico's 'ricorso' theory and its relation to Byron, see for example Frederick W. Shilstone, *Byron and the Myth of Tradition* (Lincoln: University of Nebraska Press, 1988), pp. 240–1.

25. See Peter L. Thorslev, 'Byron and Bayle: Biblical Scepticism and Romantic Irony', in Hirst, *Byron, the Bible and Religion*, pp. 58–76; and Roy E. Acock, 'Lord Byron and Bayle's Dictionary', *The Yearbook of English Studies, Modern Humanities Research Association*, 5 (1975) 142–52.

26. James Kennedy, *Conversations on Religion with Lord Byron* (London: John Murray, 1830), p. 89.

27. See for example Michael Macovski, 'Byron, Bakhtin, and the Translation of History', in *Re-Reading Byron: Essays Selected from Hofstra University's Byron Bicentennial Conference*, ed. by Alice Levine and Robert N. Keane (New York: Garland, 1993), pp. 21–41; and J.J. McGann, 'Byron's Ideal of Immediacy', in *The Romantic Ideology: A Critical Investigation* (Chicago: Chicago University Press, 1983), pp. 123–30. For Byron's 'increasing distrust of the authenticity of history', see Shilstone, p. 228; and for Byron's scepticism see Terence Allan Hoagwood, *Byron's Dialectic: Scepticism and the Critique of Culture* (London and Toronto: Associated University Presses, 1993).

28. For the notion of dramatising history, see Vincent Newey, 'Authoring the Self: *Childe Harold* III and IV', *Byron and the Limits of Fiction*, ed. by Bernard Beatty and Vincent Newey (Liverpool: Liverpool University Press, 1988), pp. 148–90: 'History is perceived as a drama against which it is pointless to complain, not simply because the plot always ends in death, but because it is a drama, a pageant without purpose beyond that of its own self-sufficient spectacle' (p. 172). See also Peter J. Manning: 'Byron habitually saw history as he saw his own life, and precisely because his expression in *Don Juan* is unrestricted he goes beyond mere self expression to illuminate the cultural situation in which he is placed, remaking and exploiting tradition as he remakes and exploits the self. In *Don Juan* Byron opposes the burdens of the past with the resources of drama, and combats his isolation by inviting the reader into his theatre', *Byron and His Fictions* (Detroit: Wayne State University Press, 1978), p. 17.

29. The phrase is from Eliot's 'Marina'. In a sense my study is following in the footsteps of Bernard Blackstone's *Byron: A Survey* (London: Longman, 1975), with its exploration of a topocriticism alive to the quasi-religious element in Byron's experience of place.

1   Being There, 1807–12

1. *Lord Byron: The Complete Poetical Works*, ed. by J.J. McGann (Oxford: Clarendon Press, 1980–86), I, p. 364. (Hereafter *BCPW*). For Macpherson's poem see *The Poems of Ossian and Related Works*, ed. by Howard Gaskill (Edinburgh: Edinburgh University Press, 1996), pp. 127–34.

2. *Byron's Letters and Journals*, ed. by Leslie A. Marchand, 12 vols (London: John Murray, 1973–82), I, p. 131. (Hereafter *BLJ*).

3. *BLJ*, I, p. 131.

4. *BLJ*, I, p. 133.

5. These are the questions Jerome Christensen suggests are both posited and answered through Byron's 'strength'. *Lord Byron's Strength: Romantic Writing and Commercial Society* (London and Baltimore: Johns Hopkins University Press, 1993), p. xvii.

6. Donald H. Reiman (ed.), *The Romantics Reviewed: Contemporary Reviews of British Romantic Writers* (New York: Garland, 1972), Part B, vol. 2, p. 835. (Hereafter *RR*).

7. *BCPW*, I, p. 373. Brougham seized on this poem too: 'There is a good deal also about his maternal ancestors, in a poem on Lachin-y-gair, a mountain where he spent part of his youth, and might have learnt that *pibroch* is not a bagpipe, any more than duet means a fiddle', *RR*, Part B, vol. 2, p. 835. This was a strike against authenticity that Byron would have found particularly stinging.

8. The preface to Murray's third edition, which included poetic extracts, promised increased enjoyment, 'knowing how much the perusal of [such extracts] on the spot, where the works themselves are not to be procured, will enhance the interest of seeing the objects described', *A Handbook for Travellers on the Continent* (London: Murray, 1842), no page number. See also Malcolm Andrews, *The Search for the Picturesque: Landscape, Aesthetics and Tourism in Britain, 1760–1800* (Aldershot: Scolar Press, 1989), pp. 79–80.

9. *BLJ*, I, pp. 195–6. See also, II, pp. 28, 32, 35, 39, 41, 45, 57, 94, 115.

10. Ida is the lofty peak from which the Gods watch over the battles of Troy. The phrase is from 'Childish Recollections' and is echoed in a letter to Edward Noel Long: 'Is your Brother at Harrow? If he is I shall *tip* the youth, on my visit to the *Blest Spot*', *BLJ*, I, p. 119. 'Lines Written Beneath an Elm, in the Churchyard of Harrow on the Hill' begin: 'Spot of my youth !'. *BCPW*, I, p. 123.

11. See letter to John Ridge, *BLJ*, I, p. 138.

12. See letter to Edward Noel Long, *BLJ*, I, p. 150.

13. Recently, close critical attention has been paid to Byron's speech-day performances as King Latinus from *The Aeneid*, King Lear, and most crucially Zanga the Moor's speech over the body of Alonso in Edward Young's *The Revenge*, revealing the ways in which these performances are in many ways rehearsals of the later strategies of authorship. See Paul Elledge, *Lord Byron at Harrow School: Speaking Out, Talking Back, Acting Up, Bowing Out* (Baltimore: Johns Hopkins University Press, 2000). See also C.J. Tyerman, 'Byron's Harrow', *The Byron Journal*, 17 (1989) 17–39. The private theatricals Byron organised at Newstead in September 1808 included Young's *The Revenge*.

14.   See, for example, the letter to William Harness, the same friend who received the nostalgic account of Arcadia I discuss below. *BLJ*, I, p. 193: 'I am obsolete among Harrow men.'

15.   *BLJ*, II, p. 137. In fact Byron had been disappointed by the 'real' Arcadia, and again returns to the line from Virgil in his notes to *Childe Harold*: 'I heard much of the beauty of Arcadia, but excepting the view from the monastery of Megaspelion (which is inferioir to Zitza in a command of the country) and the descent from the mountains on the way from Tripolitza to Argos, Arcadia has little to recommend it beyond the name. "Sternitur, et *dulces* moriens reminiscitur Argos." Virgil could have put this into the mouth of none but an Argive; and (with reverence be it spoken) it does not deserve the epithet', *BCPW*, II, p. 200.

16.   See letter to Charles Robert Dallas, *BLJ*, II, p. 111. Stephen Bann contrasts the example of Byron with that of Scott in 'The Historical Composition of Place: Byron and Scott', in *The Clothing of Clio: A Study of the Representation of History in Nineteenth Century Britain and France* (Cambridge: Cambridge University Press, 1984), pp. 93–111. Bann draws distinctions between Byron's relation to Newstead, and Scott's to Abbotsford. The kind of synecdochic method I have been ascribing to Byron's *Hours of Idleness* Bann sees as more aptly describing Scott's Abbotsford: 'part-objects which are linked synecdochically both to an architectural whole and to the mythic system of "History"', whereas Byron's representations of Newstead (in *Childe Harold* and *Don Juan*) offer 'part-objects which are disjoined from each other and from any transcendent whole' (p. 108).

17.   *BCPW*, I, p. 427.

18.   For many of the details in this chapter I am indebted to Timothy Webb's essay 'Appropriating the Stones: the "Elgin Marbles" and English National Taste', in Elazar Barkan and Ronald Bush (eds), *Claiming the Stones/ Naming the Bones: Cultural Property and Group Identity* (Oxford and California: Oxford University Press and J. Paul Getty Foundation, 2000). See also Timothy Webb, '"Branding Pages and Burning Lines": Re-visiting *The Curse of Minerva*', Marios Byron Raizis (ed.), *Byron: A Poet for All Seasons: Proceedings of the 25th International Byron Conference* (Messolonghi: Messolonghi Byron Society, 2000), pp. 12–52.

19.   *BLJ*, II, p. 37.

20.   *BCPW*, I, p. 446.

21.   'The poem presents an account of nationality which is confused or subtly evasive or perhaps fashionably fluid since it includes "England", "Albion", "Free Britannia" and "British Hands" yet clearly distinguishes between such apparently inclusive titles and Elgin's own narrow Scottishness which personifies the land which it seems to represent' (Webb, p. 13). Angus Calder has pointed out that this anti-Scottishness was something of a stock literary theme among the Augustan poets Byron admired, and so represents something not entirely heart-felt: '*English Bards and Scotch Reviewers* and *The Curse of Minerva* reveal no serious anti-Scottish animus, rather a young poet's emulation of his predecessor: he drew from a bank of anti-Caledonian jibes', Angus Calder (ed.), *Byron and Scotland: Radical or Dandy?* (Edinburgh: Edinburgh University Press, 1989), p. 2. Timothy Webb points out that Scottishness

is presented as a 'fate' in the poem in which Elgin is trapped. See '"Branding Pages and Burning Lines"', p. 26. For Scotland as a symbol of exile in European novels by female writers, see April Alliston, 'Of Haunted Highlands: Mapping a Geography of Gender in the Margins of Europe', in Gregory Maertz (ed.), *Cultural Interactions in the Romantic Age: Critical Essays in Comparative Literature* (Albany: State University of New York Press, 1998). Byron returns to the subject of Scotland (and the Jeffrey incident) in the tenth canto of *Don Juan*, stanzas 12–19.

22. *BCPW*, I, p. 450. Webb argues that the elusive grammatical shifts towards the end of the poem allow a certain open-endedness, in which the doom predicted for the city of London could still be avoided. 'For all the ferocious emphases of its perspective, and for all the violence of its attacks on the plunderers of Athens and particularly on Elgin, *The Curse* stops short of fully endorsing the apocalyptic visions which it presents', '"Branding Pages and Burning Lines"', p. 49.

23. See Webb, p. 11. In the 'Letter to John Murray Esq' of 1821, Byron's intervention in the Bowles/Pope controversy, a section analysing the distinction between Art and Nature takes the example of the Parthenon marbles and the importance of viewing them in their original context. Byron employs the trope of the *spot* of earth to emphasise that mere geography without the adornment of Art (or the associations of history) amounts to little:

> There are a thousand rocks and capes – far more picturesque than those of the Acropolis and Cape Sunium – in themselves, – what are they to a thousand Scenes in the wilder parts of Greece? of Asia Minor? Switzerland, – or even of Cintra in Portugal, or to many scenes of Italy – and the Sierras of Spain? – But it is the '*Art*' – the Columns – the temples – the wrecked vessel – which give them their antique and modern poetry – and not the spots themselves. – Without them the *Spots* of earth would be unnoticed and unknown – buried like Babylon and Nineveh in indistinct confusion – without poetry – as without existence – but to whatever spot of earth these ruins were transported if they were *capable* of transportation – like the Obelisk and the Sphinx – and the Memnon's head – *there* they would still exist in the perfection of their beauty – and in the pride of their poetry. – I opposed – and will ever oppose – the robbery of ruins – from Athens to instruct the English in Sculpture – (who are as capable of Sculpture – as the Egyptians are of skating) but why did I do so? – the *ruins* are as poetical in Piccadilly as they were in the Parthenon – but the Parthenon and it's [sic] rock are less so without them.—Such is the Poetry of Art. –

> *Lord Byron: The Complete Miscellaneous Prose*, ed. by Andrew Nicholson (Oxford: Clarendon Press, 1991), p. 133. [Hereafter *CMP*].

24. *BCPW*, II, p. 191. Richard Cronin has drawn attention to the symbolic significance of Lord Elgin in this broader historical context:

> The ideal of art, unlike the ideal of national independence, might seem immune from the war between Britain and France. Lord Elgin's

function within the poem is to demonstrate that this is not the case. In stripping the Parthenon of its friezes, Elgin offered a lively demonstration that art offers no sanctuary from a world of power. In Greece Elgin did no more than imitate what Napoleon had done in Italy. The Porte in Constantinople was too reliant on the power of British arms to deny Elgin the permission he needed. ...Lord Elgin's activities, the fact itself that the marbles were transported to Britain by warships, afforded an ample proof that art could no longer claim to transcend politics in a world in which the work of art had become the most prized trophy of success.

Richard Cronin, 'Mapping *Childe Harold* I and II', *The Byron Journal*, 22 (1994) 14–30; (23). Jerome McGann has argued that the vision of *Don Juan* in particular takes European history of 1787–1820 as being 'all of a piece' and that within this coherence 'the condition of Greece during the period is the very symbol of the condition of Europe', *The Beauty of Inflections*, p. 283.

25. 'I was fortunate enough to engage a very superior German artist; and hope to renew my acquaintance with this and many other Levantine scenes, by the arrival of his performances', *BCPW*, II, p. 285. Webb points out the 'delicious irony' of the fact that the ship carrying part of Lord Elgin's hoard back to England by way of Malta also carried Lord Byron and the unfinished manuscript of *The Curse of Minerva*. (Webb, p. 6).

26. A note in Italian on the wrapper of a letter to Hobhouse from Malta, 15 May 1811, explains that Byron has found his friend's missing marbles: 'Li Marmi sono trovati; – dopo [cercando] tutto la Citta, furono [scoperti insie] me col'li al[tre ?]. Milordo [Elgin ?] Li portaro al [T-vra ?]'. Marchand translates and deciphers thus: 'the marbles are found; after [searching] throughout the city, they were [discovered together] with the other [marbles of] Lord [Elgin ?]. They will be carried to [?]', *BLJ*, II, p. 47. The possibility that this might be Lord Elgin's name, along with the Italian (coded ?) nature of the note, are intriguing. Byron stole Meletius' *Ancient and Modern Geography* (Venice, 1728), from the Bishop of Chrisso during his tour of Parnassus in December 1810. See *BLJ*, II, pp. 59–60, p. 114. Christensen reads the ambivalence of Lord Byron's relation to Elgin as a 'displacement...of his own anxieties over spoiling the femininely gendered scenes his poems compulsively review', *Lord Byron's Strength*, p. 73.

27. See Webb, p. 25.

28. *BCPW*, II, pp. 191–2.

29. For arguments about the possible restoration of the marbles, see Webb, p. 12.

30. William Hazlitt, 'Byron and Wordsworth', *CWWH*, vol. 20, p. 156. Hazlitt had reworked this sentence from the earlier critique of Byron for *The Spirit of the Age*: '*Childe Harold* contains a lofty and impassioned review of the great events of history, of the mighty objects left as wrecks of time, but he dwells chiefly on what is familiar to the mind of every schoolboy', *CWWH*, vol. 11, p. 73. Hazlitt often repeated the accusation that Byron's writing consisted of 'a tissue of superb common-places; even

his paradoxes are *common-place*. They are familiar in the schools'; 'That where the face of nature has changed, time should have rolled its course, is but a common-place discovery'; 'The judgements pronounced are often more dogmatical than profound, and with all their extravagance of expression, common-place', *CWWH*, vol. 11, p. 76; vol. 20, p. 155; vol. 19, p. 36. See also Jerome Christensen, *Byron's Strength*, p. 62.

31. 'The Parthenon, before its destruction in part by fire during the Venetian siege, had been a temple, a church, and a mosque. In each point of view it is an object of regard; it changed its worshippers; but still it was a place of worship thrice sacred to devotion: its violation is a triple sacrilege' (Byron's note), *BCPW*, II, p. 190. See also stanza 3 of the second canto: 'Look on this spot – a nation's sepulchre! / Abode of gods, whose shrines no longer burn'. (II.3).

32. *BCPW*, II, p. 3.

33. *BLJ*, II, p. 165.

34. *BLJ*, II, p. 91.

35. *BLJ*, II, p. 75.

36. Byron attempted to enlist the services of his Greek servant Demo (Demetrius Zograffo) to draw up a Romaic lexicon for Hobhouse: 'I have told Demo to write 150 times, but he either dont or wont understand me, if you were on the spot, all this could be easily arranged', *BLJ*, II, p. 162. See also the letters to Hobhouse, *BLJ*, II, pp. 113; 123; 135;155.

37. *BLJ*, II, p.125.

38. *BCPW*, II, p. 192.

39. *BLJ*, I, pp. 237–8.

40. *BCPW*, II, pp. 195–6.

41. 'Five thousand Suliotes, among the rocks and in the castle of Suli, withstood 30,000 Albanians for eighteen years: the castle at last was taken by bribery. In this contest there were several acts performed not unworthy of the better days of Greece', *BCPW*, II, p. 195.

42. *BCPW*, II, p. 200. Most tellingly, Byron remembers the unexpected question he and Hobhouse had been asked at Ali Pacha's court:

> I remember Mahmout, the grandson of Ali Pacha, asking whether my fellow-traveller and myself were in the upper or lower House of Parliament. Now this question from a boy of ten years old proved that his education had not been neglected. It may be doubted if an English boy at that age knows the difference of the Divan from a College of Dervises; but I am very sure a Spaniard does not. How little Mahmout, surrounded, as he had been, entirely by his Turkish tutors, had learned that there was such a thing as a Parliament it were useless to conjecture, unless we suppose that his instructors did not confine his studies to the Koran.

> *BCPW*, II, p. 210.

43. *BLJ*, II, p. 117.

44. See, for example, the remarks on Henry Swinburne's *Travels in the Two Sicilies* (1783), *BLJ*, II, p. 155; and Byron's invective in the notes to *Childe Harold* in reaction to Thornton's derogatory remarks on the modern

Greeks in his *Present State of Turkey*: 'As to Mr. Thornton's voyages in the Black Sea with Greek vessels, they give him the same idea of Greece as a cruize to Berwick in a Scotch smack would of Johnny Grot's house', *BCPW*, II, p. 203. Of Lieutenant-Colonel William Martin Leake's *Researches in Greece* (1814) Byron had this to say: 'There [i.e. Greece] – without having carried out with us a larger share of the ancient – or acquired upon the spot much more of the modern languages than has enabled us to prove that the Major knows nothing of the one – and rather worse than nothing of the other or *just enough to blunder withal* – it was with peculiar gratification that we seized such opportunities as are offered to the traveller – of observing countries and nations where intercourse with our own shores is still partial & limited', *CMP*, p. 48.

45. *BCPW*, II, p. 204. Capuchin is a post-1528 variant of Franciscan, so called because of the capuche garment, adopted in 1525.

46. *BCPW*, II, p. 204.

47. *BCPW*, II, p. 209.

48. *BCPW*, II, p. 209.

49. *BCPW*, I, p. 33.

50. 'Byron derived his fiscally rewarding insubstantiality from the synthetic Scottishness apparent in his early reworkings of Ossian and other Highland themes', Andrew Noble, 'Byron: Radical, Scottish Aristocrat', in Calder, *Byron and Scotland*, p. 31.

51. *BCPW*, I, p. 103. Donald Reiman provides a gloss of the phrase 'Caledonian Cremona', with which Byron describes Edinburgh in a note to *Hints from Horace*, in 'Byron and the Uses of Refamiliarization', in Alice Levine and Robert N. Keane (eds), *Re-reading Byron: Essays Selected from Hofstra University's Byron Bicentennial Conference* (New York: Garland, 1993), pp. 115–16.

52. Byron would himself become embroiled in the preliminary moves of the duelling ritual with Tom Moore, later his close friend, in 1811.

53. *BCPW*, p. 409.

54. *BCPW*, I, p. 263.

55. See Andrew Nicholson's review of Angus Calder, *Byron* (Milton Keynes: Open University Press, 1987), Angus Calder (ed.), *Byron and Scotland: Radical or Dandy?* (Edinburgh: Edinburgh University Press, 1989) and Frederick W. Shilstone, *Byron and the Myth of Tradition* (Lincoln: University of Nebraska Press, 1989), in *Keats–Shelley Review*, 5 (Autumn, 1990) 118–28: 'Byron's structure of perception, and our way of reading his perception, is syncretic – whereby an identity, but *not* identicality, is revealed. Scotland and Greece do not merge, nor do they become interchangeable; they are distinct, and yet the same: we see Scotland *in* Greece, Greece *in* Scotland'. (123) Nicholson goes on to use the figure of the palimpsest to describe the kind of over-mapping of place-on-place I describe below.

56. Note to canto two, *BCPW* , II, pp. 192–3.

57. *BLJ*, I, p. 73.

58. Letter to his mother, *BLJ*, I, p. 89

59. *BLJ*, I, pp. 131–2.

60. *BLJ*, I, p. 132.

61. *BLJ*, I, p. 135.
62. *BLJ*, I, p. 151. This is the first mention of the Eastern Mediterranean and the first occasion Byron uses the word 'pilgrimage' to describe the journey.
63. *BLJ*, I, p. 172.
64. *BLJ*, I, p. 172.
65. *BLJ*, I, p. 175.
66. Letter to John Hanson, *BLJ*, I, p. 192.
67. *BLJ*, I, p. 199.
68. *BLJ*, I, p. 203.
69. *BLJ*, I, p. 206.
70. *BLJ*, I, p. 230.
71. *BLJ*, I, p. 234.
72. *BLJ*, I, p. 252.
73. Letter to Hobhouse, *BLJ*, II, p. 7.
74. Letter to Hobhouse, *BLJ*, II, p. 33.
75. *BLJ*, II, p. 38.
76. *BLJ*, II, p. 38.
77. *BLJ*, II, p. 39
78. See letter to James Cawthorn, *BLJ*, II, p. 44.
79. *BLJ*, II, p. 49.
80. *BLJ*, II, p. 54
81. *BLJ*, II, p. 63.
82. This latter point is forcefully made by Richard Cronin in his essay 'Mapping *Childe Harold* 1 and 2', *The Byron Journal*, 22 (1994), 14–30.
83. This has been the kind of reading consistently offered by Jerome McGann, from his early assertion that the narrator is 'dramatically presented to the reader in a series of virtually present moments', *Fiery Dust: Byron's Poetic Development* (Chicago: Chicago University Press, 1968), p. 40; through to his notes to *Lord Byron: The Major Works* (Oxford: Oxford World's Classics, 1986), describing the poem as 'a radical transformation of the popular genre of travelogue known as the topographical poem. Byron interiorizes the form so drastically that it mutates into a drama of personal history. The historical context in which the personal record is set is turned to a reflection of Byron's own psychological condition. ...The whole comprises an autobiographical journey into and through a deep personal malaise which Byron represents as a symbol of the condition of Europe between 1809 and 1818' (p. 1026). The phrase 'shifting sensibilites' is from *Fiery Dust*, p. 54. In the notes to the second volume of *BCPW* McGann describes the poem as 'a dramatic personal record of the growth of a poet's mind – to sorrow, even despair' (p. 271).
84. See Caroline Franklin, 'Cosmopolitan Masculinity and the British Female Reader of *Childe Harold's Pilgrimage*', in Richard A. Cardwell (ed.), *Lord Byron the European: Essays for the International Byron Society* (Lampeter: Edwin Mellen Press, 1997): 'Byron probes the relationship between European martial and poetic masculine role models and so constructs a new masculine public persona for himself' (p. 106). Frederick W. Shilstone, *Byron and the Myth of Tradition* (Lincoln: University of Nebraska Press, 1988), describes the poem as one in which Byron

'opposes the autonomous self to the inherited values that would deny its significance, even its very existence' (p. 1).

85. The first phrase is from Bernard Beatty's important essay, 'Byron and the Paradoxes of Nationalism' in Vincent Newey and Ann Thompson (eds), *Literature and Nationalism* (Liverpool: Liverpool University Press, 1991), p. 152. The second is from J.J. McGann, *The Romantic Ideology* (Chicago: Chicago University Press, 1983), p. 127. Jerome Christensen argues that 'in default of an identity, Harold gives the poet the support of an attitude', *Lord Byron's Strength*, p. 67.

86. Byron's letter to his mother, *BLJ*, II, p. 4.

87. Edward John Trelawny, *Records of Shelley, Byron, and the Author* (Middlesex: Penguin, 1973), p. 82.

88. *BLJ*, IX, p. 41. The earlier journal entry read: 'I remember, in riding from Chrisso to Castri (Delphos), along the sides of Parnassus, I saw six eagles in the air. It is uncommon to see so many together; and it was the number – not the species, which is common enough – that excited my attention', *BLJ*, III, p. 253.

89. See, for example, Roger Poole, 'What constitutes, and what is external to, the "real" text of Byron's *Childe Harold's Pilgrimage, A Romaunt: and Other Poems* (1812)', in *Lord Byron the European*, pp. 149–207. Poole extends the earlier insistences of Jerome McGann, specifically in *The Beauty of Inflections: Literary Investigations in Historical Method and Theory* (Oxford: Clarendon Press, 1985), that we should read the poem with an awareness of its surrounding apparatus of notes and appendages. See also Peter Graham, 'Byron, Hobhouse and Editorial Symbiosis', *The Byron Journal*, 23 (1995) 14–21: 'Byron and Hobhouse served each other as implicit "ideal reader" and urbane editor – whether the other wished it or not – each recognising and attempting to rectify errors of taste and strategy that, if left uncorrected, would harm the other's reputation in the eyes of the world – that is to say, the reading public' (14). Donald Reiman talks of the 'use of a separate, antiphonal voice of common sense – usually in prose notes in the earlier poetry', 'Byron and the Uses of Refamiliarization', p. 115.

90. John Cam Hobhouse, *Travels in Albania and Other Provinces of Turkey in 1809 & 1810* (London: Murray, 1813; revised edition 1858), p. 198. [Hereafter *Travels*].

91. Hobhouse mentions that Crisso is 'the residence of a Bishop, to whom we had a letter from the Consul-General at Patras' (*Travels*, p. 199). It is one of the many ironies of this visit that Byron and Hobhouse stole a book, the classic *Ancient and Modern Geography* by Meletius of Janina (1661–1714), from this same bishop. Writing to Henry Drury on his way home aboard the *Volgate* on 7 July 1811, Byron remembers his classicist friend Francis Hodgson: 'What would he give? to have seen like me the *real Parnassus*, where I robbed the Bishop of Chrisso of a book of Geography, but this I call only plagiarism, as it was done within an hour's ride of Delphi', *BLJ*, II, p. 59. Hobhouse asked to borrow this stolen book from Byron to help prepare his *Travels*, 'on account of the modern topography, a point in which I have endeavoured to be more accurate than usual with travel writers'. Letter to Byron, 13 December

1811, see *Byron's Bulldog: The Letters of John Cam Hobhouse to Lord Byron*, ed. by Peter Graham (Columbus: Ohio State University Press, 1984), p. 93. Later Byron attempted to have the inscription on the title page of the *Meletius* erased, presumably as it identified its original owner (see *BLJ*, III, p. 61).

92. *Travels*, p. 199.

93. 'Parnassus is not so much a single mountain as a vast range of hills. ... The two tops have a sort of poetical existence which one would not be inclined to dispute. ... The peak is covered with perpetual snows. ... The summits of Parnassus, says Pausanias, are above the clouds. ... At present they are the summer retreats of the Albanian robbers...'. *Travels*, pp. 208–9.

94. Hobhouse quotes from the forty-second book of Livy's *Rome and the Mediterranean* describing the topography of Delphi: 'Adscendentibus ad templum a Cirrhâ priusquam perveniretur ad frequentia aedificiis loca, maceria erat, ab laeva semitae paulum extans a fundamento, quâ singuli transirent', *Travels*, p. 200 [On the ascent from Cirrha to the temple, before the built-up district was reached, there was a wall on the left beside a path which extended only a little distance from the bottom of the wall, making a place where passengers had to go in single file], *Livy: Rome and the Mediterranean*, translated by Henry Betteson (Harmondsworth: Penguin, 1976), p. 505.

95. *BCPW*, II, p. 187. Elsewhere in the notes Byron describes a domestic dispute breaking out among his servants 'on our journey over Parnassus' (p. 194). Domestic disputes, disappointments, foul-tasting springs, and the theft of a book from a bishop: this was the kind of visit it seemed to be.

96. 'qui rore puro Castaliae lavit / crines solutos' (he who washes his flowing hair in the pure dews of Castaly): Horace, *Odes*, III, iv, ll.61–2. Hobhouse is directly (mis)quoting Edmund Spenser's *The Ruines of Time*: 'But that blinde bard did him immortall make / With verses, dipt in deaw of *Castalie*' (ll. 430–1).

97. *BCPW*, II, pp. 199–200. A footnote added by Hobhouse to the 1854 edition of the *Travels* quotes Dr Edward Daniel Clarke's description of the Castalian spring from his own *Travels* (1816): 'the *Castalian bath*, wherein the priestess used to wash her whole body, and particularly her hair, before she placed herself on the tripod in the Temple of Apollo'; Hobhouse comments that this description is 'a little too romantic' (p. 204). His later memoirs (partly based on the earlier travelogue), *Recollections of a Long Life: By Lord Broughton*, 6 vols (London: Murray, 1909), recall taking souvenirs from Castri: 'from one of the fountains of the village, believed to have been the sacred spring, we brought away a bottle of water, as also we did from the stream which flows from Parnassus' (*Recollections*, I, p. 23). Souvenir and relic-hunting, collecting actual material evidence of having been in a significant place, would become something of an obsession for Byron and Hobhouse, particularly in their travels through Italy of 1818. For Hobhouse the desire for material connection with ancient Greek culture is cruelly frustrated at Delphi. Speculating about the possible location for the Pythian games he

complains that 'divested of its ancient fame, the place would have nothing either alluring or romantic' about it (*Recollections*, I, p. 23).

98. For 'place' in *Childe Harold*, see especially Frederick Garber, *Self, Text, and Romantic Irony* (Princeton: Princeton University Press, 1988), pp. 12–13.

99. *BLJ*, VIII, pp. 21–2. Byron clung fiercely to his sense of the authenticity of the Troad despite the fact that the place itself, as he attests elsewhere, was disappointing: 'a fine field for conjecture and Snipe-shooting, and a good sportsman and an ingenious scholar may exercise their feet and faculties to great advantage upon the spot', *BLJ*, I, p. 238. The conflation of antiquarianism with traditional aristocratic leisure activity was characteristic of Byron. The Troad itself, even on the spot, offered no direct material aid to imagining what Troy was once like: 'The only vestige of Troy, or her destroyers, are the barrows supposed to contain the carcases of Achilles [,] Antilochus, Ajax &c. but Mt. Ida is still in high feather, though the shepherds are nowadays not much like Ganymede', *BLJ*, I, p. 238. This of course did not mean that the imagination would fail to supply what the place itself was lacking, as with Parnassus.

100. '[W]e *do* care about "the authenticity of the tale of Troy". I have stood upon that plain *daily*, for more than a month, in 1810; and, if any thing diminished my pleasure, it was that the blackguard Bryant had impugned its veracity', *BLJ*, VIII, pp. 21–2. Byron is referring to Jacob Bryant's *Dissertation concerning the war of Troy, and the expedition of the Grecians, as described by Homer; showing that no such expedition was ever udertaken, and that no such city of Phrigia existed* (1796).

101. See John Whale's chapter, 'Romantics, Explorers and Picturesque Travellers', in *The Politics of the Picturesque: Literature, Landscape and Aesthetics since 1770*, ed. by Stephen Copley and Peter Garside (Cambridge: Cambridge University Press, 1994), pp. 175–95. Whale discusses in detail James Bruce's disappointment at discovering the source of the Nile, an account Byron may have been familiar with since 1807.

102. See David Wright's introduction to Trelawny's *Records*, p. 27.

103. *BCPW*, II, p. 280.

104. See for example the lines on 'lonely Athos' (II, 27), or 'Monastic Zitza' (II, 48), or the more general eulogy to Greece: 'Let such approach this consecrated land, / And pass in peace along the magic waste' (II, 93).

105. If this is a play on 'still', then perhaps the same pun is there at the beginning of the poem, again recording Byron's encounter with the 'real Parnassus': 'Yet there I've wander'd by thy vaunted rill; / Yes! sigh'd o'er Delphi's long-deserted shrine, / Where, save that feeble fountain, all is still...'(I,1). 'Still' signifies dead matter *and* surviving matter; that which has survived, or is still there, is frozen or still. This reading would imply that Byron is uncertain whether the 'feeble fountain' is authentic or not.

106. *Recollections*, p. 23. Lord Aberdeen had been named as one of the despoilers of the Parthenon in the early lines (later dropped) for the second canto of *Childe Harold* discussed earlier in this chapter.

107. See, for example, Andrews, *The Search for the Picturesque*, p. 22.

108. *BLJ*, IV, p. 325. 'It is one thing to read the *Iliad* at Sigaeum and on the tumuli, or by the springs with mount Ida above, and the plains and rivers and Archipelago around you: and another to trim your taper over

it in a snug library – *this* I know', *BCPW*, II, p. 310. See also Anne Barton's 1968 Nottingham Byron Lecture *Byron and the Mythology of Fact* (Nottingham: Hawthornes, 1968).

109. *BLJ*, III, pp. 219–20. See also the Dedication to *Don Juan*: 'You're shabby fellows – true – but poets still / And duly seated on the immortal hill'. There may be a pun here on 'still' again as meaning both 'yet' and 'dead'. See also Peter T. Murphy, 'Climbing Parnassus, and Falling Off', in *At the Limits of Romanticism: Essays in Cultural, Feminist, and Materialist Criticism*, ed. by Mary A. Favret and Nicola J. Watson (Bloomington: Indiana University Press, 1994), pp. 40–58.

2   The Spirit and Body of Place: 1812–18

1. *The Works of Sir William Jones*, ed. by Lady Jones, 6 vols (London, 1799), I, p. 4. Since the late 1970s the word 'Orientalism' has of course acquired a different discursive and evaluative meaning to the one it possessed for Lord Byron at the beginning of the nineteenth century. Byron's brief appearances in the book which inaugurated the critique of Orientalism – Edward Said's *Orientalism* (London: Pantheon Books, 1978) – are as someone contributing to and confirming a pre-existent canonicity, in which the word 'Orientalism' stood for 'a separate and unchallenged coherence', a set of ideas about the East which included 'its sensuality, its tendency to despotism, its aberrant mentality, its habits of inaccuracy, its backwardness' (p. 205). Said lists Byron alongside writers such as Beckford, Goethe and Hugo who 'restructured the Orient by their art and made its colours, lights and people visible through their images, rhythms and motifs' (p. 22). The textuality of Said's Orient is clear here (in what sense is the word 'restructured' being used?), but at best Said's sense of Byron's interaction with a real geographical area is one of having been stimulated by local colour into producing cliché: 'At most the "real" Orient provoked a writer to his vision; it very rarely guided it' (p. 22). Marilyn Butler describes the setting of Byron's tales (and other Orientalist writing of the early nineteenth century) as 'exactly or approximately suggesting the Ottoman empire. By approximately, I mean that anything from Greece in the west to Moghul Delhi in the east qualified as Turkish', 'Byron and the Empire in the East', in Andrew Rutherford (ed.), *Byron: Augustan and Romantic* (London: Macmillan, 1990), p. 68. Much has been written on the textuality of the east or the 'Orient-as-text', but see for example Eric Meyer, '"I Know Thee Not, I Loathe Thy Race": Romantic Orientalism in the Eye of the Other', *ELH*, 58 (1991) 657–99, especially 695. For Byron's own early absorption in Orientalist literature see Mohammed Sharafuddin, *Islam and Romantic Orientalism: Literary Encounters with the Orient* (London: I.B. Tauris, 1994), pp. 215–16. The best study of the relation between the tales and British politics is Nigel Leask's *British Romantic Writers and the East* (Cambridge: Cambridge University Press, 1992). Leask is particularly interesting on the sense of Byron's

anxiety or sense of complicity, as I have been describing it, with British imperial power nexi:

> Byron's gaze, fixed like many of his fellow-countrymen on the collapsing fabric of the Ottoman Empire, also turned back reflectively upon his own culture as the world's dominant colonial power, and upon the significance of his own complicity in that power as a poet of orientalism. The pathos of the *Tales* lies in Byron's discovery of the extent to which English (and European) culture had become permeated and corroded by what he regarded as the pernicious influence of imperialism, consistently figured as the abandonment of an aristocratic, republican, civic, human- ist heritage. On a wider scale, Byron sought to elegize the loss of contact of modern European civilization with its classical, Hellenistic source (pp. 23–4).

> See also Daniel Watkins, *Social Relations in Byron's Eastern Tales* (London: Associated University Press, 1987). Watkins argues that the tales 'provide a systematic critique of conventional notions about society and erect a shaky but visible alternative to individualistic perspectives of society. Even if they are not confident in their assessments (as they certainly are not), and even if they do not establish a fully workable position, they offer a rough sketch of new possibilities in social imagination and analysis', p. 20.

2. Saree Makdisi describes the 'two different and mutually-exclusive spatial- temporal constructs' represented by the Levant: 'first, the Levant as the cul- tural and historical ancestor of Europe; and second, the Levant as the space and territory of the Oriental other', *Romantic Imperialism: Universal Empire and the Culture of Modernity* (Cambridge: Cambridge University Press, 1998), p. 127.
3. For all quotations from the texts of the Turkish Tales, and notes, see *BCPW*, III. For this note, see *BCPW*, III, p. 416.
4. *BLJ*, III, pp. 206–7.
5. *BLJ*, III, p. 168. Mohammed Sharafuddin coins the expression 'oriental realism' to describe the 'hard, authentic edge' to Byron's descriptions of the East as they are based in personal knowledge. *Islam and Romantic Orientalism*, pp. 229; 228.
6. *BLJ*, III, p. 58.
7. *BLJ*, III, p. 196.
8. *BLJ*, III, p. 199.
9. Byron wrote to an anxious Moore in December 1813: 'The only advantage I have is being on the spot; and that merely amounts to saving me the trouble of turning over books, which I had better read again. If *your chamber* was furnished in the same way, you have no need to *go there* to describe – I mean only as to *accuracy* – because I drew it from recollection', *BLJ*, III, p. 194.
10. *BLJ*, III, p. 246.
11. *BLJ*, V, p. 262.
12. *BLJ*, V, p. 249.

13. See *BLJ*, III, p. 324. Marilyn Butler has highlighted the ways in which *The Giaour* was written in ideological opposition to Robert Southey's *The Curse of Kehama* (1810), an Oriental poem begun in Portugal and finished in Keswick.

14. See *BCPW*, III, p. 414.

15. *BCPW*, III, p. 423. See also the letter to Edward Daniel Clarke, 15 December 1813: 'I want to show you Lord Sligo's letter to me detailing, as he heard them on the spot, the Athenian account of our adventure (a personal one) which certainly first suggested to me the story of *The Giaour*. It was a strange and not a very long story, and his report of the reports (he arrived just after my departure, and I did not know till last summer that he knew anything of the matter) is not very far from the truth. Don't be alarmed. There was nothing that led further than to the water's edge; but one part (as is often the case in life) was more singular than any of the *Giaour's* adventures. I never have, and never should have, alluded to it on my own authority, from respect to the ancient proverb on Travellers', *BLJ*, III, p. 200.

16. *BLJ*, III, p. 205. Virgil, *Aeneid*, II, 5: 'I myself saw these things in all their horror, and I bore great part in them'.

17. Byron always neglected to mention that a Mr. Ekenhead also swam with him that day and, according to Hobhouse, finished the crossing five minutes faster. See Lord Broughton, John Cam Hobhouse, *Recollections of a Long Life* (London: John Murray, 1909), p. 28.

18. *BCPW*, III, pp. 438–9.

19. This is from the Ravenna journal of 1821, *BLJ*, VIII, pp. 21–2. *Homer Travestied: Being a new translation of the great poet* was an anonymous burlesque of 1720, in fact written by T. Bridges. See also Manfred Korfmann, 'Troy: Topography and Navigation', in Machteld J. Mellink (ed.), *Troy and the Trojan War* (Bryn Mawr: Bryn Mawr College Press, 1986), pp. 1–16.

20. *BCPW*, III, pp. 449–51.

21. *BCPW*, III, pp. 454–6

22. *BCPW*, III, p. 453.

23. *BLJ*, IV, p. 146.

24. On the evening of his visit to the battlefield Byron entered two stanzas (beginning 'Stop! – for thy tread is on an Empire's dust') in an album belonging to Mrs Pryse Gordon, the wife of Byron's guide. Sir Walter Scott had already written some lines from his own poem about Waterloo, *The Field of Waterloo*, in this same album, so that Byron's 'Stop!' should be read as a direct response to Scott, which, when removed from the context of the album, gains a broader resonance. See Simon Bainbridge, *Napoleon and English Romanticism* (Cambridge: Cambridge University Press, 1995), p. 156.

25. *BLJ*, IV, p. 302. Byron later managed to gain more information about the precise circumstances of Howard's death, which he conveyed to Augusta, see *BLJ*, V, p. 70.

26. *BCPW*, II, pp. 302–3.

27. Scott's *The Field of Waterloo* (1815); Robert Southey, *The Poet's Pilgrimage to Waterloo* (1816).

28. *BLJ*, V, p. 76.

29. *BLJ*, V, p. 82.

30. *BCPW*, III, p. 475.

31. *BCPW*, III, p. 492.
32. *BCPW*, II, p. 306.
33. *BCPW*, II, p. 305.
34. *BCPW*, II, p. 305.
35. *BLJ*, V, p. 78.
36. *BCPW*, II, p. 307.
37. *BCPW*, II, p. 309.
38. This mode is at its direst in, for example, 'The Dream', written in July 1816:

> he lived
> Through that which had been death to many men,
> And made him friends of mountains: with the stars
> And the quick Spirit of the Universe
> He held his dialogues; and they did teach
> To him the magic of their mysteries;
> To him the book of Night was opened wide,
> And voices from the deep abyss reveal'd
> A marvel and a secret – Be it so.
>
> (8. ll.193–201) (*BCPW*, IV, p. 29)

Note, however, the seemingly inescapable figure of the open book, and the process of reading, even in this most nature-worshipful of passages.
39. *BLJ*, V, p. 81.
40. *BLJ*, V, p. 82.
41. Edward Duffy has observed the manner in which both Byron and Shelley 'rediscovered a Rousseau very much like themselves' in their separate rehabilitative projects. *Rousseau in England: The Context for Shelley's Critique of the Enlightenment* (Berkeley: University of California Press, 1979), p. 71. Duffy discusses Byron's stanzas in the third canto: 'Admitting all of Rousseau's faults, Byron nonetheless names the man himself "all fire" and the man's purest epiphany the passionate but ideal eroticism of *Julie*. Such a characterization reverses the usual emphasis of English opinion. It acknowledges the tainted life of the man only to exalt further the productions of the poet', p. 73. Gregory Dart argues that Byron is most interested in what Rousseau's style represents: 'transcending the bounds of eighteenth century sentimental narrative, breaking down the conventional barriers existing between writer and reader, [it functions] as an overpoweringly direct and unmediated conduit of libertarian sentiment', *Rousseau, Robespierre and English Romanticism* (Cambridge: Cambridge University Press, 1999), p. 3. This latter account has something in common with the direct and unmediated access to the spirit of place which I am arguing lies at the heart of Byron's critique of Rousseau.
42. As so often in Byron's writing, comparison with a Greek original (the type of authenticity) is used to *confirm* the heightened reality of a non-Greek place. In this case Clarens is the 'ground / Where early Love his Psyche's zone unbound', i.e. Greece. When Rousseau was inspired 'from him came, / As from the Pythian's mystic cave of yore, / Those oracles which set the world in flame' (III.81). Byron had visited the Pythian cave at Delphi, in use as a cattleshed (See previous chapter.)

43. *BCPW*, II, p. 312. Byron's lengthy description of Clarens in the notes to the third canto employ the trope of the consecrated spot in contrast to a Christianized sacred space:

> The hills are covered with vineyards, and interspersed with some small but beautiful woods; one of these was named the 'Bosquet de Julie', and it is remarkable that, though long ago cut down by the brutal selfishness of the monks of St. Bernard (to whom the land appertained), that the ground might be inclosed into a vineyard for the miserable drones of an execrable superstition, the inhabitants of Clarens still point out the spot where its trees stood, calling it by the name which consecrated and survived them. *BCPW*, II, pp. 312–13.

44. Hazlitt, *CWWH*, 20, p. 156.
45. *BLJ*, V, pp. 208–9.
46. *The Autobiography of Edward Gibbon*, ed. by Oliphant Smeaton (London: J.M. Dent, 1911), p. 166 *BLJ*, V, p. 81.
47. *BLJ*, V, p. 91.
48. *BLJ*, V, p. 114.
49. *BLJ*, V, p. 115.
50. *BLJ*, V, p. 123.
51. *BLJ*, V, p. 118. The text, in Marchand's appendix, is given as the 'American Art Assoc. Cat., Nov. 7, 1934' (*BLJ*, V, p. 286). The quotation is from Pope's *The Rape of the Lock*, II, l.28: 'And beauty draws us with a single hair'.
52. Byron's note records: 'In the cells are seven pillars, or, rather, eight, one being half-merged in the wall; in some of these are rings for the fetters and the fettered: in the pavement the steps of Bonnivard have left their traces – he was confined here several years', *BCPW*, IV, p. 452.
53. See, for example, the letter to Annabella Milbanke, 12 February 1814, *BLJ*, IV, p. 54.
54. See, for example, the letter to Hobhouse, 8 February 1816, and the letter to Samuel Rogers written on the same day, *BLJ*, V, pp. 24–5.
55. *BLJ*, V, p. 92.
56. *BLJ*, V, p. 98.
57. *BLJ*, V, p. 97.
58. *BLJ*, V, p. 108.
59. See *BLJ*, V, p. 99.
60. Letter to Moore, 25 March 1817, *BLJ*, V, p. 188. Proof B: Byron's MS. note in margin reads: 'With regard to the "pastoral life" of the Alps – there is but little – I reserve that some day or other – for another subject', *BCPW*, IV, p. 472.
61. *BCPW*, IV, p. 466. The invocation of the place-spirits in the first scene of the dramatic poem are of spirits of the 'Earth, ocean, air, night, mountains, winds, thy star...' (I.i.l.132); in other words, of the natural world rather than of any specific place. The actual scene-settings of the dramatic poem are worth listing to gain some sense of the way in which the Alps are there as *mode*: I.i. 'A Gothic Gallery', I.ii. 'The Mountain of the Jungfrau'; II.i. 'A Cottage amongst the Bernese Alps'; II.ii. 'A Lower Valley in the Alps. – A Cataract'; II.iii. 'The Summit of the Jungfrau Mountain'; II.iv. 'The Hall of

Arimanes'; III.i. 'A Hall in the Castle of Manfred'; III.ii. 'Another Chamber'; III.iii. 'The Mountains – The Castle of Manfred at some distance'; III.iv. 'Interior of the Tower'.

62. *BLJ*, V, p. 170.
63. *BLJ*, V, p. 165.
64. *BLJ*, V, p. 188. See also letter to Kinnaird, p. 196.
65. *BLJ*, V, pp. 104–5.
66. *BCPW*, IV, p. 116.
67. Letter to Moore, 11/4/17, *BLJ*, V, p. 211.
68. *BLJ*, V, p. 217. Byron sent Augusta a specimen of the Italian poet Monti's handwriting from Milan on 26 October 1816. *BLJ*, V, pp. 118–19.
69. Hobhouse, *Historical Illustrations of the Fourth Canto of Childe Harold's Pilgrimage* (London: John Murray, 1818), pp. 5–6.
70. Hobhouse, *Illustrations*, p. 27.
71. See, for example, the letters to Kinnaird, *BLJ*, V, pp. 226; 230; 247; and the letter to John Hanson, p. 236.
72. *BCPW*, II, p. 121.
73. 'I must confess I feel an affection for it [the fourth canto] more than ordinary, as part of it was begot, as it were, under my own eyes; for although your poets are as shy as elephants or camels of being seen in the act of procreation yet I have not infrequently witnessed his lordship's coupleting and some of the stanzas owe their birth to our morning walk or evening ride at La Mira', Michael Joyce, *My Friend H* (London, 1948), pp. 112–13, cited in Andrew Rutherford, 'The Influence of Hobhouse on *Childe Harold's Pilgrimage*, Canto IV', *Review of English Studies*, 12 (1961) 391–7; 391.
74. Rutherford, 39. From Hobhouse's *Italy: Remarks Made in Several Visits From the Year 1816 to 1854* (London, 1859), I.iv.
75. *BCPW*, II, p. 231.
76. *BCPW*, II, p. 233. Hobhouse's notes outline the exact topography of the battle-plains of Thrasimene, where Hannibal and the Carthaginians had defeated the Romans under Flaminius in 217 BC, and give a further example of tutelary guardianship: 'The second [rivulet], about a quarter of a mile further on, is called the "bloody rivulet", and the peasants point out an open spot to the left between the "Sanguinetto" and the hills, which, they say, was the principal scene of slaughter. ...Every district of Italy has its hero. In the north some painter is the usual genius of the place, and the foreign Julio Romano more than divides Mantua with her native Virgil. To the south we hear of Roman names. Near Thrasimene tradition is still faithful to the fame of an enemy, and Hannibal the Carthaginian is the only ancient name remembered on the banks of the Perugian lake. Flaminius is unknown; but the postilions on that road have been taught to show the very spot where *il Console romano* was slain', *BCPW*, II, p. 247.
77. Byron's note, *BCPW*, II, p. 234.
78. Byron's note is from the second canto of *Childe Harold*. *BCPW*, II, p. 189.
79. *BCPW*, II, p. 253. Hobhouse, who was Byron's guide through Rome, may have been one of the few whose 'belief' could be satisfied by what they saw, since according to Byron his friend had 'more real knowledge of Rome & its environs than any Englishman – who has been there since Gibbon'. Letter to Murray, *BLJ*, V, p. 263.

80. Hobhouse quotes a lengthy passage from Sir William Drummond's *Academical Questions* (1805), I, pp. xiv–xv: 'I trust, whatever may be the fate of my own speculations, that philosophy will regain that estimation which it ought to possess. The free and philosophic spirit of our nation has been the theme of admiration to the world. This was the proud distinction of Englishmen and the luminous source of all their glory', *BCPW*, II, p. 256. The Miltonic–Satanic boast of the mind being its own place very quickly shades into a patriotic boast for England being the particular place of liberty.

81. *BCPW*, II, pp. 253–4. Peter J. Manning, for example, suggests that 'gladiatorial combat is the paradigm of Byron's view of history as an infinite series of "second falls" caused by "vile Ambition", and the motives of self-regarding pride and hyperassertive will he discerns in history are congruent with his own oedipal resentments', *Byron and His Fictions* (Detroit: Wayne State University Press, 1978), p. 92. See also Bernard Beatty, 'Byron and the Paradoxes of Nationalism', *Literature and Nationalism*, ed. by Vincent Newey and Ann Thompson (Liverpool: Liverpool University Press, 1991), pp. 152–62.

82. *BCPW*, II, pp. 249–50. McGann comments: 'It may be of Pompey, but was not the statue at whose base Caesar was killed' (p. 330). Hobhouse expends enormous energy in discussing the different kinds of authenticites in this, and very many other disputed examples, such as Juvenal's topography; the Egerian grotto; Horace's 'ustica'; the site of Cicero's villa; the statue of the Capitoline wolf.

83. 'Moreover, Pius V. used to say, that he who wanted relics should take some earth from the arena, which was cemented with so much holy blood: and Cardinal Uderic Carpegna always stopped his coach opposite the Coliseum, and repeated the names of all the martyrs who had been sacrificed in that spot', *Historical Illustrations*, p. 281.

3   Translation: 1818–21

1. *BCPW*, IV, p. 129; see commentary p. 485. Ayscough's note comes from *The Dramatic Works of William Shakespeare, with Explanatory Notes, by Samuel Ayscough* (1807). Byron substitutes 'dissoluteness' for Ayscough's 'licentiousness'.

2. See, for example, *BLJ*, VI, pp. 23; 43–4; 65–6; 168; 192; 205; *BLJ*, VII, p. 25.

3. For Byron's own sexual profligacy during this period, see, for example, the letter to Hobhouse and Kinnaird of 19 January 1819, *BLJ*, VI, p. 92.

4. *BLJ*, VI, p. 192; p. 205.

5. *BLJ*, VI, p. 205. At the end of August 1820 Byron was sending Murray copies of an actual letter written by Count Guiccioli to his brother-in-law, concerning Byron's affair with his wife. '*You* want to know *Italy*', Byron tells Murray; '– there's more than Lady Morgan can tell me – in these sheets if carefully perused', *BLJ*, VII, p. 165.

6. See for example *BLJ*, VII, pp. 183–4 on travel-writing on Italy, such as Miss Jane Waldie's *Sketches Descriptive of Italy*: 'These fools will force me to write a book about Italy myself to give them "the loud lie".'

7. Donald H. Reiman, 'Countess Guiccioli's Byron', *Shelley and His Circle, 1773–1822*, ed. by K.N. Cameron, Donald H. Reiman, and Doucet D. Fischer, 8 vols (Cambridge, Mass.: 1961–86), VII, p. 378. [Hereafter, *SC*.] For an account of Teresa Guiccioli's liberal education, see *SC*, VII, pp. 378–80.

8. *His Very Self and Voice: Collected Conversations of Lord Byron*, ed. by Ernest J. Lovell, Jr (New York: Macmillan, 1954), pp. 247–8.

9. *SC*, VII, p. 398.

10. Lovell, p. 250. Teresa had read *Don Juan* in a French translation, and had immediately disliked it. In a letter to Murray dated 6 July 1821 Byron explains her antipathy as 'the wish of all women to exalt the *sentiment* of the passions', *BLJ*, VIII, pp. 147–8. A letter to Murray of 25 December 1822 defends *Don Juan* against the charge of being potentially corrupting : 'No girl will ever be seduced by reading DJ – no – no – she will go to Little's poems – & Rousseau's romans – for that – or even to the immaculate De Staël—they will encourage – & not the Don – who laughs at that.' *BLJ*, X, p. 68. Byron's 'Observations upon Observations of the Revd W.L.B.&^{c}&^{c}&$^{c'}$', makes the same point: 'The Sentimental Anatomy – of Rousseau & Mad.^{e} de. S. – are far more formidable than any quantity of verse.—They are so – because they sap the principles – by *reasoning* upon the *passions* – whereas poetry is in itself passion – and does not systematize', *CMP*, pp. 178–9. Lady Blessington's memoir has a long passage recording Byron's feelings about *Corinne*, including his claim to have told Madame De Staël in person that the book would 'be considered, if not cited, as an excuse for violent *passions*, by all young ladies with imaginations *exalté*, and that she had much to answer for', Ernest J. Lovell (ed.), *Lady Blessington: Conversations of Lord Byron* (Princeton: Princeton University Press, 1969), pp. 25–7. As time passed, *Corinne* became something of a bone of contention between Byron and Teresa. In August 1821, for example, Byron is wearily reassuring Teresa of his continued love for her: 'Senza tradurre tante pagine di "Corinna" – nè sforzare tanta apparanza del' romanesco – ti assicuro che ti amo come t'ho sempre amato'. ['Without translating so many pages of *Corinne*, or forcing so great a semblance of romance, I assure you that I love you as I always have loved you.'] The letter continues: 'But in eloquence I give way to you for two reasons – firstly, I don't know the language – secondly, too many words are always suspect – the great *preachers* of exaggerated sentiment limit the practice of their maxims to their pulpit; – true love says little', *BLJ*, VIII, p. 170. Sorting through Teresa's letters in September 1821, Byron comments: 'It has cost me two hours to put in order the archives of your Excellency's letters – being at least five hundred; a full translation of *Corinne* – i.e. *The Gossip*, the romance of Her Excellency Our Lady Countess Gaspara Dominica Teresa Guiccioli, born Gamba Ghiselli and Respected Gossip', *BLJ*, VIII, p. 213. In October 1821 Byron is criticising Teresa's epistolary style: 'And do not exaggerate with that turgid epistolar imagination of Santa Chiara – (blessed be the Convent) the most simple and necessary things into evil and wrongs, etc, etc, which do not exist except in your romanesque or rather *romantic* head. For it upsets all the rules of thought in order to behave *à la De Staël*', *BLJ*, VIII, p. 242.

11. *BLJ*, VI, pp. 215–16. On the same day, and in the same copy of *Corinne*, Byron also wrote the following marginalia note: 'I knew Madame de Staël

well – better than She knew Italy; – but I little thought that one day I should think with her thoughts in the country where she has laid the scene of her most attractive production. – She is sometimes right and often wrong about Italy and England – but almost always true in delineating the heart, which is of but one nation and of no country or rather of all', *CMP*, pp. 223–4.

12. Reiman discusses the influence of Teresa's Santa Chiara education and her reading of novels such as *Corinne* upon her letter-writing style. *SC*, VII, p. 388. He notes: 'how seldom laughter and irony – so prominent in most of Byron's correspondence – temper the romantic sentiment of his early letters to Teresa Guiccioli' (p. 598). Peter Vassallo comments: 'The remarkable thing about these letters in Italian is that Byron allowed himself to be influenced by the native effusiveness of the Italian amatory style', *Byron: The Italian Literary Influence* (London: Macmillan, 1984), p. 40.

13. *BLJ*, VI, p. 206. 'The whole affair could be presented in the manner of the Goldonian comedy – with the audience's sympathy focused on the two lovers, and with Count Guiccioli (the avaricious, calculating husband) as the villain, Fanny Silvistrini as the obliging confidante, Count Ruggero as the noble father, and Pietro as the young gallant. Even the minor parts could be allotted – the venal priest, the maid, the Moorish page-boy – and, in the pine forest of Ravenna, the chorus of conspirators', Iris Origo, *The Last Attachment* (New York: Charles Scribner's Sons, 1949), p. 8. Reiman uses the term 'refamiliarization' to describe Byron's experience as a *cavalier servente*, 'where Teresa Guiccioli played his mother-mistress, while Count Ruggero and Pietra Gamba became his first sympathetic father and admiring younger brother...he entered for the first time in his maturity into a familial relationship with her and the Gamba clan and found himself *within* Italian society, with his Mediterranean "other" now a part of his newly assumed identity', 'Byron and the Uses of Refamiliarization', Alice Levine and Robert N. Keane, *Essays Selected From Hofstra University's Byron Bicentennial Conference* (New York: Hofstra University Press, 1993), pp. 101; 108. Reiman's emphasis on reintegration and psycho-sexual healing is slightly different from my own, which emphasises the strangeness of this process. Reiman also observes, however, the ways in which Teresa 'enculturated' Byron 'in the ways of her region' (109).

14. *BLJ*, VI, p. 239.

15. *BLJ*, VII, pp. 42–3.

16. *BLJ*, VII, p. 138.

17. *BLJ*, VI, p. 226. On Byron's ambivalence about his role as *cavalier servente*, Teresa herself commented: 'One would almost have thought that he was a little ashamed – that in showing himself kind he was making an avowal of weakness and being deficient in that virility of soul which he admired so much.' This is quoted and translated from Teresa's *La Vie* by Iris Origo, *The Last Attachment*, p. 147.

18. *BLJ*, VII, p. 28. See also the letter to Hobhouse, 3 March 1820, *BLJ*, VII, p. 51.

19. *BLJ*, VIII, p. 78.

20. Mobility (or *mobilité*) is a crucial concept in Byron's writing, especially his later writing, and is related to what I have been describing as 'interchangeability', as well as translatability. For a discussion of Byron's and De Staël's

separate interest in mobility, see Joanne Wilkes, *Lord Byron and Madame De Staël* (Aldershot: Ashgate, 1999). The best general discussion of the subject is to be found in J.J. McGann, *The Beauty of Inflections: Literary Investigations in Historical Method and Theory* (Oxford: Clarendon Press, 1985), pp. 272–4. McGann makes the important point that the concept represents a 'structure of social relations and not simply a psychological characteristic' (p. 273).

21. See, for example, the Ravenna Journal, 5 January 1821, *BLJ*, VIII, p. 14.
22. More is made of Wordsworth's untranslatability in the rejected dedication of *Marino Faliero* to Goethe which I discuss below. Writing to Hodgson in May 1821, Byron observes of the comparative merits of the living poets: 'There is but one of your "tests" which is not infallible: Translation', *BLJ*, VIII, p. 114.
23. R.L. Brett and A.R. Jones (eds), *Wordsworth and Coleridge: Lyrical Ballads* (London: Routledge, 1991), p. 288.
24. McGann has drawn attention to the connection between *mobilité* and apostasy: 'It is mildly shocking, but quite necessary, to understand that the dark shadow cast by the mobility of the spontaneous Romantic poet is called (in *Don Juan*) Robert Southey, and sometimes William Wordsworth', McGann, *Beauty of Inflections*, p. 274. I will have more to say about apostasy in the following chapter.
25. *BLJ*, VII, p. 208; see also the letter to Augusta, 30 November 1820, *BLJ*, VII, p. 239. See also *Some Observations on an Article in Blackwood's Edinburgh Magazine* (1820), in *CMP*, p. 93.
26. Letter to Douglas Kinnaird, 24 April 1819, *BLJ*, VI, p. 115: 'She is a sort of an Italian Caroline Lamb, except that She is much prettier, and not so savage. – But She has the same red-hot head – the same noble dis*dain* of public opinion – with the superstructure of all that Italy can add to such natural dispositions.' See also the letter of 28 November 1819 to Augusta Leigh, *BLJ*, VI, p. 248: 'But the Guiccioli was romantic – and had read "*Corinna*" – in short she was a kind of Italian Caroline Lamb – but very pretty and gentle – at least to me.'
27. *CMP*, pp. 77–8.
28. During this period Byron is repeatedly urging Lady Byron to promise to teach Ada Italian when she is old enough. See, for example, *BLJ*, VII, p. 211. Allegra, Byron's child by Claire Clairmont, already seemed to be developing an Anglo-Italian hybridity: 'She is English – but speaks nothing but Venetian – "Bon *di Papa*" &c&c', *BLJ*, VI, p. 223. Byron was himself teaching Teresa French during this period. See, for example, *BLJ*, VII, p. 38. It is a poignant irony that Byron's last ever letter to Teresa Guiccioli of 17 March 1824 is in fact written in English: 'I write to you in English without apologies – as you say you have become a great proficient in that language of birds. — To the English and Greeks – I generally write in Italian – from a Spirit of contradiction, I suppose – and to show that I am Italianized by my long stay in your Climate', *BLJ*, XI, p. 137.
29. Occasionally parts of Byron's letters to Teresa would resemble an entirely private language, as they employed a secret code. See, for example, *BLJ*, VII, p. 26.
30. *BCPW*, IV, p. 214.

31. 'Transplantation' is the term Timothy Webb uses, *The Violet in the Crucible: Shelley and Translation* (Oxford: Clarendon Press, 1976), p. 326. See also Drummond Bone, 'On "Influence", and on Byron's and Shelley's Use of Terza Rima in 1819', *K-SMB*, 32 (1981) 38–48. Shelley's other experiments in *terza rima* include, of course, *The Triumph of Life* (1822), 'The Tower of Famine' (1821); a fragment, 'The false laurel and the True' (1821/22?); 'The Woodman and the Nightingale' (1821); and two translations from Virgil in *terza rima* (See Webb, pp. 329–36.)

32. In this respect Byron's method belongs to translation theories which emphasise the participation of the translation in the after-life (Benjamin's 'überleben', for example), of the source text, interpreting that text in the light of its reception history. Byron perhaps goes even further in that his translation (or imitation) purports to bring out prophetic elements latent within the original text. See Lawrence Venuti (ed.), *The Translation Studies Reader* (London and New York: Routledge, 2000), p. 11.

33. See, for example, the letter of 28 February 1818 to Hoppner, *BLJ*, VI, p. 15.

34. *BLJ*, VI, p. 15.

35. See *BLJ*, VI, p. 42. Byron seems to have believed that the Italian language, like the country itself, could provide a refuge from his own literary fame – a place where he would not be followed. This was certainly not to be the case. Byron's attitude to Leoni, however, altered over the course of the next two years as he became aware of the persecution his translator had received at the hands of the authorities, for his version of the fourth canto. See, for example, the letter to Murray of 8 May 1820 describing Leoni's persecution, and quoting an extract from Leoni himself, in Italian (*BLJ*, VII, p. 97). Leoni's fate further accelerated Byron's involvement in Italian politics, and marked the beginning of his journey into the interior of Italian society. This is coincident and bound up with the beginnings of Byron's imitations of Italian poetic models, and his own translations from Italian. A short poem in rhyming couplets of 1818 ('E Nihilo Nihil; or an Epigram Bewitched') is a facetious commentary on his own translation history to that date, directly mapping such a history alongside a change in his own poetic models: 'For *my* part, all men must allow/ Whate'er I was – I'm classic now – / I saw & left my fault in time' [*BCPW*, IV, pp. 208–9.]. Byron's increasing militancy in the classic/ romantic debate, which would eventually manifest itself in his ferocious entry into the Bowles/Pope controversy is a process wholly involved with his own acculturation during these years. Byron was also very conscious of the fierce debate in Italian literary circles prompted by the essay on contemporary Italian literature (co-written by Foscolo) which appeared in Hobhouse's notes to the fourth canto of *Childe Harold*. See *BLJ*, VI, pp. 51; 90; 96.

36. *BLJ*, VII, p. 104. See also pp. 127; 201.

37. *BLJ*, VII, pp. 201; 207. During this same period German interest in Byron began to come to his attention. See, for example, *BLJ*, VII, pp. 106; 113; 203. Again his response seems to have been bewilderment, particularly as he had a very limited knowledge of German literature: 'what have *I* to do with Germany or Germans neither my subjects nor my language having anything in common with that Country?' (*BLJ*, VIII, pp. 166–7).

Nevertheless, the fact that he had been translated into German was not only the source of some pride for him, but is used against Wordsworth in particular, in the abandoned dedication to Goethe written for *Marino Faliero* (1821) (see below).

38. See Vassallo, pp. 147–8. Byron wrote to John Murray in February 1820: 'I think my translation of Pulci will make you stare – it must be put by the original stanza for stanza and verse for verse – and you will see what was permitted in a Catholic country and a bigotted age to a Churchman on the score of religion', *BLJ*, VII, p. 35.

39. *BLJ*, VII, p. 39.

40. *BCPW*, IV, p. 248.

41. Letter to Murray 21/2/1820, *BLJ*, VII, p. 42.

42. *BLJ*, VII, p. 54; see also the letter to John Murray of 1 March 1820, *BLJ*, VII, p. 47.

43. *BCPW*, IV, p. 248.

44. The limited reputations Wordsworth and Southey had in a broader European context which was a central joke in the preface to *Don Juan*, were recycled in the dedication to Goethe of *Marino Faliero* (eventually dropped): 'It is owing to this neglect on the part of your German translators that you are not aware of the works of William Wordsworth – who has a baronet in London who draws him <front> frontispieces and leads him about to dinners and to the play; and a Lord in the country who gave him a place in the Excise – and <a pla> a cover at his table...There is also another – named Southey – who is more than a poet – being actually poet *Laureate* – a post which corresponds with <that of what> what we call in Italy '*Poeta Cesareo*' and which you call in German – I know not what – but as you have a 'Caesar' probably you have a name for it...they form but two bricks of our <poetical> Babel – (*Windsor* bricks by the way) but may serve for a Specimen of the building', *BCPW*, IV, p. 545.

45. *BLJ*, VII, p. 150; p. 182; VIII, p. 65; XI, p. 118. A letter to Murray of 12 September 1821 describes the Pulci translation as 'the very best thing I ever wrote', *BLJ*, VIII, p. 206.

46. See Frederick L. Beaty, 'Byron and the Story of Francesca da Rimini', *PMLA*, 75 (1960) 395–401. Byron and Hobhouse had briefly collaborated on a translation of Silvio Pellico's tragedy *Francesca da Rimini* in Milan 1816 (Byron's contribution probably being confined to the first act). Pellico would later translate *Manfred* into Italian. See N.R. Havely, 'Francesca Frustrated: New Evidence about Hobhouse's and Byron's Translation of Pellico's *Francesca da Rimini*', *Romanticism*, 1:1 (1995) 106–20. Byron planned to write a five-act tragedy based on the story of Francesca, and had visited Rimini in 1819 to try to gather information about the historical Francesca for Leigh Hunt, but had been unable to find anything. Typically though he had observed that Hunt had made a 'sad mistake' in his description of Ravenna in *The Story of Rimini*, and Byron was able to correct Hunt's topography, having observed the facts himself: 'about "old Ravenna's *clear-shewn towers* and *bay*" the city Lies so low that you must be close upon it before it is "shewn" at all – and the sea had retired *four miles* at least, long before Francesca was born – and as far back as the Exarchs and Emperors', *BLJ*, VI, p. 181.

47. 'The terms of fidelity used in discussions of translation may differ (whether it is the spirit or the letter that one must serve, whether it is best to be servile before the original or to dominate it as one would a captive slave), but the marked term is usually gendered female. Thus, theories of translation have been peopled, metaphorically, with chaste maidens, mistresses, and unfaithful lovers. Translators have worried that the process of translation may violate the purity of the mother tongue, and that bastards may be bred. Translators have worried equally over the virility of the original, and the complaint is frequently that the original has been emasculated. The act of translation has been compared to sex, and to rape.' Lori Chamberlain, 'Gender Metaphorics in Translation', in *Encyclopaedia of Translation Studies*, ed. by Mona Baker (London and New York: Routledge, 1998), p. 94. See also Edwin Gentzler, who writes of 'the epistemological strait-jacket that the power of the original text retains over the translation...[in the] ideal of a "faithful" version', *Contemporary Translation Theories* (London and New York: Routledge, 1993), p. 144.

48. *BLJ*, VII, p. 58. Byron tried to find a publisher in England for John Taafe's translation and commentary on Dante, even though he privately thought of the former as a 'traduction' (See the letter to Moore, *BLJ*, IX, p. 63.)

49. *BCPW*, IV, pp. 280–5. For the textual history of the translation, see McGann, *BCPW*, IV, pp. 514–17.

50. The bracketed translations are those of John D. Sinclair, *Dante: The Divine Comedy: Inferno* (Oxford: Oxford University Press, 1961), p. 79. During a domestic quarrel with Teresa in October 1820, Byron had accused her servant Fanny of spying on him. Fanny's letter of self-defence prompted Byron to recall Francesca's contempt for the author of the story of Lancilot: 'La lettera della F[anni] è un'ritratto del'carattere di quella "Galeotta che la scrisse,"* – Falsa – furba – arrogante – venale – pedantesca – adulante – bugiarda', *BLJ*, VII, p. 209. * 'the procuress [Galeotto] who wrote it', *Inferno*, 5, l.137.

51. The first six lines of stanza 108 of the third canto of *Don Juan* are a translation of the famous opening to the eighth canto of Dante's *Purgatorio* ('era gia l'ora che volge il disio / ai navicanti'). The subject is separation, wandering, homesickness.

52. *BLJ*, VII, p. 170.

53. *BLJ*, VI, pp. 236; 226.

54. *BLJ*, VI, p. 183.

55. *BLJ*, VI, p. 244.

56. *BLJ*, VI, p. 262.

57. See the letter to Murray from Ravenna 21 February 1820, *BLJ*, VII, pp. 42–3. Writing to Murray in September 1820 to pour scorn on the evidence gathered against Queen Caroline in Italy (which the Italians had informed Byron could be bought at no great price), Byron draws a distinction between his kind of insider-knowledge, and the information reported by travellers: 'as to what travellers report – *what are travellers?* – now I have *lived* among the Italians – not *Florenced* and *Romed* – and Galleried – and Conversationed it for a few months – and then home again – but been of their families – and friendships and feuds – and loves – and councils – and correspondence in a part of Italy least known to foreigners – and have been amongst them of all classes – from the Conte to the Contadino – and you may be sure of what I say to you', *BLJ*, VII, p. 180.

58. *BLJ*, VI, pp. 147–8. In a letter to Murray of October 1820 Byron recounts a story of an 1810 doppleganger. *BLJ*, VII, p. 192.
59. *BLJ*, VII, pp. 207–8.
60. By late December 1820 Byron is writing to Francis Hodgson: 'what I have been doing would but little interest you, as it regards another country and another people, & would be almost speaking another language, for my own is not quite so familiar to me as it used to be', *BLJ*, VII, p. 253. This claim to have become less articulate in English is repeated in letters during this period, and is sometimes accompanied with the declared intention of giving up writing in English altogether and producing future work in Italian. See for example, *BLJ*, VI, p. 105.
61. Letter to Augusta, *BLJ*, VI, p. 229.
62. Letter to Hobhouse, *BLJ*, VII, p. 81. See also the letter to Hobhouse, 11 May 1819, *BLJ*, VII, p. 99.
63. A letter to Douglas Kinnaird of April 1820 expresses Byron's sense of in-betweenness and uncertainty: 'I sometimes think of going to England after the Coronation, and sometimes not, – I have no thoughts at least no wish – of coming before – & not much after, but I am very undecided & uncertain, & have quite lost all *local* feeling for England without having acquired any *local* attachment for any other spot, except in the occasional admiration of fine landscapes – & goodly cities', *BLJ*, VII, p. 86.
64. *BLJ*, VII, p. 187: 'Un'Inglese – amico della Libertà – avendo sentito che i Napolitani permettono anche ai stranieri di contribuire all buona causa – bramerebbe l'onore di aver' accettata l'offerta di mille Luigi – la quale egli azzarda di fare.' ['An Englishman, a friend to Liberty, having understood that the Neapolitans permit even foreignors to contribute to the good cause, is desirous that they should do him the honour of accepting a thousand louis, which he takes the liberty of offering.'] (Moore's translation).
65. *BLJ*, VII, p. 76. Byron's interesting use of the word 'inoculation' to mean, not to be strengthened against, but to have been introduced *into*, in the sense of cross-fertilisation, implantation, or acculturation, may have derived from an anecdote of Grimm's about Louis XV. Grimm's review of the *Memoirs of the History, Sciences, Arts, Manners, Usages &c. of the Chinese; by the Missionaries of Peking* records a conversation between Louis XV and M. Bertin about the best way to re-shape and strengthen the French nation. Bertin's advice is this: '"*Sire, it is to inoculate the French with the Chinese character.*"' Andrew Nicholson has suggested that Byron read this review in Grimm's and Diderot's *Correspondence Litteraire*, and that it may have influenced his short anti-travel prose fragment, 'Italy', or not *Corinna'* (1820). See *CMP*, pp. 85–7; 357–8.
66. See, for example, *BLJ*, VII, pp. 77; 136; 155; 172.
67. See, for example, *BLJ*, VII, p. 205: 'Now is a good time for the Prophecy of Dante; – Events have acted as an Advertisement thereto. – Egad – I think I am as good a vates (prophet videlicet) as Fitzgerald of the Morning Post.'
68. Writing to Murray in September 1820:

> I suspect that in Marino Faliero you and yours won't like the *politics* which are perilous to you in these times – but recollect that it is *not* a *political* play & that I was obliged to put into the mouths of the

Characters the sentiments upon which they acted. – I hate all things written like Pizarro to represent france [sic] England & so forth – all I have done is meant to be purely Venetian – even to the very prophecy of its present state.

BLJ, VII, p. 184. This is partly to appease Murray, although Byron's sense of being faithful to the Venetian context (as I shall argue) is an important one. Nevertheless, the play interacts with contemporary political events in England in extremely suggestive ways. As John Kerrigan observes: 'The politics of *Marino Faliero* interact so richly with the events of that year that it is hard to determine which factors stimulated, and which merely lent significance to, the evolving text of a play which had been on Byron's mind since 1817', 'Revolution, Revenge, and Romantic Tragedy', *Romanticism*, 1:1 (1995) 121–40; 121.

69. *BCPW*, IV, p. 548.
70. *BCPW*, IV, p. 301; p. 539.
71. *BCPW*, IV, p. 541. It was during this period that the Pope granted Teresa permission to separate from her husband.
72. *BCPW*, IV, p. 302. In the first scene of the fifth act when Angiolina addresses the Council of Ten and responds to Steno's public apology, she puts this passage into verse.
73. See note 57, and *BLJ*, VII, pp. 42–3.
74. *BLJ*, VII, p. 175. The preface to the play observes that 'whether I have succeeded or not in the tragedy, I have at least transferred to our language an historical fact worthy of commemoration'. Writing to Hodgson in May 1821, Byron informs him: 'I have just published a drama, which is at least good English – I presume – for Gifford lays great stress on the purity of its diction', *BLJ*, VIII, p. 114.
75. *BLJ*, VII, p. 194–5.
76. An entry in the Ravenna journal makes a connection between the 'bastardy' of the Italian language, and their ability as translators: 'they are the very worst of translators, except from the Classics – Annibale Caro, for instance – and *there*, the bastardy of their language helps them, as, by way of *looking legitimate*, they ape their fathers' tongue', *BLJ*, VIII, p. 25.
77. Letter to Teresa, 24 July 1820, *BLJ*, VII, pp. 140–1. See also *Don Juan*, V, 61.
78. Letter to Moore, 5 November 1820, *BLJ*, VII, p. 220. Byron repeats the joke in a letter to Douglas Kinnaird of 9 November 1820: 'I see that her Majesty the *Queen* is likely to triumph over her Tory opponents. — It is a good thing in more ways than one – and the reading of the Evidence will greatly multiply our stock of Grandchildren', *BLJ*, VII, p. 220.
79. *BLJ*, VII, p. 237.
80. *BLJ*, VII, p. 255.
81. *BLJ*, VIII, pp. 87; 192. Byron uses the centaur figure again in canto fourteen to describe the curious mix of the sensual and the sentimental often found in love, certainly in his relationship withTeresa: 'But both together form a kind of centaur, / Upon whose back 'tis better not to venture.' (XIV.73)
82. The etymological root of 'centaur' is 'poke-wind', as the horse-men are traditionally said to have been the offspring of Ixion and a cloud. I am suggesting a semantic train of association rather than a pun. Interestingly,

the word 'chevalier' is almost always used by Byron in an ironic or tongue-in-cheek way, usually as a means of ridiculing quixotic aristocratic figures and very often as part of a compound such as 'preux-chevalier', or as Byron describes the luckless Wedderburn Webster to Lady Hardy, a 'Chevalier errant', *BLJ*, X, p. 101. Reiman discusses an unpublished memorandum entitled 'Some recollections of my acquaintance with Madame De Staël' dated from Ravenna 1821, in which Byron responds to the news he had just received that August Wilhelm von Schlegel was planning to write a hostile article against him. In it Schlegel is referred to as the 'Chevalier–Professor'. Reiman, 'Byron and the Uses of Refamiliarisation', p. 116.

83. George Steiner, *After Babel* (Oxford: Oxford University Press, 3rd edn; 1998), p. 332.

84. Jacques Derrida, *Monolingualism of the Other, or The Prothesis of Origin*, translated by Patrick Mensah (Stanford: Stanford University Press, 1998), p. 57.

4   Nostalgia, 1821–24

1. McGann describes 'that large recollective writing project, which B opened in July 1818 when he began both *DJ* and his *Memoirs*. His letters and Journals of 1821–2 demonstrate an increasing turn to memorial materials, and *DJ* itself would eventually culminate in the "English cantos"', *BCPW*, VI, p. 665.

2. See, for example, *BLJ*, VIII, p. 226. Donald Reiman talks of Byron's 'rapprochement in 1821–23 with his national heritage'. 'Byron and the Uses of Refamiliarisation', p. 102.

3. The poem beginning 'Oh! Talk not to me of a name great in story / The days of our Youth, are the days of our Glory' appears in 'Detached Thoughts', dated 'Pisa Novr. 6th. 1821'. See *BLJ*, IX, p. 51.

4. Byron's Journal of 14 November 1813–19 April 1814 records an evening dining with 'Rogers, – Mackintosh, Sheridan, Sharpe', in which there was much talk 'of old times – Horne Tooke – the Trials – evidence of Sheridan, and anecdotes of those times when *I*, alas! Was an infant', *BLJ*, III, pp. 248–9. A letter to Samuel Rogers, whom Byron thought of as himself belonging to the 'old school', from Ravenna in October 1821, looks back in sorrow at the deaths of Lady Melbourne, Grattan, Sheridan and Curran, 'almost every body of much name of the old School', *BLJ*, VIII, p. 246.

5. See Asa Briggs, *The Age of Improvement: 1783–1867* (London: Longmans, 1959), p. 150.

6. *CMP*, pp. 184–5.

7. In a letter to Hobhouse from Pisa in May 1821, Byron observes: 'As to Johnson and Pope – surely *your* admiration cannot surpass *mine* of them – and had they lived now – I would not have published a line of anything I have ever written', *BLJ*, IX, p. 68. Byron frequently records his opinion that the it was a 'great error to suppose the *present* a *high* age of English poetry', *BLJ*, VIII, p. 200. See also, for example, the entry in 'Detached Thoughts': 'One of my notions different from my contemporaries is, that the present is

not a high age of English poetry', *BLJ*, IX, p. 35. In the 'Letter to John Murray Esqre' (1821), Byron's intervention in the Bowles/Pope controversy, he reiterates this sentiment:

> I have loved and honoured the fame and name of that illustrious and unrivalled man [i.e. Alexander Pope] – far more than my own paltry renown – and the trashy Jingle of the crowd of "Schools" and upstarts – who pretend to rival – or even surpass him. – Sooner than a single leaf should be torn from his laurel – it were better that all which these men – and that I as one of their set – have ever written, should
> "Line trunks – clothe spice – or fluttering in a row
> Befringe the rails of Bedlam – or Soho.—"   [*CMP*, pp. 148–9]

Byron is quoting Pope's *The First Epistle of the Second Book of Horace*, ll.418–19.

8. I will have more to say about Cuvier later in this chapter. For the future-orientations of nostalgia, see, for example, J.M. Fritzman's meditation on the subject, 'The Future of Nostalgia and the Time of the Sublime', *Clio*, 23:2 (1994), 167–89: 'The lost homeland only ever existed in a future, and nostalgia seeks to remember what has yet to be imagined'. [169]

9. The fullest account of the poem is that of Timothy Webb, '"The Bastinadoed Elephant": Byron and the Rhetoric of Irish Servility', in *Byron: East and West*, edited by Martin Prochazka (Prague: Univerzita Karlova v Praze, 2000), pp. 29–62.

10. *BLJ*, VIII, p. 225.

11. 'Detached Thoughts' describes Grattan's oratory in these terms: 'I have never heard any one who fulfilled my Ideal of an Orator. – Grattan would have been near it but for his Harlequin delivery', *BLJ*, IX, p. 13. *The Irish Avatar* puts it like this:

> Ever glorious GRATTAN! the best of the Good!
>   So simple in heart, so sublime in the rest!
> With all which Demosthenes wanted endued,
>   And his rival or victor in all he possess'd.
>
> Ere Tully arose in the zenith of Rome,
>   Though unequall'd, preceded, the task was begun –
> But GRATTAN sprung up like a God from the tomb
>   Of ages, the first, last, the Saviour, the *One*!
>
>   (ll.37–44).

This is part of the poem's conscious method of hyperbole or 'ferocious phantasy' whereby Byron's high opinion of men such as Grattan is worked up into apotheoses.

12. See *BLJ*, VIII, pp. 19; 29–30. For doubts about the age of Samuel Rogers see *BLJ*, VIII, p. 218.

13. See *BLJ*, IX, pp. 11–52 inclusive. Curran and Erskine are also remembered in *Don Juan*, XIII, stanzas 92 and 93, as 'Longbow from Ireland, Strongbow from the Tweed'(l.730).

14. *BLJ*, IX, p. 14. Thomas Moore was Sheridan's biographer, as well as Byron's, and records the illustrious dinner party from the year 1813 at the home of Samuel Rogers, when Byron met Sheridan: 'The company consisted but of Mr. Rogers himself, Lord Byron, Mr. Sheridan, and the writer of this Memoir. Sheridan knew the admiration his audience felt for him; the presence of the young poet, in particular, seemed to bring back his own youth and wit; and the details he gave of his early life were not less interesting and animating to himself than delightful to us', Thomas Moore, *Memoirs of the Life of the Right Honourable Richard Brinsley Sheridan* (1825), p. 683. For Sheridan's wish for Byron to write his biography, see Jack C. Wills, 'Lord Byron and "Poor Dear Sherry", Richard Brinsley Sheridan', in Charles E. Robinson (ed.), *Lord Byron and His Contemporaries: Essays for the Sixth International Byron Seminar* (Newark: University of Delaware Press, 1982), pp. 85–104. Wills observes that 'Probably more than any other person of his time Byron perceived and understood the paradox that was Richard Brinsley Sheridan. ...Byron saw Sheridan as the living repository of the eighteenth century manners and ethos he so revered' (pp. 88/94).

15. *BLJ*, III, p. 129. At the age of thirty-four Byron felt (or enjoyed pretending to feel) as old as these 'Immortals' had been when he had known them. In a letter to Tom Moore of October 1821, describing a half-hearted attempt to woo an Italian lady, Byron quotes Curran (who had died in 1817): 'I feel as your poor friend Curran said, before his death, "a mountain of lead upon my heart", which I believe to be constitutional', *BLJ*, VIII, p. 230. This kind of statement was typical of Byron in a certain senescent mode, imitated in part from the older (and he believed grander) men he had 'seen' in the days of his glory. A journal entry for 1813 captures the sentimental element to the friendship:

> Lord Holland told me a curious piece of sentimentality in Sheridan. The other night we were all delivering our respective and various opinions on him and other *hommes marquans*, and mine was this. 'Whatever Sheridan has done or has chosen to do has been, *par excellence*, always the *best* of its kind. He has written the *best* comedy (School for Scandal) the *best* drama (in my mind, far before that St. Giles's lampoon, the Beggar's Opera), the best farce (the *Critic* – it is only too good for a farce), and the best Address (Monologue on Garrick), and, to crown all, delivered the very best Oration (the famous Begum Speech) ever conceived or heard in this country.' Somebody told S. this the next day, and on hearing it he burst into tears!
>
> Poor Brinsley! If they were tears of pleasure, I would have rather have said these few, but most sincere, words than have written the Iliad or made his own celebrated Philippic. Nay, his own comedy never gratified me more than to hear he had derived a moment's gratification from any praise of mine, humble as it must appear to my 'elders and my betters'.

BLJ, III, p. 239.

16. *Lady Blessington's Conversations of Lord Byron*, ed. Ernest J. Lovell, Jr (Princeton: Princeton University Press, 1969), p. 141. [Hereafter, *Blessington.*]

17. '"The Blues" foregrounds its memorial character precisely because, as a satire, it seems so anachronistic', McGann, *BCPW*, VI, p. 665.
18. *Poetical Works of Robert Southey* (London: Longman's, 1884), pp. 766/9.
19. *CMP*, p. 224.
20. *CMP*, p. 554.
21. The story of the disagreement between Byron and Teresa Guiccioli about the status of 'love' as a tragic subject – Teresa contested Byron's claim that it 'was *not the loftiest* theme for true tragedy', and so Byron was persuaded to introduce Myrrha into the drama – is retold by the play itself in the struggle between the two main protagonists, which is essentially about the meaning of love as suffering. *BLJ*, VIII, p. 26.

> Oh mighty Jove!
> Forgive this monstrous love for a barbarian,
> Who knows not of Olympus...

> (III.i.ll.182–4.)

The notion of a 'monstrous' love ties in with the 'moral centaur' figure for the *cavalier servente*, explored in the last chapter. Myrrha defines her love specifically in the negative terms of place (Sardanapalus 'knows not of Olympus').

22. *BLJ*, V, p. 99. An entry in the Ravenna Journal for 2 February 1821, meditating upon Swift's last years ('Swift had hardly *begun life* at the very period (thirty-three) when I feel quite an *old sort* of feel'), suddenly breaks off:

> Oh! There is an organ playing in the street – a waltz, too! I must leave off to listen. They are playing a waltz which I have heard ten thousand times at the balls in London, between 1812 and 1815. Music is a strange thing.

(*BLJ*, VIII, p. 43).
23. *Blessington*, p. 32.
24. *Blessington*, pp. 34–5.
25. Byron uses the Scala dei Giganti as a symbol and spectacle of Venetian state power in both *The Two Foscari* and *Marino Faliero*, even though the staircase wasn't built until the late fifteenth century (i.e. after the periods of the Foscari and Faliero). The anachronism perhaps fits in with the play's prophetic vision.
26. 'Existential' seems the most useful umbrella term for the inter-related areas of morality, philosophy, theology, ontology and phenomenology that fall within the scope of Byron's remarkably suggestive mystery play.
27. Letter to Murray, 3 November 1821, *BLJ*, IX, p. 53.
28. *BCPW*, VI, p. 689.
29. *CMP*, p. 150.
30. *Don Juan* 'is always about England – and never more so than when at its most exotic', Peter Graham, *Don Juan and Regency England* (Virginia: University Press of Virginia, 1990), p. 4.
31. From Genoa in March 1823 Byron wrote to Bryan Waller Procter: 'As to what D[on] J[uan] may do in England – you will see. If you had had the experience which I have had of the *grande monde* in that and other coun-

tries, you would be aware that there is no society so intrinsically (though hypocritically) *intrigante* and profligate as English high life', *BLJ*, X, p. 116.

32. Peter Graham invokes Bakhtin's notion of the 'chronotope': 'a place permitting us to range through time in space, to see the past in the present. The chronotopic nature of *Don Juan* blends a time when the narrative is taking place (1792 or so), a period from which most of the real details are drawn (1811–16, Byron's years in the Great World), and the moment of composition (1822–3)', *Don Juan and Regency England*, p. 163. Jerome McGann distinguishes the 'immediate context' (1818–24) from the narrative time (1780s and 1790s), and from that of Byron's English recollections (1808–16), and reflects upon the meaning of these distinctions in *The Beauty of Inflections: Literary Investigations in Historical Method and Theory* (Oxford: Clarendon Press, 1985).

33. Writing to Tom Moore from Ravenna in June 1822, Byron comments: 'I do not see an Englishman in half a year, and, when I do, I turn my horse's head the other way', *BLJ*, VIII, p. 141. For being out of touch with England, see for example, the letter to John Murray, from Ravenna 24 September 1821: 'For *two years* (except two or three articles cut out & sent by *you* – by the post) I never read a newspaper – which was not forced upon me by some accident – & know upon the whole as little of England – as you all do of Italy – & God knows – *that* is little enough with all your travels &c. &c. &c.', *BLJ*, VIII, p. 220. See also, *BLJ*, IX, p. 126.

34. 'That you shall *not* send me any modern or (as they are called) *new* publications in *English – whatsoever* – save and excepting any writing prose or verse of (or reasonably presumed to be of) Walter Scott – Crabbe – Moore – Campbell – Rogers – Gifford – Joanna Baillie – *Irving* (the American) Hogg – Wilson (Isle of Palms Man) or any especial *single* work of fancy which is thought to be of considerable merit', *BLJ*, VIII, p. 219.

35. Other such moments might include, for example, the direct address to Mrs Fry in canto X (stanza 85) whose visits to Newgate had made the news in 1812. Fry is asked to concentrate on reforming the contemporary British court rather than female prisoners, and to tell them 'William Curtis is a bore', or *was* a bore as Lord Mayor in 1795, and MP from 1790 to 1818.

36. 'The end of war, which is the condition for the retrospect on its unfolding as a narrative of violent ruptures and collective delusion, coincides with the foreclosure of a future that is anything more than that condition of normal change which Immanuel Wallerstein has described as the temporal modality of modern liberalism. The historical advent of aftermath made it possible for Coleridge, Constant, Scott, Wordsworth, and Byron to think the posthistorical', Jerome Christensen, *Romanticism at the End of History* (Baltimore: Johns Hopkins University Press, 2000), p. 7.

37. Malcolm Kelsall, for example, comments: 'It would be clumsy to gloss each allusion because the function of the rhetoric is to rush over the territory, to bring together matters major and minor – and by jumbling them in a catalogue to devalue them... . Yet, paradoxically, the recitation of the changes in the larger context of the poem indicates *idem semper*. For, if the issues change with meaningless rapidity, the social structure of British society beneath them does not alter', *Byron's Politics* (Brighton: Harvester, 1987), p. 187.

38. Byron is conflating two lines from Virgil's *Aeneid* II, 6 and 91: 'et quorum pars magna fui...(haud ignota loquor)...'. Byron's Latin would translate as 'I speak of what I know; these are trivial things with which I had some small a part'.

Afterword: Dying in Greece

1. For the response to Byron's death, see William St Clair, *That Greece Might Still Be Free: The Philhellenes in the War of Independence* (London: Oxford University Press, 1972), pp. 173–276.
2. All three of these quotations are from Frederick Prokosch's novel *The Missolonghi Manuscript* (London: W.H. Allen, 1968), which I take to be an example of the mud-and-fever cliché of imagining Byron's death. Prokosch's novel tells the story of Byron's life, and his last days, through a manuscript in Byron's hand discovered in a house in Missolonghi (belonging to Dr Vaya), which passes through the possession of a Baron von Haugwitz, Colonel Eppingham, the Marchesa del Rosso, to T.H. Applebee of Bryn Mawr College, who presents his discovery to the world (pp. 9/331/333).
3. Stephen Minta, *On a Voiceless Shore: Byron in Greece* (New York: Henry Holt, 1998), p. 208.
4. St Clair, p. 177. Stephen Minta is particularly subtle on this subject: 'But there was nothing inevitable about his death in Mesolongi. That, in the end, was simply bad luck, perhaps simply the chance of the weather. Once he was dead, however, everything begins to look fated', Minta, p. 255. Naturally, the idea of fate, or a plot working itself out, is central to Prokosch's novel. Andrew Rutherford talks of the 'extra-literary radiance' cast by his death in Missolonghi upon earlier poems on the subject of Greece. See Andrew Rutherford, 'Byron of Greece and Lawrence of Arabia', *The Byron Journal*, 16 (1988) 29–46 (34).
5. *BLJ*, XI, p. 83
6. *BLJ*, XI, p. 20.
7. *BLJ*, XI, p. 107.
8. *BLJ*, XI, p. 22.
9. *BLJ*, XI, p. 33. On 12 October 1823 Byron writes to Augusta that 'things are in such a state among them [i.e. the Greeks] – that it is difficult to conjecture where one could be useful to them', *BLJ*, XI, p. 45. On 16 October Byron is writing to Hobhouse from Cephalonia: 'I shall continue here till I see when and where I can be of use', *BLJ*, XI, p. 50.
10. Joan Blythe draws attention to the Miltonic echo in her essay, 'Byron and Greek Independence: The Miltonic Vision', M.B. Raizis (ed.), *Byron: A Poet for All Seasons*, pp. 178–87 (185).

Select Bibliography

Acock, R.E. 'Lord Byron and Bayle's Dictionary', *The Yearbook of English Studies, Modern Humanities Research Association*, 5 (1975) 142–52

Andrews, M. *The Search for the Picturesque: Landscape, Aesthetics and Tourism in Britain, 1760–1800* (Aldershot: Scolar Press, 1989)

Bachelard, G. *The Poetics of Space*, translated by M. Jolas (Boston: Orion, 1964)

Bainbridge, S. *Napoleon and English Romanticism* (Cambridge: Cambridge University Press, 1995)

Baker, M. (ed.), *Encyclopedia of Translation Studies* (London and New York: Routledge, 1998)

Bann, S. *Romanticism and the Rise of History* (New York: Twayne Publishers, 1995)

Bann, S. *The Clothing of Clio: A Study of the Representation of History in Nineteenth Century Britain and France* (Cambridge: Cambridge University Press, 1984)

Barkan, E. and Bush, R. (eds), *Claiming the Stones / Naming the Bones: Cultural Property and Group Identity* (Oxford and California: Oxford University Press and J. Paul Getty Foundation, 2000)

Barnes, T.J. and Duncan, J. (eds), *Writing Worlds: Discourse, Text and Metaphor in the Representation of Landscape* (London and New York: Routledge, 1992)

Barton, A. *Byron and the Mytholgy of Fact* (Nottingham: Hawthornes, 1968)

Beatty, B. and Newey, V. (eds), *Byron and the Limits of Fiction* (Liverpool: Liverpool University Press, 1988)

Beatty, B. 'Byron and the Paradoxes of Nationalism', *Literature and Nationalism*, ed. by Vincent Newey and Anne Thompson (Liverpool: Liverpool University Press, 1991)

Beaty, F. L. 'Byron and the Story of Francesca da Rimini', *PMLA*, 75 (1960) 395–401

Blair, S. 'Cultural Geography and the Place of the Literary', *American Literary History*, 10:3 (1998) 544–67

Brett, R.L. and Jones, A.R. (eds), *Wordsworth and Coleridge: Lyrical Ballads* (London: Routledge, 1991)

Briggs, A. *The Age of Improvement: 1783–1867* (London: Longmans, 1959)

Buzard, J. *The Beaten Track: European Tourism, Literature, and the Ways to 'Culture' 1800–1918* (Oxford: Oxford University Press, 1993)

Cameron, K.N., Reiman, D.H. and Fischer, D.D. (eds), *Shelley and His Circle, 1773–1822*, 8 vols (Cambridge Mass.: Harvard University Press, 1961–86)

Casey, E. *Getting Back Into Place: Toward a Renewed Understanding of the Place-World* (Bloomington and Indianopolis: Indiana Unversity Press, 1993)

Casey, E. *The Fate of Place: A Philosophical History* (Berkeley and Los Angeles: University of California Press, 1997)

Calder, A. (ed.), *Byron and Scotland: Radical or Dandy?* (Edinburgh: Edinburgh University Press, 1989)

Cardwell, R.A. (ed.), *Lord Byron the European: Essays for the International Byron Society* (Lampeter: Edwin Mellen Press, 1997)

233

Christensen, J. *Lord Byron's Strength: Romantic Writing and Commercial Society* (London and Baltimore: Johns Hopkins University Press, 1993)

Christensen. J. *Romanticism at the End of History* (Baltimore: Johns Hopkins University Press, 2000)

Copley, S. and Garside, P. (eds), *The Politics of the Picturesque: Literature, Landscape and Aesthetics since 1770* (Cambridge: Cambridge University Press, 1994)

Crang, M. and Thrift, N. (eds), *Thinking Space* (London and New York: Routledge, 2000)

Cronin, R. 'Mapping *Childe Harold* I and II', *The Byron Journal*, 22 (1994) 14–30

Daly, K. 'Worlds Beyond England: *Don Juan* and the Legacy of Enlightenment Cosmopolitanism', *Romanticism*, 4:2 (1998) 189–201

Dart, G. *Rousseau, Robespierre and English Romanticism* (Cambridge: Cambridge University Press, 1999)

Deleuze, G. and Guattari, F. (eds), *A Thousand Plateaus*, translated by B. Massumi (Minneapolis: University of Minnesota Press, 1987)

Derrida, J. *Monolingualism of the Other, or The Prothesis of Origin*, translated by Patrick Mensah (Stanford: Stanford University Press, 1998)

Duffy, E. *Rousseau in England: The Context for Shelley's Critique of the Enlightenment* (Berkeley: University of California Press, 1979)

Duncan, J. and Ley, D. (eds), *Place/Culture/Representation* (London: and New York: Routledge, 1993)

Elledge, P. *Lord Byron at Harrow School: Speaking Out, Talking Back, Acting Up, Bowing Out* (Baltimore: Johns Hopkins University Press, 2000)

Foote, K.E. and Mathewson, K. (eds), *Re-reading Cultural Geography* (Austin: University of Texas Press, 1994)

Freud, S. *Civilization and its Discontents*, vol. 12 of *The Penguin Freud Library* (Harmondsworth: Penguin, 1991)

Fritzman, J.M. 'The Future of Nostalgia and the Time of the Sublime', *Clio*, 23:2 (1994) 167–89

Garber, F. *Byron: Self, Text, and Romantic Irony* (Princeton: Princeton University Press, 1988)

Gaskill, H. (ed.), *The Poems of Ossian and Related Works* (Edinburgh: Edinburgh University Press, 1996)

Gentzler, E. *Contemporary Translation Theories* (London and New York: Routledge, 1993)

Gilroy, A. (ed.), *Romantic Geographies: Discourses of Travel 1775–1844* (Manchester: Manchester University Press, 2000)

Graham, P. (ed.), *Byron's Bulldog: The Letters of John Cam Hobhouse to Lord Byron* (Columbus: Ohio State University Press, 1984)

Graham, P. *Don Juan and Regency England* (Virginia: University Press of Virginia, 1990)

Graham, P. 'Byron, Hobhouse and Editorial Symbiosis', *The Byron Journal*, 23 (1995) 14–21

Harbinson, R. *Eccentric Spaces* (Cambridge Mass.: MIT Press, 1977)

Havely, N.R. 'Francesca Frustrated: New Evidence about Hobhouse's and Byron's Translation of Pellico's *Francesca da Rimini*', *Romanticism*, 1:1 (1995) 106–20

Hirst, W.Z. (ed.), *Byron, the Bible, and Religion: Essays from the Twelfth International Byron Seminar* (Newark: University of Delaware Press, 1991)

Hoagwood, T.A. *Byron's Dialectic: Scepticism and the Critique of Culture* (London and Toronto: Associated University Presses, 1993)

Hobhouse, J.C. *Travels in Albania and Other Provinces of Turkey in 1809 & 1810* (London: John Murray, 1813)

Hobhouse, J.C. *Recollections of a Long Life: By Lord Broughton*, 6 vols (London: John Murray, 1909)

Howe, P.P. (ed.), *The Complete Works of William Hazlitt*, 21 vols (London and Toronto: J.M. Dent, 1932)

Jamison, K.R. *Touched with Fire: Manic Depressive Illness and the Artistic Temperament* (New York: Free Press, 1993)

Jones, A.M. *The Works of Sir William Jones*, 6 vols (London: G.G. and J. Robinson, 1799)

Joseph, M.K. *Byron the Poet* (London: Victor Gollancz, 1964)

Kelsall, M. 'The Sense of Place and the Romantic Cosmopolite', *Literaria Pragensia*, 3:5 (1993) 28–41

Kelsall, M. *Byron's Politics* (Brighton: Harvester Press, 1987)

Kennedy, J. *Conversations on Religion with Lord Byron* (London: John Murray, 1830)

Kerrigan, J. 'Revolution, Revenge, and Romantic Tragedy', *Romanticism*, 1:1 (1995) 121–40

Korfmann, M. 'Troy: Topography and Navigation', in Machteld J. Mellink (ed.), *Troy and the Trojan War* (Bryn Mawr: Bryn Mawr College Press, 1986)

Leask, N. *British Romantic Writers and the East* (Cambridge: Cambridge University Press, 1992)

Lefebvre, H. *The Production of Space*, translated by Donald Nicholson-Smith (Oxford: Blackwell, 1991)

Levine, A. and Keane, R.N. (eds), *Re-reading Byron: Essays Selected from Hofstra University's Byron Bicentenial Conference* (New York: Garland, 1993)

Liu, A. 'Local Transcendence: Cultural Criticism, Postmodernism, and the Romanticism of Detail', *Representations*, 32 (Fall, 1990) 75–113

Lovell, E.J., Jr (ed.), *His Very Self and Voice: Collected Conversations of Lord Byron* (New York: Macmillan, 1954)

Lovell, E.J., Jr *Lady Blessington's Conversations of Lord Byron* (Princeton: Princeton University Press, 1969)

Makdisi, S. *Romantic Imperialism: Universal Empire and the Culture of Modernity* (Cambridge: Cambridge University Press, 1998)

Mallory, W.E. and Housley, P.S. (eds), *Geography and Literature: A Meeting of the Disciplines* (Syracuse, NY: Syracuse University Press, 1987)

Malpas, J.E. *Place and Experience: A Philosophical Topography* (Cambridge: Cambridge University Press, 1999)

Manning, P. *Byron and His Fictions* (Detroit: Wayne State University Press, 1978)

Marchand, L. (ed.), *Byron's Letters and Journals*, 12 vols (London: John Murray, 1973–82)

May, J. and Thrift, N. (eds), *Timespace: Geographies of Temporality* (London and New York: Routledge, 2001)

McGann, J.J. (ed.), *The Complete Poetical Works of Lord Byron*, 7 vols (Oxford: Clarendon Press, 1980–86)

McGann, J.J. *Fiery Dust: Byron's Poetic Development* (Chicago: Chicago University Press, 1968)

McGann, J.J. *The Romantic Ideology: A Critical Investigation* (Chicago: Chicago University Press, 1983)

McGann, J. *The Beauty of Inflections: Literary Investigations in Historical Method and Theory* (Oxford: Clarendon Press, 1985)

Eric Meyer, '"I Know Thee Not, I Loathe Thy Race": Romantic Orientalism in the Eye of the Other', *ELH*, 58 (1991) 657–99

Thomas Moore, *Memoirs of the Life of the Right Honourable Richard Brinsley Sheridan* (London: Longman,1825)

Mulhauser, F.L. (ed.), *The Correspondence of Arthur Hugh Clough*, 2 vols (Oxford: Clarendon Press, 1957)

Murphy, P.T. 'Climbing Parnassus and Falling Off', *At the Limits of Romanticism: Essays in Cultural, Feminist, and Materialist Criticism*, ed. by Mary A. Favret and Nicola J. Watson (Bloomington: Indiana University Press, 1994)

Nicholson, A. (ed.), *Lord Byron: The Complete Miscellaneous Prose* (Oxford; Clarendon Press, 1991)

Origo, I. *The Last Attachment* (New York: C. Scribner's Sons, 1949)

Pile, S. and Thrift, N. (eds), *Mapping the Subject: Geographies of Cultural Transformation* (London and New York: Routledge, 1995)

Quinones, R.J. 'Byron's Cain: Between History and Theology', *Byron, the Bible, and Religion: Essays from the Twelfth International Byron Seminar*, ed. Wolf Z. Hirst (Newark: University of Delaware Press, 1991)

Raizis, M.B. (ed.), *Byron: A Poet for All Seasons: Proceedings of the 25th International Byron Conference* (Messolonghi: Messolonghi Byron Society, 2000)

Reiman, D.H. (ed.), *The Romantics Reviewed: Contemporary Reviews of British Romantic Writers* (New York: Garland, 1972)

Robinson, C. (ed.), *Lord Byron and His Contemporaries: Essays for the Sixth International Byron Seminar* (Newark: University of Delaware Press, 1982)

Rutherford, A. (ed.), *Byron: Augustan and Romantic* (London: Macmillan, 1990)

Rutherford, A. 'The Influence of Hobhouse on *Childe Harold's Pilgrimage*, Canto IV', *Review of English Studies*, 12 (1961) 391–7

Said, E. *Orientalism* (London: Pantheon Books, 1978)

Sharafuddin, M. *Islam and Romantic Orientalism: Literary Encounters with the Orient* (London: I.B. Tauris, 1994)

Shilstone, W. *Byron and the Myth of Tradition* (Lincoln: University of Nebraska Press, 1988)

Simpson, D. *The Academic Postmodern and The Rule of Literature: A Report on Half-Knowledge* (Chicago: Chicago University Press, 1995)

Sinclair, J.D. *Dante: The Divine Comedy: Inferno* (Oxford: Oxford University Press, 1961)

Steiner, G. *After Babel* 3rd edn (Oxford: Oxford University Press, 1998)

Trelawny, E.J. *Records of Shelley, Byron, and the Author* (Harmondsworth: Penguin, 1973)

Tuan, T. *Topophilia* (Englewood Cliffs, NJ.: Prentice Hall, 1974)

Vassallo, P. *Byron: The Italian Literary Influence* (London: Macmillan, 1984)

Venuti, L. (ed.), *The Translation Studies Reader* (London and New York: Routledge, 2000)

Watkins, D. *Social Relations in Byron's Eastern Tales* (London: Associated University Press, 1987)

Webb, T. *The Violet in the Crucible: Shelley and Translation* (Oxford: Clarendon Press, 1976)

Webb, T. '"The Bastinadoed Elephant": Byron and the Rhetoric of Irish Servility', in *Byron: East and West* ed. by Martin Prochazka (Prague: Univerzita Karlova v Praze, 2000)

Wilkes, J. *Lord Byron and Madame De Staël* (Aldershot: Ashgate, 1999)

Yaeger, P. *The Geography of Identity* (Ann Arbor: University of Michigan Press, 1996)

Index